INFLUENCE

❃

INFLUENCE

*How and why
people agree to
things*

❋

ROBERT B. CIALDINI, PH.D.

QUILL
New York

Grateful acknowledgment is made for permission to reprint the following:

Figure 1-1 Courtesy of Dansk International Designs
Figure 2-1 Group photograph courtesy of United Press International; photograph of woman and man by Harry Goodman, *The Washington Star*
Figure 2-2 Wide World Photos
Figure 2-3 Photograph by UPI; Dennis the Menace used by permission of Hank Ketcham and Field Enterprises, Inc.
Figure 3-1 Courtesy of Schieffelin & Co.
Figure 3-2 Artist Maria Picardi; copyright © by Robert B. Cialdini
Figure 4-1 Jan Halaska/Photo Researchers Inc.
Figure 4-2 Eric Knoll/Taurus Photos
Figure 4-3 UPI
Figure 5-1 from *Penguin Leunig*, copyright © by Michael Leunig, courtesy of Penguin Books Australia
Figure 5-2 David L. Langford, Associated Press
Figure 5-4 UPI
Figure 5-5 Tug McGraw courtesy of Walter Iooss, Jr./*Sports Illustrated;* victory parade courtesy of Heinz Kluetmeier/*Sports Illustrated*
Figure 6-1 Stanley Milgram, 1965. From the film *Obedience,* distributed by the University of Pennsylvania, PCR
Figure 6-2 Courtesy of General Foods Corporation
Figure 7-1 UPI
Figure 7-2 Peter Kerr, *The New York Times*
Figure 7-3 Robert B. Cialdini
Figure 7-4 UPI

Library of Congress Cataloging in Publication Data

Cialdini, Robert B.
  Influence : the new psychology of modern persuasion.

  Reprint. Originally published: Influence—how and
why people agree to things. New York : Morrow, 1984.
  Bibliography: p.
  Includes index.
  1. Persuasion (Psychology) 2. Influence (Psychology)
I. Title.
[BF637.P4C5 1985]   153.8'52   84-24791
ISBN 0-688-04107-8 (pbk.)

Printed in the United States of America

14   15   16   17   18   19   20

This book is dedicated to Chris, who glows in his father's eye.

ACKNOWLEDGMENTS

✳

An array of people deserve and have my appreciation for their aid in making this book possible. Several of my academic colleagues read and provided perceptive comments on the entire manuscript in its initial draft form, greatly strengthening the subsequent version. They are Gus Levine, Doug Kenrick, Art Beaman, and Mark Zanna. In addition, the first draft was read by a few family members and friends—Richard and Gloria Cialdini, Bobette Gorden, and Ted Hall—who offered not only much-needed emotional support but insightful substantive commentary as well.

A second, larger group provided helpful suggestions for selected chapters or groups of chapters: Todd Anderson, Sandy Braver, Catherine Chambers, Judy Cialdini, Nancy Eisenberg, Larry Ettkin, Joanne Gersten, Jeff Goldstein, Betsy Hans, Valerie Hans, Joe Hepworth, Holly Hunt, Ann Inskeep, Barry Leshowitz, Darwyn Linder, Debbie Littler, John Mowen, Igor Pavlov, Janis Posner, Trish Puryear, Marilyn Rall, John Reich, Peter Reingen,

8

INFLUENCE

Diane Ruble, Phyllis Sensenig, Roman Sherman, and Henry Wellman.

Certain people were instrumental at the beginning stages. John Staley was the first publishing professional to recognize the project's potential. Jim Sherman, Al Goethals, John Keating, and Dan Wegner provided early, positive reviews that encouraged author and editors alike. William Morrow and Company's president, Larry Hughes, sent a small but enthusiastic note that fortified me importantly for the task that lay ahead. Last and hardly least, Maria Guarnaschelli believed with me from the start in the book I wanted to write. It is to her editorial credit that the finished product remains that book, much improved. For her insightful direction and her potent efforts in the book's behalf, I am most grateful.

In addition, I would be remiss if I did not recognize the skill and efficiency of Sally Carney at manuscript preparation and the sound counsel of my attorney, Robert Brandes.

Finally, throughout the project, no one was more on my side than Bobette Gorden, who lived every word with me.

CONTENTS

❋

INTRODUCTION

❋

I can admit it freely now. All my life I've been a patsy. For as long as I can recall, I've been an easy mark for the pitches of peddlers, fund raisers, and operators of one sort or another. True, only some of these people have had dishonorable motives. The others—representatives of certain charitable agencies, for instance—have had the best of intentions. No matter. With personally disquieting frequency, I have always found myself in possession of unwanted magazine subscriptions or tickets to the sanitation workers' ball. Probably this long-standing status as sucker accounts for my interest in the study of compliance: Just what are the factors that cause one person to say yes to another person? And which techniques most effectively use these factors to bring about such compliance? I wondered why it is that a request stated in a certain way will be rejected, when a request that asks for the same favor in a slightly different fashion will be successful.

So in my role as an experimental social psychologist, I began to do research into the psychology of compliance. At first the research took the form of experiments performed, for the most part, in my laboratory and on college students. I wanted to find out which psychological principles influence the tendency to comply with a request. Right now, psychologists know quite a bit about these principles—what they are and how they work. I have characterized such principles as weapons of influence and will report on some of the most important in the upcoming chapters.

After a time, though, I began to realize that the experimental work, while necessary, wasn't enough. It didn't allow me to judge the importance of the principles in the world beyond the psychology building and the campus where I was examining them. It became clear that if I was to understand fully the psychology of compliance, I would need to broaden my scope of investigation. I would need to look to the compliance professionals—the people who had been using the principles on me all my life. They know what works and what doesn't; the law of survival of the fittest assures it. Their business is to make us comply, and their livelihoods depend on it. Those who don't know how to get people to say yes soon fall away; those who do, stay and flourish.

Of course, the compliance professionals aren't the only ones who know about and use these principles to help them get their way. We all employ them and fall victim to them to some degree in our daily interactions with neighbors, friends, lovers, and offspring. But the compliance practitioners have much more than the vague and amateurish understanding of what works than the rest of us have. As I thought about it, I knew that they represented the richest vein of information about compliance available to me. For the past three years, then, I have combined my experimental studies with a decidedly more entertaining program of systematic immersion into the world of compliance professionals—sales operators, fund raisers, con artists, and advertisers.

The purpose was to observe, from the inside, the techniques and strategies most commonly and effectively used by a broad range of compliance practitioners. That program of observation

INTRODUCTION

has sometimes taken the form of interviews with the practitioners themselves and sometimes with the natural enemies (for example, police bunco-squad officers, consumer agencies) of certain of the practitioners. At other times it has involved an intensive examination of the written materials by which compliance techniques are passed down from one generation to another—sales manuals and the like.

Most frequently, though, it has taken the form of participant observation. Participant observation is a research approach in which the researcher becomes a spy of sorts. With disguised identity and intent, the investigator infiltrates the setting of interest and becomes a full-fledged participant in the group to be studied. So when I wanted to learn about the compliance tactics of encyclopedia (or vacuum-cleaner, or portrait-photography, or dance-lesson) sales organizations, I would answer a newspaper ad for sales trainees and have them teach me their methods. Using similar but not identical approaches, I was able to penetrate advertising, public-relations, and fund-raising agencies to examine their techniques. Much of the evidence presented in this book, then, comes from my experience posing as a compliance professional, or aspiring professional, in a large variety of organizations dedicated to getting us to say yes.

One aspect of what I learned in this three-year period of participant observation was most instructive. Although there are thousands of different tactics that compliance practitioners employ to produce yes, the majority fall within six basic categories. Each of these categories is governed by a fundamental psychological principle that directs human behavior and, in so doing, gives the tactics their power. The book is organized around these six principles, one to a chapter. The principles—consistency, reciprocation, social proof, authority, liking, and scarcity—are each discussed in terms of their function in the society and in terms of how their enormous force can be commissioned by a compliance professional who deftly incorporates them into requests for purchases, donations, concessions, votes, assent, etc. Finally, each principle is examined as to its ability to produce a distinct kind of automatic, mindless compliance from people, that is, a willingness to say yes without thinking first. The evi-

INFLUENCE

dence suggests that the ever-accelerating pace and informational crush of modern life will make this particular form of unthinking compliance more and more prevalent in the future. It will be increasingly important for the society, therefore, to understand the how and why of automatic influence.

1

WEAPONS OF
INFLUENCE

✻

I got a phone call one day from a friend who had recently opened an Indian jewelry store in Arizona. She was giddy with a curious piece of news. Something fascinating had just happened, and she thought that, as a psychologist, I might be able to explain it to her. The story involved a certain allotment of turquoise jewelry she had been having trouble selling. It was the peak of the tourist season, the store was unusually full of customers, the turquoise pieces were of good quality for the prices she was asking; yet they had not sold. My friend had attempted a couple of standard sales tricks to get them moving. She tried calling attention to them by shifting their location to a more central display area; no luck. She even told her sales staff to "push" the items hard, again without success.

Finally, the night before leaving on an out-of-town buying trip, she scribbled an exasperated note to her head saleswoman, "Everything in this display case, price × ½," hoping just to be rid of the offending pieces, even if at a loss. When she returned a few days later, she was not surprised to find that every article had been sold. She was shocked, though, to discover that, because the employee had read the "½" in her scrawled message as a "2," the entire allotment had sold out at twice the original price!

That's when she called me. I thought I knew what had happened but told her that, if I were to explain things properly, she would have to listen to a story of mine. Actually, it isn't my story; it's about mother turkeys, and it belongs to the relatively new science of ethology—the study of animals in their natural settings. Turkey mothers are good mothers—loving, watchful, and protective. They spend much of their time tending, warming, cleaning, and huddling the young beneath them. But there *is* something odd about their method. Virtually all of this mothering is triggered by one thing: the "cheep-cheep" sound of young turkey chicks. Other identifying features of the chicks, such as their smell, touch, or appearance, seem to play minor roles in the mothering process. If a chick makes the "cheep-cheep" noise, its mother will care for it; if not, the mother will ignore or sometimes kill it.

The extreme reliance of maternal turkeys upon this one sound was dramatically illustrated by animal behaviorist M. W. Fox in his description of an experiment involving a mother turkey and a stuffed polecat.[1] For a mother turkey, a polecat is a natural enemy whose approach is to be greeted with squawking, pecking, clawing rage. Indeed, the experimenters found that even a stuffed model of a polecat, when drawn by a string toward a mother turkey, received an immediate and furious attack. When, however, the same stuffed replica carried inside it a small recorder that played the "cheep-cheep" sound of baby turkeys, the mother not only accepted the oncoming polecat but gathered it underneath her. When the machine was turned off, the polecat model again drew a vicious attack.

How ridiculous a female turkey seems under these circumstances: She will embrace a natural enemy just because it goes "cheep-cheep," and she will mistreat or murder one of her own chicks just because it does not. She looks like an automaton whose maternal instincts are under the automatic control of that single sound. The ethologists tell us that this sort of thing is far from unique to the turkey. They have begun to identify regular, blindly mechanical patterns of action in a wide variety of species.

Called fixed-action patterns, they can involve intricate sequences of behavior, such as entire courtship or mating rituals. A fundamental characteristic of these patterns is that the behaviors that comprise them occur in virtually the same fashion and in the same order every time. It is almost as if the patterns were recorded on tapes within the animals. When the situation calls for courtship, the courtship tape gets played; when the situation calls for mothering, the maternal behavior tape gets played. *Click* and the appropriate tape is activated; *whirr* and out rolls the standard sequence of behaviors.

The most interesting thing about all this is the way the tapes are activated. When a male animal acts to defend his territory, for instance, it is the intrusion of another male of the same species that cues the territorial-defense tape of rigid vigilance, threat, and, if need be, combat behaviors. But there is a quirk in the system. It is not the rival male as a whole that is the trigger; it is some specific feature of him, the *trigger feature*. Often the trigger feature will be just one tiny aspect of the totality that is the approaching intruder. Sometimes a shade of color is the trigger feature. The experiments of ethologists have shown, for instance, that a male robin, acting as if a rival robin had entered its territory, will vigorously attack nothing more than a clump of robin-red breast feathers placed there. At the same time, it will virtually ignore a perfect stuffed replica of a male robin *without* red breast feathers; similar results have been found in another species of bird, the bluethroat, where it appears that the trigger for territorial defense is a specific shade of blue breast feathers.[2]

Before we enjoy too smugly the ease with which lower animals can be tricked by trigger features into reacting in ways wholly inappropriate to the situation, we might realize two things. First, the automatic, fixed-action patterns of these animals work very well the great majority of the time. For example, because only healthy, normal turkey chicks make the peculiar sound of baby turkeys, it makes sense for mother turkeys to respond maternally to that single "cheep-cheep" noise. By reacting to just that one stimulus, the average mother turkey will nearly always behave correctly. It takes a trickster like a scientist to make her tapelike response seem silly. The second important thing to understand is that we, too, have our preprogrammed tapes; and, although they usually work to our advantage, the trigger features that activate them can be used to dupe *us* into playing them at the wrong times.[3]

This parallel form of human automatic action is aptly demonstrated in an experiment by Harvard social psychologist Ellen Langer. A well-known principle of human behavior says that when we ask someone to do us a favor we will be more successful if we provide a reason. People simply like to have reasons for what they do. Langer demonstrated this unsurprising fact by asking a small favor of people waiting in line to use a library copying machine: *Excuse me, I have five pages. May I use the Xerox machine because I'm in a rush?* The effectiveness of this request-plus-reason was nearly total: ninety-four percent of those asked let her skip ahead of them in line. Compare this success rate to the results when she made the request only: *Excuse me, I have five pages. May I use the Xerox machine?* Under those circumstances only 60 percent of those asked complied. At first glance, it appears that the crucial difference between the two requests was the additional information provided by the words "because I'm in a rush." But a third type of request tried by Langer showed that this was not the case. It seems that it was not the whole series of words, but the first one, "because," that made the difference. Instead of including a real reason for compliance, Langer's third type of request used the word "because" and then, adding nothing new, merely restated the obvious: *Excuse me, I have five pages. May I use the Xerox machine because I have to make some copies?* The result was that once again nearly all (93 percent) agreed, even though no real reason, no new information was added to justify their compliance. Just as the "cheep-cheep" sound of turkey chicks triggered an automatic mothering response from maternal turkeys, even when it emanated from a stuffed polecat, so the word "because" triggered an automatic compliance response from Langer's subjects, even when they were given no subsequent reason to comply. *Click, whirr!*[4]

*   *   *

WEAPONS OF INFLUENCE

Although some of Langer's additional findings show that there are many situations in which human behavior does not work in a mechanical, tape-activated way, what is astonishing is how often it does. For instance, consider the strange behavior of those jewelry store customers who swooped down on an allotment of turquoise pieces only after the items had been mistakenly offered at double their original price. I can make no sense of their behavior unless it is viewed in *click, whirr* terms.

The customers, mostly well-to-do vacationers with little knowledge of turquoise, were using a standard principle—a stereotype—to guide their buying: "expensive = good." Thus the vacationers, who wanted "good" jewelry, saw the turquoise pieces as decidedly more valuable and desirable when nothing about them was enhanced but the price. Price alone had become a trigger feature for quality; and a dramatic increase in price alone had led to a dramatic increase in sales among the quality-hungry buyers. *Click, whirr!*

It is easy to fault the tourists for their foolish purchase decisions. But a close look offers a kinder view. These were people who had been brought up on the rule "You get what you pay for" and who had seen that rule borne out over and over in their lives. Before long, they had translated the rule to mean "expensive = good." The "expensive = good" stereotype had worked quite well for them in the past, since normally the price of an item increases along with its worth; a higher price typically reflects higher quality. So when they found themselves in the position of wanting good turquoise jewelry without much knowledge of turquoise, they understandably relied on the old standby feature of cost to determine the jewelry's merits.

Although they probably did not realize it, by reacting solely to the price feature of the turquoise, they were playing a shortcut version of betting the odds. Instead of stacking all the odds in their favor by trying painstakingly to master each of the things that indicate the worth of turquoise jewelry, they were counting on just one—the one they knew to be usually associated with the quality of any item. They were betting that price alone would tell them all they needed to know. This time, because someone mistook a "½" for a "2," they bet wrong. But in the long run, over all the past and future situations of their lives, betting those

INFLUENCE

Expensive...By Design

Teak Bread Board
Hand assembled endwood....designed by Jens Quistgaard
DANSK
Dansk International Designs
Mt. Kisco, New York 10549, Box 712
Write for free color brochure

FIGURE 1-1

CAVIAR AND CRAFTSMANSHIP

The message to be communicated by this ad is, of course, that expensive equals good. (Courtesy of Dansk International Designs)

shortcut odds may represent the most rational approach possible.

In fact, automatic, stereotyped behavior is prevalent in much of human action because in many cases it is the most efficient form of behaving, and in other cases it is simply necessary. You and I exist in an extraordinarily complicated stimulus environment, easily the most rapidly moving and complex that has ever existed on this planet. To deal with it, we *need* shortcuts. We can't be expected to recognize and analyze all the aspects in each person, event, and situation we encounter in even one day. We haven't the time, energy, or capacity for it. Instead, we must very often use our stereotypes, our rules of thumb to classify things according to a few key features and then to respond mindlessly when one or another of these trigger features is present.

Sometimes the behavior that unrolls will not be appropriate for the situation, because not even the best stereotypes and trigger features work every time. But we accept their imperfection, since there is really no other choice. Without them we would stand frozen—cataloging, appraising, and calibrating—as the time for action sped by and away. And from all indications, we will be relying on them to an even greater extent in the future. As the stimuli saturating our lives continue to grow more intricate and variable, we will have to depend increasingly on our shortcuts to handle them all.

It is odd that despite their current widespread use and looming future importance, most of us know very little about our automatic behavior patterns. Perhaps that is so precisely because of the mechanistic, unthinking manner in which they occur. Whatever the reason, it is vital that we clearly recognize one of their properties: They make us terribly vulnerable to anyone who does know how they work.

To understand fully the nature of our vulnerability, another glance at the work of the ethologists is in order. It turns out that these animal behaviorists with their recorded "cheep-cheeps" and their clumps of colored breast feathers are not the only ones who have discovered how to activate the behavior tapes of various species. There is a group of organisms, often termed mimics, that copy the trigger features of other animals in an attempt to trick these animals into mistakenly playing the right behavior tapes at the wrong times. The mimic will then exploit this altogether inappropriate action for its own benefit.

Take, for example, the deadly trick played by the killer females of one genus of firefly *(Photuris)* on the males of another firefly genus *(Photinus)*. Understandably, the *Photinus* males scrupulously avoid contact with the bloodthirsty *Photuris* females. But through centuries of experience, the female hunters have located a weakness in their prey—a special blinking courtship code by which members of the victims' species tell one another they are ready to mate. Somehow, the *Photuris* female has cracked the *Photinus* courtship code. By mimicking the flashing mating signals of her prey, the murderess is able to feast on the bodies of males whose triggered courtship tapes cause them to fly mechanically into death's, not love's, embrace.

Insects seem to be the most severe exploiters of the automaticity of their prey; it is not uncommon to find their victims duped to death. But less uncompromising forms of exploitation occur as well. There is, for instance, a little fish, the saber-toothed blenny, that takes advantage of an unusual program of cooperation worked out by members of two other species of fish. The cooperating fish form a Mutt and Jeff team consisting of a large grouper fish on the one hand and a much smaller type of fish on the other. The smaller fish serves as a cleaner to the larger one, which allows the cleaner to approach it and even enter its mouth to pick off fungus and other parasites that have attached themselves to the big fish's teeth or gills. It is a beautiful arrangement: The big grouper gets cleaned of harmful pests, and the cleaner fish gets an easy dinner. The larger fish normally devours any other small fish foolish enough to come close to it. But when the cleaner approaches, the big fish suddenly stops all movement and floats open-mouthed and nearly immobile in response to an undulating dance that the cleaner performs. This dance appears to be the trigger feature of the cleaner that activates the dramatic passivity of the big fish. It also provides the saber-toothed blenny with an angle—a chance to take advantage of the cleaning ritual of the cooperators. The blenny will approach the large predator, copying the undulations of the cleaner's dance and automatically producing the tranquil, unmoving posture of the big fish. Then, true to its name, it will quickly rip a mouthful from the larger fish's flesh and dart away before its startled victim can recover.[5]

There is a strong but sad parallel in the human jungle. We too have exploiters who mimic trigger features for our own brand of automatic responding. Unlike the mostly instinctive response sequences of nonhumans, our automatic tapes usually develop from psychological principles or stereotypes we have learned to accept. Although they vary in their force, some of these principles possess a tremendous ability to direct human action. We have been subjected to them from such an early point in our lives, and they have moved us about so pervasively since then, that you and I rarely perceive their power. In the eyes of others, though, each such principle is a detectable and ready weapon, a weapon of automatic influence.

There is a group of people who know very well where the weapons of automatic influence lie and who employ them regularly and expertly to get what they want. They go from social encounter to social encounter requesting others to comply with their wishes; their frequency of success is dazzling. The secret of their effectiveness lies in the way they structure their requests, the way they arm themselves with one or another of the weapons of influence that exist within the social environment. To do this may take no more than one correctly chosen word that engages a strong psychological principle and sets an automatic behavior tape rolling within us. And trust the human exploiters to learn quickly exactly how to profit from our tendency to respond mechanically according to these principles.

Remember my friend the jewelry-store owner? Although she benefited by accident the first time, it did not take her long to begin exploiting the "expensive = good" stereotype regularly and intentionally. Now during the tourist season, she first tries to speed the sale of an item that has been difficult to move by increasing its price substantially. She claims that this is marvelously cost-effective. When it works on the unsuspecting vacationers— as it frequently does—it results in an enormous profit margin. And even when it is not initially successful, she can mark the article "Reduced from _____" and sell it at its original price while still taking advantage of the "expensive = good" reaction to the inflated figure.

There are several components shared by most of the weapons of automatic influence to be described in this book. We have already discussed two of them—the nearly mechanical process by which the power within these weapons can be activated, and the consequent exploitability of this power by anyone who knows how to trigger them. A third component involves the way that the weapons of automatic influence lend their force to those who use them. It's not that the weapons, like a set of heavy clubs, provide a conspicuous arsenal to be used by one man to bludgeon another into submission.

The process is much more sophisticated and subtle. With proper execution, the exploiter need hardly strain a muscle to get his way. All that is required is to trigger the great stores of influence that already exist in the situation and direct them toward the intended target. In this sense, the approach is not unlike that of the Japanese martial-art form called jujitsu. A woman employing jujitsu would utilize her own strength only minimally against an opponent. Instead, she would exploit the power inherent in such naturally present principles as gravity, leverage, momentum and inertia. If she knows how and where to engage the action of these principles, she can easily defeat a physically stronger rival. And so it is for the exploiters of the weapons of automatic influence that exist naturally around us. The exploiters can commission the power of these weapons for use against their targets while exerting little personal force. This last feature of the process allows the exploiters an enormous additional benefit—the ability to manipulate without the appearance of manipulation. Even the victims themselves tend to see their compliance as due to the action of natural forces rather than to the designs of the person who profits from that compliance.

An example is in order. There is a principle in human perception, the contrast principle, that affects the way we see the difference between two things that are presented one after another. Simply put, if the second item is fairly different from the first, we will tend to see it as more different than it actually is. So if we lift a light object first and then lift a heavy object, we will estimate the second object to be heavier than if we had lifted it without first trying the light one. The contrast principle is well established in the field of psychophysics and applies to all sorts of perceptions besides weight. If we are talking to a beautiful woman at a cocktail party and are then joined by an unattractive one, the second woman will strike us as less attractive than she actually is.

In fact, studies done on the contrast principle at Arizona State and Montana State universities suggest that we may be less satisfied with the physical attractiveness of our own mates because of the way the popular media bombard us with examples of unrealistically attractive models. In one study college students rated a picture of an average-looking member of the opposite sex as less attractive if they had first looked through the ads in some popular magazines. In another study, male college dormitory residents rated the photo of a potential blind date. Those who did so while watching an episode of the *Charlie's Angels* TV series viewed the blind date as a less attractive woman than those who rated her while watching a different show. Apparently it was the uncommon beauty of the *Angels* female stars that made the blind date seem less attractive.[6]

A nice demonstration of perceptual contrast is sometimes employed in psychophysics laboratories to introduce students to the principle firsthand. Each student takes a turn sitting in front of three pails of water—one cold, one at room temperature, and one hot. After placing one hand in the cold water and one in the hot water, the student is told to place both in the lukewarm water simultaneously. The look of amused bewilderment that immediately registers tells the story: Even though both hands are in the same bucket, the hand that has been in the cold water feels as if it is now in hot water, while the one that was in the hot water feels as if it is now in cold water. The point is that the same thing—in this instance, room-temperature water—can be made to seem very different depending on the nature of the event that precedes it.

Be assured that the nice little weapon of influence provided by the contrast principle does not go unexploited. The great advantage of this principle is not only that it works but also that it is virtually undetectable. Those who employ it can cash in on its influence without any appearance of having structured the situation in their favor. Retail clothiers are a good example. Suppose a man enters a fashionable men's store and says that he wants to buy a three-piece suit and a sweater. If you were the salesperson, which would you show him first to make him likely to spend the most money? Clothing stores instruct their sales personnel to sell the costly item first. Common sense might suggest the reverse: If a man has just spent a lot of money to purchase a suit, he may be reluctant to spend very much more on the purchase of a sweater.

But the clothiers know better. They behave in accordance with what the contrast principle would suggest: Sell the suit first, because when it comes time to look at sweaters, even expensive ones, their prices will not seem as high in comparison. A man might balk at the idea of spending $75 for a sweater, but if he has just bought a $275 suit, a $75 sweater does not seem excessive. The same principle applies to a man who wishes to buy the accessories (shirt, shoes, belt) to go along with his new suit. Contrary to the commonsense view, the evidence supports the contrast-principle prediction. As sales motivation analysts Whitney, Hubin, and Murphy state in their book, "The interesting thing is that even when a man enters a clothing store with the express purpose of purchasing a suit, he will almost always *pay more* for whatever accessories he buys if he buys them *after* the suit purchase than before."

It is much more profitable for salespeople to present the expensive item first, not only because to fail to do so will lose the influence of the contrast principle; to fail to do so will also cause the principle to work actively against them. Presenting an inexpensive product first and following it with an expensive one will cause the expensive item to seem even more costly as a result—hardly a desirable consequence for most sales organizations. So, just as it is possible to make the same bucket of water appear to be hotter or colder depending on the temperature of previously presented water, it is possible to make the price of the same item seem higher or lower depending on the price of a previously presented item.

Clever use of perceptual contrast is by no means confined to clothiers. I came across a technique that engaged the contrast principle while I was investigating, undercover, the compliance tactics of real-estate companies. To "learn the ropes," I was accompanying a company realty salesman on a weekend of showing houses to prospective home buyers. The salesman—we can call him Phil—was to give me tips to help me through my break-in period. One thing I quickly noticed was that whenever Phil began showing a new set of customers potential buys, he would start with a couple of undesirable houses. I asked him about it, and he laughed. They were what he called "setup" properties. The company maintained a rundown house or two on its lists at inflated prices. These houses were not intended to be sold to customers but to be shown to them, so that the genuine properties in the company's inventory would benefit from the comparison. Not all the sales staff made use of the setup houses, but Phil did. He said he liked to watch his prospects' "eyes light up" when he showed the place he really wanted to sell them after they had seen the rundown houses. "The house I got them spotted for looks really great after they've first looked at a couple of dumps."

Automobile dealers use the contrast principles by waiting until the price for a new car has been negotiated before suggesting one option after another that might be added. In the wake of a ten-thousand-dollar deal, the hundred or so dollars required for a nicety like an FM radio seems almost trivial in comparison. The same will be true of the added expense of accessories like tinted windows, dual side-view mirrors, white-wall tires, or special trim that the salesman might suggest in sequence. The trick is to bring up the extras independently of one another so that each small price will seem petty when compared to the already-determined much larger one. As the veteran car buyer can attest, many a budget-sized final price figure has ballooned out of proportion from the addition of all those seemingly little options. While the customer stands, signed contract in hand, wondering what happened and finding no one to blame but himself, the car dealer stands smiling the knowing smile of the jujitsu master.

INFLUENCE

Dear Mother and Dad:

Since I left for college I have been remiss in writing and I am sorry for my thoughtlessness in not having written before. I will bring you up to date now, but before you read on, please sit down. You are not to read any further unless you are sitting down, okay?

Well, then, I am getting along pretty well now. The skull fracture and the concussion I got when I jumped out the window of my dormitory when it caught on fire shortly after my arrival here is pretty well healed now. I only spent two weeks in the hospital and now I can see almost normally and only get those sick headaches once a day. Fortunately, the fire in the dormitory, and my jump, was witnessed by an attendant at the gas station near the dorm, and he was the one who called the Fire Department and the ambulance. He also visited me in the hospital and since I had nowhere to live because of the burntout dormitory, he was kind enough to invite me to share his apartment with him. It's really a basement room, but it's kind of cute. He is a very fine boy and we have fallen deeply in love and are planning to get married. We haven't got the exact date yet, but it will be before my pregnancy begins to show.

Yes, Mother and Dad, I am pregnant. I know how much you are looking forward to being grandparents and I know you will welcome the baby and give it the same love and devotion and tender care you gave me when I was a child. The reason for the delay in our marriage is that my boyfriend has a minor infection which prevents us from passing our pre-marital blood tests and I carelessly caught it from him. I know that you will welcome him into our family with open arms. He is kind and, although not well educated, he is ambitious. Although he is of a different race and religion than ours, I know your often expressed tolerence will not permit you to be bothered by that.

Now that I have brought you up to date, I want to tell you that there was no dormitory fire, I did not have a concussion or skull fracture, I was not in the hospital, I am not pregnant, I am not engaged, I am not infected, and there is no boyfriend. However, I am getting a "D" in American History, and an "F" in Chemistry and I want you to see those marks in their proper perspective.

Your loving daughter,
Sharon

FIGURE 1-2

PERCEPTUAL CONTRAST AND THE
COLLEGE   GIRL

Sharon may be failing chemistry, but she gets an "A" in psychology.

2

RECIPROCATION
The old give and take
. . . and take

❋

A few years ago, a university professor tried a little experiment. He sent Christmas cards to a sample of perfect strangers. Although he expected some reaction, the response he received was amazing—holiday cards addressed to him came pouring back from the people who had never met nor heard of him. The great majority of those who returned a card never inquired into the identity of the unknown professor. They received his holiday greeting card, *click,* and, *whirr,* they automatically sent one in return. While small in scope, this study nicely shows the action of one of the most potent of the weapons of influence around us—the rule for reciprocation.[1] The rule says that we should try to repay, in kind, what another person has provided us. If a woman does us a favor, we should do her one in return; if a man sends us a birthday present, we should remember his birthday with a gift of our own; if a couple invites us to a party, we should be sure to invite them to one of ours. By virtue of the reciprocity rule, then, we are *obligated* to the future repayment of favors, gifts, invitations, and the like. So typical is it for indebtedness to accompany the receipt of such things that a term like "much obliged" has become a synonym for "thank you," not only in the English language but in others as well.

The impressive aspect of the rule for reciprocation and the sense of obligation that goes with it is its pervasiveness in human culture. It is so widespread that, after intensive study, sociologists such as Alvin Gouldner can report that there is no human society that does not subscribe to the rule.[2] And within each society it seems pervasive also; it permeates exchanges of every kind. Indeed, it may well be that a developed system of indebtedness flowing from the rule for reciprocation is a unique property of human culture. The noted archaeologist Richard Leakey ascribes the essence of what makes us human to the reciprocity system: "We are human because our ancestors learned to share their food and their skills in an honored network of obligation,"[3] he says. Cultural anthropologists Lionel Tiger and Robin Fox view this "web of indebtedness" as a unique adaptive mechanism of human beings, allowing for the division of labor, the exchange of diverse forms of goods, the exchange of different services (making it possible for experts to develop), and the creation of a cluster of interdependencies that bind individuals together into highly efficient units.[4]

It is the future orientation inherent in a sense of obligation that is critical to its ability to produce social advances of the sort described by Tiger and Fox. A widely shared and strongly held feeling of future obligation made an enormous difference in human social evolution because it meant that one person could give something (for example, food, energy, care) to another with confidence that it was not being lost. For the first time in evolutionary history, one individual could give away any of a variety of resources without actually giving them away. The result was the lowering of the natural inhibitions against transactions that must be *begun* by one person's providing personal resources to another. Sophisticated and coordinated systems of aid, gift giving, defense, and trade became possible, bringing immense benefit to the societies that possessed them. With such clearly adaptive consequences for the culture, it is not surprising that the

RECIPROCATION

rule for reciprocation is so deeply implanted in us by the process of socialization we all undergo.

Make no mistake, human societies derive a truly significant competitive advantage from the reciprocity rule and consequently they make sure their members are trained to comply with and believe in it. Each of us has been taught to live up to the rule, and each of us knows about the social sanctions and derision applied to anyone who violates it. The labels we assign to such a person are loaded with negativity—moocher, ingrate, welsher. Because there is general distaste for those who take and make no effort to give in return, we will often go to great lengths to avoid being considered one of their number. It is to those lengths that we will often be taken and, in the process, be "taken" by individuals who stand to gain from our indebtedness.

To understand how the rule for reciprocation can be exploited by one who recognizes it as the source of influence it certainly is, we might closely examine an experiment performed by Professor Dennis Regan of Cornell University.[5] A subject who participated in the study found himself rating, along with another subject, the quality of some paintings as part of an experiment on "art appreciation." The other rater—we can call him Joe—was only posing as a fellow subject and was actually Dr. Regan's assistant. For our purposes, the experiment took place under two different conditions. In some cases, Joe did a small, unsolicited favor for the true subject. During a short rest period, he left the room for a couple of minutes and returned with two bottles of Coca-Cola, one for the subject and one for himself, saying, "I asked him [the experimenter] if I could get myself a Coke, and he said it was okay, so I bought one for you, too." In other cases, Joe did not provide the subject with a favor; he simply returned from the two-minute break empty-handed. In all other respects, however, Joe behaved identically.

Later on, after the paintings had all been rated and the experimenter had momentarily left the room, Joe asked the subject to do *him* a favor. He indicated that he was selling raffle tickets for a new car and that if he sold the most tickets, he would win a fifty-dollar prize. Joe's request was for the subject to buy some raffle tickets at twenty-five cents apiece: "Any would help, the more the better." The major finding of the study concerns the number of tickets subjects purchased from Joe under the two conditions. Without question, Joe was more successful in selling his raffle tickets to the subjects who had received his earlier favor. Apparently feeling that they owed him something, these subjects bought twice as many tickets as the subjects who had not been given the prior favor. Although the Regan study represents a fairly simple demonstration of the workings of the rule for reciprocation, it illustrates several important characteristics of the rule that, upon further consideration, help us to understand how it may be profitably used.

The rule is overpowering

One of the reasons reciprocation can be used so effectively as a device for gaining another's compliance is its power. The rule possesses awesome strength, often producing a "yes" response to a request that, except for an existing feeling of indebtedness, would have surely been refused. Some evidence of how the rule's force can overpower the influence of other factors that normally determine whether a request will be complied with can be seen in a second result of the Regan study. Besides his interest in the impact of the reciprocity rule on compliance, Regan was also interested in how liking for a person affects the tendency to comply with that person's request. To measure how liking toward Joe affected the subjects' decisions to buy his raffle tickets, Regan had them fill out several rating scales indicating how much they liked Joe. He then compared their liking responses with the number of tickets they had purchased from Joe. There was a significant tendency for subjects to buy more raffle tickets from Joe the more they liked him. But this alone is hardly a startling finding. Most of us would have guessed that people are more willing to do a favor for someone they like.

The interesting thing about the Regan experiment, however, is that the relationship between liking and compliance was completely wiped out in the condition under which subjects had been given a Coke by Joe. For those who owed him a favor, it made no difference whether they liked him or not; they felt a sense of

RECIPROCATION

obligation to repay him, and they did. The subjects in that condition who indicated that they disliked Joe bought just as many
of his tickets as did those who indicated that they liked him. The
rule for reciprocity was so strong that it simply overwhelmed the
influence of a factor—liking for the requester—that normally affects the decision to comply.

Think of the implications. People we might ordinarily dislike—unsavory or unwelcome sales operators, disagreeable
acquaintances, representatives of strange or unpopular organizations—can greatly increase the chance that we will do what they
wish merely by providing us with a small favor prior to their
requests. Let's take an example that by now many of us have
encountered. The Hare Krishna Society is an Eastern religious
sect with centuries-old roots traceable to the Indian city of Cal-
cutta. But its spectacular modern-day story occurred in the 1970s
when it experienced a remarkable growth not only in followers
but also in wealth and property. The economic growth was
funded through a variety of activities, the principal and still most
visible of which is the request for donations by society members
from passersby in public places. During the early history of the
group in this country, the solicitation for contributions was attempted in a fashion memorable for anyone who saw it. Groups
of Krishna devotees—often with shaved heads, and wearing ill-
fitting robes, leg wrappings, beads, and bells—would canvass a
city street, chanting and bobbing in unison while begging for
funds.

Although highly effective as a technique for gaining attention, this form of fund raising did not work especially well. The
average American considered the Krishnas weird, to say the
least, and was reluctant to provide money to support them. It
quickly became clear to the society that it had a considerable
public-relations problem. The people being asked for contributions did not like the way the members looked, dressed, or acted.
Had the society been an ordinary commercial organization, the
solution would have been simple—change the things the public
does not like. But the Krishnas are a religious organization; and
the way members look, dress, and act is partially tied to religious
factors. Because, in any denomination, religious factors are typically resistant to change because of worldly considerations, the

INFLUENCE

Krishna leadership was faced with a real dilemma. On the one hand were beliefs, modes of dress and hairstyles that had, religious significance. On the other hand, threatening the organization's financial welfare, were the less-than-positive feelings of the American public toward these things. What's a sect to do?

The Krishnas' resolution was brilliant. They switched to a fund-raising tactic that made it unnecessary for target persons to have positive feelings toward the fund raisers. They began to employ a donation-request procedure that engaged the rule for reciprocation, which, as demonstrated by the Regan study, is strong enough to overcome the factor of dislike for the requester. The new strategy still involves the solicitation of contributions in public places with much pedestrian traffic (airports are a favor-

FIGURE 2–1

THEN AND NOW

In the 1960s and early 1970s (left), the Krishnas solicited in a much more conspicuous way than today (right). Note the flight-bag disguise carried by the modern-day solicitor to help her trap airport visitors like the obviously unhappy man depicted above. (Source: left, UPI; right, Harry Goodman, The Washington Star*)*

ite), but now, before a donation is requested, the target person is given a "gift"—a book (usually the *Bhagavad Gita*), the *Back to Godhead* magazine of the society, or, in the most cost-effective version, a flower. The unsuspecting passerby who suddenly finds a flower pressed into his hands or pinned to his jacket is under no circumstances allowed to give it back, even if he asserts that he does not want it. "No, it is our gift to you," says the solicitor, refusing to accept it. Only after the Krishna member has thus brought the force of the reciprocation rule to bear on the situation is the target asked to provide a contribution to the society. This benefactor-before-beggar strategy has been wildly successful for the Hare Krishna Society, producing large-scale economic gains and funding the ownership of temples, businesses, houses, and property in 108 centers in the United States and overseas.

As an aside, it is instructive that the reciprocation rule has begun to outlive its usefulness for the Krishnas, not because the rule itself is any less potent societally, but because we have found ways to prevent the Krishnas from using it on us. After once falling victim to their tactic, many travelers are now alert to the presence of robed Krishna Society solicitors in airports and train stations, adjusting their paths to avoid an encounter and preparing beforehand to ward off a solicitor's "gift." Although the Society has tried to counter this increased vigilance by instructing members to be dressed and groomed in modern styles to avoid immediate recognition when soliciting (some actually carry flight bags or suitcases, Figure 2-1), even disguise has not worked especially well for the Krishnas. Too many individuals now know better than to accept unrequested offerings in public places like airports. Furthermore, airport administrators have initiated a number of procedures designed to forewarn us of the Krishnas' true identity and intent. Thus, it is now common airport practice to restrict the Krishnas' soliciting activity to certain areas of the airport and to announce via signs and the public address system that the Krishnas are soliciting there. It is a testament to the societal value of reciprocation that we have chosen to fight the Krishnas mostly by seeking to avoid rather than to withstand the force of their gift giving. The reciprocity rule that empowers their tactic is too strong—and socially beneficial—for us to want to violate it.

INFLUENCE

FIGURE 2–2

KRISS KRISHNA

Taking disguise to its limits but still employing the reciprocity rule as an ally, these Krishna members were arrested for soliciting without a license when they pressured Christmas shoppers for donations after first pushing candy canes on them. (Source: Wide World Photos)

RECIPROCATION

Politics is another arena in which the power of the reciprocity rule shows itself. Reciprocation tactics appear at every level:

□ At the top, elected officials engage in "logrolling" and the exchange of favors that makes politics the place of strange bedfellows, indeed. The out-of-character vote of one of our elected representatives on a bill or measure can often be understood as a favor returned to the bill's sponsor. Political analysts were amazed at Lyndon Johnson's ability to get so many of his programs through Congress during his early administration. Even congressmembers who were thought to be strongly opposed to the proposals were voting for them. Close examination by political scientists has found the cause to be not so much Johnson's political savvy as the large score of favors he had been able to provide to other legislators during his many years of power in the House and Senate. As President, he was able to produce a truly remarkable amount of legislation in a short time by calling in those favors. It is interesting that this same process may account for the problems Jimmy Carter had in getting his programs through Congress during his early administration, despite heavy Democratic majorities in both House and Senate. Carter came to the presidency from outside the Capitol Hill establishment. He campaigned on his outside-Washington identity, saying that he was indebted to no one there. Much of his legislative difficulty upon arriving may be traced to the fact that no one there was indebted to *him*.

□ At another level, we can see the recognized strength of the reciprocity rule in the desire of corporations and individuals to provide judicial and legislative officials with gifts and favors, and in the series of legal restrictions against such gifts and favors. Even with legitimate political contributions, the stockpiling of obligations often underlies the stated purpose of supporting a favorite candidate. One look at the lists of companies and organizations that contribute to the campaigns of *both* major candidates in important elections gives evidence of such motives.

□ At the grass-roots level, local political organizations have learned that a principal way to keep their candidates in office is to make sure they provide a wide range of little favors to the voters. The "ward heelers" of many cities still operate effectively in this fashion. The capacity of a small personal favor to produce or even change a vote is documented in the report of a student in one of my compliance seminars.

While campaigning for presidential hopeful George McGovern, my GI veteran's check became delayed, and I was unable to obtain it. Since I was then a staunch supporter of the Democratic party, I was reluctant to contact my local representative, the incumbent Republican senator for Arizona. When I did, he secured my check for me and with it, my vote in the subsequent election. I returned the favor.

Of course, the power of reciprocity can be found in the merchandising field as well. Although the number of possible examples is large, let's examine a pair of familiar ones deriving from the "free sample." As a marketing technique, the free sample has a long and effective history. In most instances, a small amount of the relevant product is provided to potential customers for the stated purpose of allowing them to try it to see if they like it. And certainly this is a legitimate desire of the manufacturer—to expose the public to the qualities of the product. The beauty of the free sample, however, is that it is also a gift and, as such, can engage the reciprocity rule. In true jujitsu fashion, the promoter who gives free samples can release the natural indebting force inherent in a gift while innocently appearing to have only the intention to inform. A favorite place for free samples is the supermarket, where customers are frequently provided with small cubes of a certain variety of cheese or meat to try. Many people find it difficult to accept a sample from the always-smiling attendant, return only the toothpick, and walk away. Instead, they buy some of the product, even if they might not have liked it especially well. A highly effective variation on this marketing procedure is illustrated in the case, cited by Vance Packard in *The Hidden Persuaders,* of the Indiana supermarket operator who sold an astounding one thousand pounds of cheese in a few hours one day by putting out the cheese and inviting customers to cut off slivers for themselves as free samples.

A different version of the free-sample tactic is used by the Amway Corporation, a rapid-growth company that manufactures and distributes household and personal-care products in a vast national network of door-to-door neighborhood sales. The company, which has grown from a basement-run operation a few years ago to a one and a half billion-dollar yearly sales business, makes use of the free sample in a device called the BUG. The BUG consists of a collection of Amway products—bottles of furniture polish, detergent, or shampoo, spray containers of deodorizers, insect killers, or window cleaners—carried to the customer's home in a specially designed tray or just a polyethylene bag. The confidential Amway Career Manual then instructs the salesperson to leave the BUG with the customer "for 24, 48, or 72 hours, at no cost or obligation to her. Just tell her you would like her to try the products. . . . That's an offer no one can refuse." At the end of the trial period, the Amway representative returns and picks up orders for those of the products the customer wishes to purchase. Since few customers use up the entire contents of even one of the product containers in such a short time, the salesperson may then take the remaining product portions in the BUG to the next potential customer down the line or across the street and start the process again. Many Amway representatives have several BUGS circulating in their districts at one time.

Of course, by now you and I know that the customer who has accepted and used the BUG products has been trapped into facing the influence of the reciprocity rule. Many such customers yield to a sense of obligation to order those of the salesperson's products that they have tried and thereby partially consumed. And, of course, by now the Amway Corporation knows that to be the case. Even in a company with as excellent a growth record as Amway, the BUG device has created a big stir. Reports by state distributors to the parent company record a remarkable effect:

Unbelievable! We've never seen such excitement. Product is moving at an unbelievable rate, and we've only just begun. . . . [Local] distributors took the BUGS, and we've had an unbelievable increase in sales [from Illinois distributor]. The most fantastic retail idea we've ever had! . . . On the average, customers purchased about half the total amount of the BUG when it is picked up. . . . In one word, tremendous! We've never seen a response within our entire organization like this [from Massachusetts distributor].

The Amway distributors appear to be bewildered—happily so, but nonetheless bewildered—by the startling power of the BUG. Of course, by now you and I should not be.

The reciprocity rule governs many situations of a purely interpersonal nature where neither money nor commercial exchange is at issue. Perhaps my favorite illustration of the enormous force available from the reciprocation weapon of influence comes from such a situation. The European scientist, Eibel-Eibesfeldt, provides the account of a German soldier during World War I whose job was to capture enemy soldiers for interrogation. Because of the nature of the trench warfare at that time, it was extremely difficult for armies to cross the no-man's-land between opposing front lines; but it was not so difficult for a single soldier to crawl across and slip into an enemy trench position. The armies of the Great War had experts who regularly did so to capture an enemy soldier, who would then be brought back for questioning. The German expert of our account had often successfully completed such missions in the past and was sent on another. Once again, he skillfully negotiated the area between fronts and surprised a lone enemy soldier in his trench. The unsuspecting soldier, who had been eating at the time, was easily disarmed. The frightened captive with only a piece of bread in his hand then performed what may have been the most important act of his life. He gave his enemy some of the bread. So affected was the German by this gift that he could not complete his mission. He turned from his benefactor and recrossed the no-man's-land empty-handed to face the wrath of his superiors.

The rule enforces uninvited debts

Earlier we suggested that the power of the reciprocity rule is such that by first doing us a favor, strange, disliked, or unwelcome others can enhance the chance that we will comply with one of their requests. However, there is another aspect of the rule, besides its power, that allows this phenomenon to occur. Another person can trigger a feeling of indebtedness by doing us an uninvited favor. Recall that the rule only states that we should provide to others the kind of actions they have provided us; it does not require us to have asked for what we have received in order to feel obligated to repay. This is not to say that we might not feel a stronger sense of obligation to return a favor we have requested, only that such a request is not necessary to produce our indebtedness.

If we reflect for a moment about the social purpose of the reciprocity rule, we can see why this should be so. The rule was established to promote the development of reciprocal relationships between individuals so that one person could *initiate* such a relationship without the fear of loss. If the rule is to serve that purpose, then, an uninvited first favor must have the ability to create an obligation. Recall, also, that reciprocal relationships confer an extraordinary advantage upon cultures that foster them and that, consequently, there will be strong pressures to ensure that the rule does serve its purpose. Little wonder, then, that the influential French anthropologist Marcel Mauss, in describing the social pressures surrounding the gift-giving process in human culture, can state, "There is an obligation to give, an obligation to receive, and an obligation to repay."[6]

Although the obligation to repay constitutes the essence of the reciprocity rule, it is the obligation to receive that makes the rule so easy to exploit. The obligation to receive reduces our ability to choose whom we wish to be indebted to and puts that power in the hands of others. Let's reexamine a pair of earlier examples to get a sense of how the process works. First, let's return to the Regan study, where we find that the favor causing subjects to double the number of raffle tickets purchased from

Joe was not one they had requested. Joe had voluntarily left the room and returned with one Coke for himself and one for the subject. There was not a single subject who refused the Coke. It is easy to see why it would have been awkward to turn down Joe's favor: Joe had already spent his money; a soft drink was an appropriate favor in the situation, especially since Joe had one himself; it would have been considered impolite to reject Joe's thoughtful action. Nevertheless, receipt of that Coke produced an indebtedness that manifested itself clearly when Joe announced his desire to sell some raffle tickets. Notice the important asymmetry here—all the genuinely free choices were Joe's. He chose the form of the initial favor, and he chose the form of the return favor. Of course, one could say that the subject had the choice of saying no to both of Joe's offers. But those would have been tough choices. To have said no at either point would have required the subject to go against the natural cultural forces favoring reciprocation arrangements that Jujitsu Joe had aligned himself with.

The extent to which even an unwanted favor, once received, can produce indebtedness is aptly illustrated in the soliciting technique of the Hare Krishna Society. During systematic observation of the airport soliciting strategy of the Krishnas, I have recorded a variety of responses from target persons. One of the most regular occurs as follows. An airport visitor—a businessman, let's say—is hurriedly walking along through a densely peopled area. The Krishna solicitor steps in front of him and hands him a flower. The man, reacting with surprise, takes it.[7] Almost immediately, he tries to give it back, saying that he does not want the flower. The Krishna member responds that it is a gift from the Krishna Society and that it is the man's to keep . . . however, a donation to further the Society's good works would be appreciated. Again the target protests, "I don't want this flower. Here, take it." And again the solicitor refuses, "It's our gift to you, sir." There is visible conflict on the businessman's face. Should he keep the flower and walk away without giving anything in return, or should he yield to the pressure of the deeply ingrained reciprocity rule and provide a contribution? By now, the conflict has spread from his face to his posture. He leans away from his benefactor, seemingly about to break free, only to be drawn back again by the pull of the rule. Once more his body tilts away, but it's no use; he cannot disengage. With a nod of resignation, he fishes in his pocket and comes up with a dollar or two that is graciously accepted. Now he can walk away freely, and he does, "gift" in hand, until he encounters a waste container—where he throws the flower.

Purely by accident, I happened to witness a scene that demonstrates that the Krishnas know very well how frequently their gifts are unwanted by the people who receive them. While spending a day observing a soliciting Krishna group at Chicago's O'Hare International Airport a few years ago, I noticed that one of the group members would frequently leave the central area and return with more flowers to resupply her companions. As it happened, I had decided to take a break just as she was leaving on one of her supply missions. Having nowhere to go, I followed. Her journey turned out to be a garbage route. She went from trash can to trash can beyond the immediate area to retrieve all the flowers that had been discarded by Krishna targets. She then returned with the cache of recovered flowers (some that had been recycled who knows how many times) and distributed them to be profitably cycled through the reciprocation process once more. The thing that really impressed me about all this was that most of the discarded flowers had brought donations from the people who had cast them away. The nature of the reciprocity rule is such that a gift so unwanted that it was jettisoned at the first opportunity had nonetheless been effective and exploitable.

The ability of uninvited gifts to produce feelings of obligation is recognized by a variety of organizations besides the Krishnas. How many times have each of us received small gifts through the mail—personalized address labels, greeting cards, key rings—from charity agencies that ask for funds in an accompanying note? I have received five in just the past year, two from disabled veterans' groups and the others from missionary schools or hospitals. In each case, there was a common thread in the accompanying message. The goods that were enclosed were to be considered a gift from the organization; and any money I wished to send should not be regarded as payment but rather as a return offering. As the letter from one of the missionary programs stated, the packet of greeting cards I had been sent was not to be directly paid for, but was designed "to encourage your kindness." If we look past the obvious tax advantage, we can see a reason why it would be beneficial for the organization to have the cards viewed as a gift instead of merchandise: There is a strong cultural pressure to reciprocate a gift, even an unwanted one; but there is no such pressure to purchase an unwanted commercial product.

The rule can trigger unfair exchanges

There is yet one other feature of the reciprocity rule that allows it to be exploited for profit. Paradoxically, the rule developed to promote equal exchanges between partners, yet it can be used to bring about decidedly unequal results. The rule demands that one sort of action be reciprocated with a similar sort of action. A favor is to be met with another favor; it is not to be met with neglect, and certainly not with attack. But within the similar-action boundaries, considerable flexibility is allowed. A small initial favor can produce a sense of obligation to agree to a substantially larger return favor. Since, as we have already seen, the rule allows one person to choose the nature of the indebting-first favor *and* the nature of the debt-cancelling return favor, we could easily be manipulated into an unfair exchange by those who might wish to exploit the rule.

Once again, we can turn to the Regan experiment for evidence. Remember in that study that Joe gave one group of subjects a bottle of Coca-Cola as an initiating gift and later asked all subjects to buy some of his raffle tickets at twenty-five cents apiece. What I have so far neglected to mention is that the study was done in the late 1960s, when the price of a Coke was a dime. The average subject who had been given a ten-cent drink bought two of Joe's raffle tickets, although some bought as many as seven. Even if we look just at the average subject, though, we can tell that Joe made quite a deal. A 500 percent return on investment is respectable indeed!

But in Joe's case, even a 500 percent return amounted to only fifty cents. Can the reciprocity rule produce meaningfully large differences in the sizes of the exchanged favors? Under the right circumstances, it certainly can. Take, for instance, the account of a student of mine concerning a day she remembers ruefully:

> About one year ago, I couldn't start my car. As I was sitting there, a guy in the parking lot came over and eventually jump started the car. I said thanks, and he said you're welcome; as he was leaving, I said that if he ever needed a favor to stop by. About a month later, the guy knocked on my door and asked to borrow my car for two hours as his was in the shop. I felt somewhat obligated but uncertain, since the car was pretty new and he looked very young. Later, I found out that he was underage and had no insurance. Anyway, I lent him the car. He totaled it.

How could it happen that an intelligent young woman would agree to turn over her new car to a virtual stranger (and a youngster at that) because he had done her a small favor a month earlier? Or, more generally, why should it be that small first favors often stimulate larger return favors? One important reason concerns the clearly unpleasant character of the feeling of indebtedness. Most of us find it highly disagreeable to be in a state of obligation. It weighs heavily on us and demands to be removed. It is not difficult to trace the source of this feeling. Because reciprocal arrangements are so vital in human social systems, we have been conditioned to be uncomfortable when beholden. If we were to ignore breezily the need to return another's initial favor, we would stop one reciprocal sequence dead and would make it less likely that our benefactor would do such favors in the future. Neither event is in the best interests of society. Consequently, we are trained from childhood to chafe, emotionally, under the saddle of obligation. For this reason alone, then, we may be willing to agree to perform a larger favor than we received, merely to relieve ourselves of the psychological burden of debt.

But there is another reason as well. A person who violates the reciprocity rule by accepting without attempting to return the good acts of others is actively disliked by the social group. The exception, of course, is when the person is prevented from repayment by reasons of circumstance or ability. For the most part, however, there is a genuine distaste for individuals who fail to conform to the dictates of the reciprocity rule.[8] Moocher and welsher are unsavory labels to be scrupulously shunned. So undesirable are they that we will sometimes agree to an unequal exchange in order to dodge them.

In combination, the reality of internal discomfort and the possibility of external shame can produce a heavy psychological cost. When seen in the light of this cost, it is not so puzzling that we will often give back more than we have received in the name of reciprocity. Neither is it so odd that, as was shown in an experiment conducted at the University of Pittsburgh, people will often avoid asking for a needed favor if they will not be in a position to repay it.[9] The psychological cost may simply outweigh the material loss. An illustration of how frustratingly bothersome an unrepaid favor can be is given in the report of another student of mine who seems to understand quite well the workings of the reciprocity rule:

> I met a fellow through a mutual friend and spent half an hour talking things over with him. When I left the state a week later, I had completely forgotten the incident. Then, several months later, I received a call from this guy, saying he was in town and could we get together? I invited him over and learned he was hitching across country with a friend. Well, I put them up for a few days and showed them around town, introducing them to people and having a good time. Ever since he's been falling over backward trying to reciprocate, but I haven't been able to take him up on any offers. I don't doubt that he will feel a need to reciprocate for years if he doesn't get the chance. So I'm content to wait until the right offer comes along.

※

RECIPROCAL CONCESSIONS

There is a second way to employ the reciprocity rule to get someone to comply with a request. It is more subtle than the direct route of providing that person with a favor and then asking for one in return; yet in some ways it is more devastatingly effective than the straightforward approach. A personal experience I had a few years ago gave me firsthand evidence of just how well this compliance technique works.

I was walking down the street when I was approached by an eleven- or twelve-year-old boy. He introduced himself and said that he was selling tickets to the annual Boy Scouts circus to be held on the upcoming Saturday night. He asked if I wished to buy any at five dollars apiece. Since one of the last places I wanted to spend Saturday evening was with the Boy Scouts, I declined. "Well," he said, "if you don't want to buy any tickets, how about buying some of our big chocolate bars? They're only a dollar each." I bought a couple and, right away, realized that something noteworthy had happened. I knew that to be the case because: (a) I do not like chocolate bars; (b) I do like dollars; (c) I was standing there with two of his chocolate bars; and (d) he was walking away with two of my dollars.

To try to understand precisely what had happened, I went to my office and called a meeting of my research assistants. In discussing the situation, we began to see how the reciprocity rule was implicated in my compliance with the request to buy the candy bars. The general rule says that a person who acts in a certain way toward us is entitled to a similar return action. We have already seen that one consequence of the rule is an obligation to repay favors we have received. Another consequence of the rule, however, is an obligation to make a concession to someone who has made a concession to us. As my research group thought about it, we realized that was exactly the position the Boy Scout had put me in. His request that I purchase some one-dollar chocolate bars had been put in the form of a concession on his part; it was presented as a retreat from his request that I buy some five-dollar tickets. If I were to live up to the dictates of the reciprocation rule, there had to be a concession on my part. As we have seen, there was such a concession: I changed from noncompliant to compliant when he changed from a larger to a smaller request, even though I was not really interested in *either* of the things he offered.

It was a classic example of how a weapon of automatic influence can infuse a compliance request with its power. I had been moved to buy something not because of any favorable feelings toward the item but because the purchase request had been presented in a way that drew force from the reciprocity rule. It had not mattered that I do not like chocolate bars; the Boy Scout had made a concession to me, *click,* and, *whirr,* I responded with a concession of my own. Of course, the tendency to reciprocate a concession is not so strong that it will invariably work in all instances on all people; none of the weapons of influence considered in this book is *that* strong. However, in my exchange with the Boy Scout, the tendency had been sufficiently potent to leave me in mystified possession of a pair of unwanted and overpriced candy bars.

Why should I feel a strain to reciprocate a concession? The answer rests once again in the benefit of such a tendency to the society. It is in the interests of any human group to have its members working together toward the achievement of common goals. However, in many social interactions the participants begin with requirements and demands that are unacceptable to one another. Thus the society must arrange to have these initial, incompatible desires set aside for the sake of socially beneficial cooperation. This is accomplished through procedures that promote compromise. Mutual concession is one important such procedure.

The reciprocation rule brings about mutual concession in two ways. The first is obvious. It pressures the recipient of an already-made concession to respond in kind. The second, while not so obvious, is pivotally important. Just as in the case of favors, gifts, or aid, the obligation to reciprocate a concession encourages the creation of socially desirable arrangements by ensuring that anyone seeking to *start* such an arrangement will not be exploited. After all, if there were no social obligation to reciprocate a concession, who would want to make the first sacrifice? To do so would be to risk giving up something and getting nothing back. However, with the rule in effect, we can feel safe making the first sacrifice to our partner, who is obligated to offer a return sacrifice.

Because the rule for reciprocation governs the compromise process, it is possible to use an initial concession as part of a highly effective compliance technique. The technique is a simple one that we can call the rejection-then-retreat technique. Suppose you want me to agree to a certain request. One way to increase your chances would be first to make a larger request of me, one that I will most likely turn down. Then, after I have refused, you would make the smaller request that you were really interested in all along. Provided that you have structured your requests skillfully, I should view your second request as a concession to me and should feel inclined to respond with a concession of my own, the only one I would have immediately open to me—compliance with your second request.

Was that how the Boy Scout got me to buy his candy bars? Was his retreat from the five-dollar request to the one-dollar request an artificial one that was intentionally designed to sell candy bars? As one who has still refused to discard even his first Scout merit badge, I genuinely hope not. But whether or not the large-request-then-smaller-request sequence was planned, its effect was the same. It worked. And because it works, the rejection-then-retreat technique can and will be used *purposely* by certain people to get their way. First let's examine how this tactic can be used as a reliable compliance device. Later we will see how it is already being used. Finally we can turn to a pair of little-known features of the technique that make it one of the most pervasively influential compliance tactics available.

Remember that after my encounter with the Boy Scout, I called my research assistants together to try to understand what had happened to me and, as it turned out, to eat the evidence. Actually, we did more than that. We designed an experiment to test the effectiveness of the procedure of moving to a desired request after a larger preliminary request had been refused. We had two primary purposes in conducting the experiment. First, we wanted to see whether this procedure worked on people besides myself. That is, it certainly seemed that the tactic had been effective on me earlier in the day; but then, I have a history of falling for compliance tricks of all sorts. So the question remained, "Does the rejection-then-retreat technique work on enough people to make it a useful procedure for gaining compliance?" If so, it would definitely be something to be aware of in the future.

Our second reason for doing the study was to determine how powerful a compliance device the technique was. Could it bring about compliance with a genuinely sizable request? In other words, did the *smaller* request to which the requester retreated have to be a *small* request? If our thinking about what caused the technique to be effective was correct, the second request did not actually have to be small; it only had to be smaller than the initial one. It was our suspicion that the critical thing about a requester's retreat from a larger to a smaller favor was its appearance as a concession. So the second request could be an objectively large one—as long as it was smaller than the first request—and the technique would still work.

After a bit of thought, we decided to try the technique on a request that we felt few people would agree to perform. Posing as representatives of the "County Youth Counseling Program," we approached college students walking on campus and asked if they would be willing to chaperon a group of juvenile delinquents on a day trip to the zoo. The idea of being responsible for a group of juvenile delinquents of unspecified age for hours in a public place without pay was hardly an inviting one for these students. As we expected, the great majority (83 percent) refused. Yet we obtained very different results from a similar sample of college students who were asked the very same question with one difference. Before we invited them to serve as unpaid chaperons on the zoo trip, we asked them for an even larger favor—to spend two hours per week as a counselor to a juvenile delinquent for a minimum of two years. It was only after they refused this extreme request, as all did, that we made the smaller, zoo-trip request. By presenting the zoo trip as a retreat from our initial request, our success rate increased dramatically. Three times as many of the students approached in this manner volunteered to serve as zoo chaperons.[10]

Be assured that any strategy able to triple the percentage of compliance with a substantial request (from 17 percent to 50 percent in our experiment) will be frequently employed in a variety of natural settings. Labor negotiators, for instance, often use the tactic of beginning with extreme demands that they do not actually expect to win but from which they can retreat in a series of seeming concessions designed to draw real concessions from the opposing side. It would appear, then, that the procedure would be more effective the larger the initial request, since there would be more room available for illusory concessions. This is true only up to a point, however. Research conducted at Bar-Ilan University in Israel on the rejection-then-retreat technique shows that if the first set of demands is so extreme as to be seen as unreasonable, the tactic backfires.[11] In such cases, the party who has made the extreme first request is not seen to be bargaining in good faith. Any subsequent retreat from that wholly unrealistic initial position is not viewed as a genuine concession and thus is not reciprocated. The truly gifted negotiator, then, is one whose initial position is exaggerated enough to allow for a series of reciprocal concessions that will yield a desirable final offer from the opponent, yet is not so outlandish as to be seen as illegitimate from the start.

It seems that certain of the most successful television producers, such as Grant Tinker and Gary Marshall, are masters of this art in their negotiations with network censors. In a candid interview with *TV Guide* writer Dick Russell, both admitted to "deliberately inserting lines into scripts that a censor's sure to ax" so that they could then retreat to the lines they really wanted included. Marshall appears especially active in this regard. Consider, for example, the following quotes from Russell's article:

> But Marshall . . . not only admits his tricks . . . he seems to revel in them. On one episode of his [then] top-rated *Laverne and Shirley* series, for example, he says, "We had a situation where Squiggy's in a rush to get out of his apartment and meet some girls upstairs. He says: 'Will you hurry up before I

lose my lust?' But in the script we put something even stronger, knowing the censors would cut it. They did; so we asked innocently, well, how about 'lose my lust'? 'That's good,' they said. Sometimes you gotta go at 'em backward."

On the *Happy Days* series, the biggest censorship fight was over the word "virgin." That time, says Marshall, "I knew we'd have trouble, so we put the word in seven times, hoping they'd cut six and keep one. It worked. We used the same pattern again with the word 'pregnant.'"[12]

I witnessed another form of the rejection-then-retreat technique in my investigations of door-to-door sales operations. These organizations used a less engineered, more opportunistic version of the tactic. Of course, the most important goal for a door-to-door salesperson is to make the sale. However, the training programs of each of the companies I investigated emphasized that a second important goal was to obtain from prospects the names of referrals—friends, relatives, or neighbors on whom we could call. For a variety of reasons we will discuss in Chapter 5, the percentage of successful door-to-door sales increases impressively when the sales operator is able to mention the name of a familiar person who "recommended" the sales visit.

Never as a sales trainee was I taught to get the sales pitch refused so that I could then retreat to a request for referrals. In several such programs, though, I was trained to take advantage of the opportunity to secure referrals offered by a customer's purchase refusal: "Well, if it is your feeling that a fine set of encyclopedias is not right for you at this time, perhaps you could help me by giving me the names of some others who might wish to take advantage of our company's great offer. What would be the names of some of these people you know?" Many individuals who would not otherwise subject their friends to a high-pressure sales presentation do agree to supply referrals when the request is presented as a concession from a purchase request they have just refused.

We have already discussed one reason for the success of the rejection-then-retreat technique—its incorporation of the reciprocity rule. This larger-then-smaller-request strategy is effective for a pair of other reasons as well. The first concerns the perceptual contrast principle we encountered in Chapter 1. That principle accounted for, among other things, the tendency of a man to spend more money on a sweater following his purchase of a suit than before: After being exposed to the price of the large item, the price of the less expensive one *appears* smaller by comparison. In the same way, the larger-then-smaller-request procedure makes use of the contrast principle by making the smaller request look even smaller by comparison with the larger one. If I want you to lend me five dollars, I can make it seem like a smaller request by first asking you to lend me ten dollars. One of the beauties of this tactic is that by first requesting ten dollars and then retreating to five dollars, I will have simultaneously engaged the force of the reciprocity rule and the contrast principle. Not only will my five-dollar request be viewed as a concession to be reciprocated, it will also look to you like a smaller request than if I had just asked for it straightaway.

In combination, the influences of reciprocity and perceptual contrast can present a fearsomely powerful force. Embodied in the rejection-then-retreat sequence, their conjoined energies are capable of genuinely astonishing effects. It is my feeling that they provide the only really plausible explanation of one of the most baffling political actions of our time: the decision to break into the Watergate offices of the Democratic National Committee that led to the ruin of Richard Nixon's presidency. One of the participants in that decision, Jeb Stuart Magruder, upon first hearing that the Watergate burglars had been caught, responded with appropriate bewilderment, "How could we have been so stupid?" Indeed, how?

To understand how enormously ill conceived an idea it was for the Nixon administration to undertake the break-in, it is necessary to review a few facts:

□ The idea was that of G. Gordon Liddy, who was in charge of intelligence-gathering operations for the Committee to Re-elect the President (CRP). Liddy had

INFLUENCE

gained a reputation among administration higher-ups as something of a flake, and there were questions about his stability and judgment.

◻ Liddy's proposal was extremely costly, requiring a budget of $250,000 in untraceable cash.

◻ In late March, when the proposal was approved in a meeting of the CRP director, John Mitchell, and his assistants Magruder and Frederick LaRue, the outlook for a Nixon victory in the November election could not have been brighter. Edmund Muskie, the only announced candidate the early polls had given a chance of unseating the President, had done poorly in the primaries. It looked very much as though the most defeatable candidate, George McGovern, would win his party's nomination. A Republican victory seemed assured.

◻ The break-in plan itself was a highly risky operation requiring the participation and discretion of ten men.

◻ The Democratic National Committee and its chairman, Lawrence O'Brien, whose Watergate office was to be burglarized and bugged, had no information damaging enough to defeat the encumbent President. Nor were they likely to get any, unless the administration did something *very, very* foolish.

Despite the obvious counsel of the above reasons, the expensive, chancy, pointless, and potentially calamitous proposal of a man whose judgment was known to be questionable was approved. How could it be that intelligent men of the attainment of Mitchell and Magruder would do something so *very, very* foolish? Perhaps the answer lies in a little-discussed fact: The $250,000 plan they approved was not Liddy's first proposal. In fact, it represented a significant concession on his part from two earlier proposals, of immense proportions. The first of these plans, made two months earlier in a meeting with Mitchell, Magruder, and John Dean, described a $1 million program that included (in addition to the bugging of the Watergate) a specially equipped communications "chase plane," break-ins, kidnaping and mugging squads, and a yacht featuring "high-class call girls" to blackmail Democratic politicians. A second Liddy plan, presented a week later to the same group of Mitchell, Magruder, and Dean, eliminated some of the program and reduced the cost to $500,000. It was only after these initial proposals had been rejected by Mitchell that Liddy submitted his "bare-bones" $250,000 plan, in this instance to Mitchell, Magruder, and Frederick LaRue. This time the plan, still stupid but less so than the previous ones, was approved.

Could it be that I, a longtime patsy, and John Mitchell, a hardened and canny politician, might both have been so easily maneuvered into bad deals by the same compliance tactic—I by a Boy Scout selling candy, and he by a man selling political disaster?

If we examine the testimony of Jeb Magruder, considered by most Watergate investigators to provide the most faithful account of the crucial meeting at which Liddy's plan was finally accepted, there are some instructive clues. First, Magruder reports that "no one was particularly overwhelmed with the project"; but "after starting at the grandiose sum of $1 million, we thought that probably $250,000 would be an acceptable figure. . . . We were reluctant to send him away with nothing." Mitchell, caught up in the "feeling that we should leave Liddy a little something . . . signed off on it in the sense of saying, 'Okay, let's give him a quarter of a million dollars and let's see what he can come up with.'"

In the context of Liddy's initial extreme requests, it seems that "a quarter of a million dollars" had come to be "a little something" to be left as a return concession. With the clarity afforded by two years' hindsight, Magruder has recalled Liddy's approach in as succinct an illustration of the rejection-then-retreat technique as I have ever heard. "If he had come to us at the outset and said, 'I have a plan to burglarize and wiretap Larry O'Brien's office,' we might have rejected the idea out of hand. Instead he came to us with his elaborate call-girl/kidnaping/mugging/sabotage/wiretapping scheme. . . . He had asked for the whole loaf when he was quite content to settle for half or even a quarter."[13]

It is also instructive that, although he finally deferred to his

FIGURE 2–3

G. GORDON THE MENACE?

Do similar styles lead to similarly satisfied smiles? So it appears, so it appears. (Dennis the Menace used by permission of Hank Ketcham and Field Enterprises, Inc.; Photo: UPI)

boss's decision, only one member of the group, Frederick LaRue, expressed any direct opposition to the proposal. Saying with obvious common sense, "I don't think it's worth the risk," he must have wondered why his colleagues, Mitchell and Magruder, did not share his perspective. Of course, there could be many differences between LaRue and the other two men that may have accounted for their differing opinions regarding the advisability of Liddy's plan. But one stands out: Of the three, only LaRue had not been present at the prior two meetings, where Liddy had outlined his much more ambitious programs. Perhaps, then, only LaRue was able to see the third proposal for the clunker that it was and to react to it objectively, uninfluenced by the reciprocity and perceptual contrast forces acting upon the others.

A bit earlier we said that the rejection-then-retreat technique had, in addition to the reciprocity rule, a pair of other factors working in its favor. We have already discussed the first of those factors, the perceptual contrast principle. The additional advantage of the technique is not really a psychological principle, as in the case of the other two factors, it is more of a purely structural feature of the request sequence. Let's once again say that I wish to borrow five dollars from you. By beginning with a ten-dollar request, I really can't lose. If you agree to it, I will have gotten twice the amount from you I would have settled for. If, on the other hand, you turn down my initial request, I can retreat to the five-dollar favor that I desired from the outset and, through the action of the reciprocity and contrast principles, greatly enhance my likelihood of success. Either way, I benefit; it's a case of heads I win, tails you lose.

The clearest utilization of this aspect of the large-then-smaller-request sequence occurs in the retail store sales practice of "talking the top of the line." Here the prospect is invariably shown the deluxe model first. If the customer buys, there is frosting on the store's cake. However, if the customer declines, the salesperson effectively counteroffers with a more reasonably priced model. Some proof of the effectiveness of this procedure comes from a report in *Sales Management* magazine, reprinted without comment in *Consumer Reports:*

If you were a billiard-table dealer, which would you advertise—the $329 model or the $3,000 model? The chances are you would promote the low-priced item and hope to trade the customer up when he comes to buy. But G. Warren Kelley, new business promotion manager at Brunswick, says you could be wrong. . . . To prove his point, Kelley has actual sales figures from a representative store. . . . During the first week, customers . . . were shown the low end of the line . . . and then encouraged to consider more expensive models—the traditional trading-up approach. . . . The average table sale that week was $550. . . . However, during the second week, customers . . . were led instantly to a $3,000 table, regardless of what they wanted to see . . . and then allowed to shop the rest of the line, in declining order of price and quality. The result of selling down was an average sale of over $1,000.[14]

Given the remarkable effectiveness of the rejection-then-retreat technique, one might think that there could be a substantial disadvantage as well. The victims of the strategy might resent having been cornered into compliance. The resentment could show itself in a couple of ways. First, the victim might decide not to live up to the verbal agreement made with the requester. Second, the victim might come to distrust the manipulative requester, deciding never to deal with him again. If either or both of these events occurred with any frequency, a requester would want to give serious second thought to the use of the rejection-then-retreat procedure. Research indicates, however, that these victim reactions do not occur with increased frequency when the rejection-then-retreat technique is used. Somewhat astonishingly, it appears that they actually occur *less* frequently! Before trying to understand why this should be as it is, let's first look at the evidence.

A study published in Canada throws light on the question of whether a victim of the rejection-then-retreat tactic will follow through with the agreement to perform the requester's second favor. In addition to recording whether target persons said yes or no to the desired request (to work for two unpaid hours one day in a community mental-health agency), this experiment also recorded whether they showed up to perform their duties as promised. As usual, the procedure of starting with a larger request (to volunteer for two hours of work per week in the agency for at least two years) produced more verbal agreement to the smaller, retreat request (76 percent) than did the procedure of asking for the smaller request alone (29 percent). The important result, though, concerned the show-up rate *of those who volunteered;* and, again, the rejection-then-retreat procedure was the more effective one (85 percent vs. 50 percent).[15]

A different experiment examined whether the rejection-then-retreat sequence caused victims to feel so manipulated that they would refuse any further requests. In this study, the targets were college students who were each asked to give a pint of blood as part of the annual campus blood drive. One group of targets was first asked to give a pint of blood every six weeks for a minimum of three years. The other targets were asked only to give the single pint of blood. Those of both groups who agreed to give a pint of blood and who later appeared at the blood center were then asked if they would be willing to give their phone numbers so they could be called upon to donate again in the future. Nearly all the students who were about to give a pint of blood as a result of the rejection-then-retreat technique agreed to donate again later (84 percent), while less than half of the other students who appeared at the blood center did so (43 percent). Even for future favors, the rejection-then-retreat strategy proved superior.[16]

Strangely enough, then, it seems that the rejection-then-retreat tactic not only spurs people to agree to a desired request but actually to carry out the request and, finally, to volunteer to perform further requests. What could there be about the technique that makes people who have been duped into compliance so bewilderingly likely to continue to comply? For an answer, we might look at the requester's act of concession, which is the heart of the procedure. We have already seen that as long as it is not viewed to be a transparent trick, the concession will likely stimulate a return concession. But what we have not yet examined is a little-known pair of positive by-products of the act of concession: feelings of greater responsibility for and satisfaction with the arrangement. It is this set of sweet side effects that enables the technique to move its victims to fulfill their agreements and to engage in further such agreements.

The desirable side effects of making a concession during an interaction with another person are nicely shown in studies of the way people bargain with each other. One experiment, conducted by social psychologists at UCLA, offers an especially apt demonstration.[17] A subject in that study faced a "negotiation opponent" and was told to bargain with the opponent concerning how to divide between themselves a certain amount of money provided by the experimenters. The subject was also informed that if no mutual agreement could be reached after a certain period of bargaining, no one would get any money. Unknown to the subjects, the opponent was really an experimental assistant who had been previously instructed to bargain with the subject in one of three ways. With some of the subjects, the opponent made an extreme first demand, assigning virtually all of the money to himself, and stubbornly persisted in that demand throughout the negotiations. With another group of subjects, the opponent began with a demand that was moderately favorable to himself; he, too, steadfastly refused to move from that position during the negotiations. With a third group, the opponent began with the extreme demand and then gradually retreated to the more moderate one during the course of the bargaining.

There were three important findings in this experiment that help us to understand why the rejection-then-retreat technique is so effective. First, compared to the two other approaches, the strategy of starting with an extreme demand and then retreating to the more moderate one produced the most money for the person using it. But this result is not very surprising in light of the previous evidence we have seen for the power of larger-then-smaller-request tactics to bring about profitable agreements. It is the two additional findings of the study that are more striking.

Responsibility. Those subjects facing the opponent who used the retreating strategy felt most responsible for the final deal. Much more than the subjects who faced a nonchanging negotiation opponent, these subjects reported that they had successfully influenced the opponent to take less money for himself. Of course, we know that they hadn't done any such thing. The experimenter had instructed their opponent to retreat gradually from his initial demand no matter what the subjects did. But it appeared to these subjects that they had made the opponent change, that they had *produced* his concessions. The result was that they felt more responsible for the final outcome of the negotiations. It does not require much of a leap from this finding to clarify the previous mystery of why the rejection-then-retreat technique causes its targets to live up to their agreements with such astounding frequency. The requester's concession within the technique not only causes targets to say yes more often, it also causes them to feel more responsible for having "dictated" the final agreement. Thus the uncanny ability of the rejection-then-retreat technique to make its targets meet their commitments becomes understandable: A person who feels responsible for the terms of a contract will be more likely to live up to that contract.

Satisfaction. Even though, on the average, they gave the most money to the opponent who used the concessions strategy, the subjects who were the targets of this strategy were the most satisfied with the final arrangement. It appears that an agreement that has been forged through the concessions of one's opponent is quite satisfying. With this in mind, we can begin to explain the second previously puzzling feature of the rejection-then-retreat tactic—the ability to prompt its victims to agree to further requests. Since the tactic uses a concession to bring about compliance, the victim is likely to feel more satisfied with the arrangement as a result. And it stands to reason that people who are satisfied with a given arrangement are more likely to be willing to agree to further such arrangements.

※

HOW TO SAY NO

Up against a requester who employs the rule for reciprocation, you and I face a formidable foe. Whether by presenting us with an initial favor or initial concession, the requester will have enlisted a powerful ally in the campaign for our compliance. At first glance, our fortunes in such a situation would appear dismal. We could comply with the requester's wish and, in so doing, succumb to the reciprocity rule. Or, we could refuse to comply and thereby suffer the brunt of the rule's force upon our deeply conditioned feelings of fairness and obligation. Surrender or suffer heavy casualties. Cheerless prospects indeed.

Fortunately, these are not our only choices. With the proper understanding of the nature of our opponent, we can come away from the compliance battlefield unhurt and sometimes even better off than before. It is essential to recognize that the requester who invokes the reciprocation rule (or any other weapon of influence) to gain our compliance is not the real opponent. Such a requester has chosen to become a jujitsu warrior who aligns himself with the sweeping power of reciprocation and then merely releases that power by providing a first favor or concession. The real opponent is the rule. If we are not to be abused by it, we must take steps to defuse its energy.

But how does one go about neutralizing the effect of a social rule like that for reciprocation? It seems too widespread to escape and too strong to overpower once it is activated. Perhaps the answer, then, is to prevent its activation. Perhaps we can avoid a confrontation with the rule by refusing to allow the requester to commission its force against us in the first place. Perhaps by rejecting the requester's initial favor or concession to us, we can evade the problem. Perhaps; but then, perhaps not. Invariably declining the requester's initial offer of a favor or sacrifice works better in theory than in practice. The major problem is that when it is first presented, it is difficult to know whether such an offer is honest or whether it is the initial step in an exploitation attempt. If we always assume the worst, it would not be possible to receive the benefits of any legitimate favors or concessions offered by individuals who had no intention of exploiting the reciprocity rule.

I have a colleague who remembers with anger how his ten-year-old daughter's feelings were terribly hurt by a man whose method of avoiding the jaws of the reciprocity rule was to refuse abruptly her kindness. The children of her class were hosting an open house at school for their grandparents, and her job was to give a flower to each visitor entering the school grounds. But the first man she approached with a flower growled at her, "Keep it." Not knowing what to do, she extended it toward him again only to have him demand to know what he had to give in return. When she replied weakly, "Nothing. It's a gift," he fixed her with a disbelieving glare, insisted that he recognized "her game," and brushed on past. The girl was so stung by the experience that she could not approach anyone else and had to be removed from her assignment—one she had anticipated fondly. It is hard to know whom to blame more here, the insensitive man or the exploiters who had abused his mechanical tendency to reciprocate a gift until his response had soured to a mechanical refusal. No matter whom you find more blameworthy, the lesson is clear. We will always encounter authentically generous individuals as well as many people who try to play fairly by the reciprocity rule rather than to exploit it. They will doubtless become insulted by someone who consistently rejects their efforts; social friction and isolation could well result. A policy of blanket rejection, then, seems ill advised.

Another solution holds more promise. It advises us to accept the desirable first offers of others but to accept those offers only for what they fundamentally are, not for what they are represented to be. If a person offers us a nice favor, let's say, we might well accept, recognizing that we have obligated ourselves to a return favor sometime in the future. To engage in this sort of arrangement with another is not to be exploited by that person through the rule for reciprocation. Quite the contrary; it is to participate fairly in the "honored network of obligation" that has served us so well, both individually and societally, from the dawn of humanity. However, if the initial favor turns out to be a device, a trick, an artifice designed specifically to stimulate our compliance with a larger return favor, that is a different story. Here our partner is not a benefactor but a profiteer. And it is here that we should respond to his action on precisely those terms. Once we have determined that his initial offer was not a favor but a compliance tactic, we need only react to it accordingly to be free of its influence. As long as we perceive and define his action as a compliance device instead of a favor, he no longer has the reciprocation rule as an ally: The rule says that favors are to be met with favors; it does not require that tricks be met with favors.

A practical example may make things more concrete. Let's suppose that a woman phoned one day and introduced herself as a member of the Home Fire Safety Association in your town. Suppose she then asked if you would be interested in learning about home fire safety, having your house checked for fire hazards, and receiving a home fire extinguisher, all free of charge. Let's suppose further that you were interested in these things and made an evening appointment to have one of the association's inspectors come over to provide them. When he arrived, he gave you a small hand extinguisher and began examining the possible fire hazards of your home. Afterward he gave you some interesting, though frightening information about general fire dangers, along with an assessment of your home's vulnerability. Finally he suggested that you get a home fire warning system and left.

Such a set of events is not implausible. Various cities and towns have nonprofit associations, usually made up of Fire Department personnel working on their own time, that provide free home fire-safety inspections of this sort. Were these events to occur, you would clearly have been done a favor by the inspector. In accordance with the reciprocation rule, you should stand more ready to provide a return favor if you were to see him in need of aid at some point in the future. An exchange of favors of this kind would be in the best tradition of the reciprocity rule.

A similar set of events with, however, a different ending would also be possible—in fact, more likely. Rather than leaving after recommending a fire-alarm system, the inspector would launch into a sales presentation intended to persuade you to buy an expensive, heat-triggered alarm system manufactured by the company he represented. Door-to-door home fire-alarm companies will frequently use this approach. Typically, their product, while effective enough, will be overpriced. Trusting that you will not be familiar with the retail costs of such a system and that, if you decide to buy one, you will feel obligated to the company that provided you with a free extinguisher and home inspection, these companies will pressure you for an immediate sale. Using this free-information-and-inspection gambit, fire-protection sales organizations have flourished around the country.[18]

If you were to find yourself in such a situation with the realization that the primary motive of the inspector's visit was to sell you a costly alarm system, your most effective next action would be a simple, private maneuver. It would involve the mental act of redefinition. Merely define whatever you have received from the inspector—extinguisher, safety information, hazard inspection—not as gifts but as sales devices, and you will be free to decline (or accept) his purchase offer without even a tug from the reciprocity rule: A favor rightly follows a favor—not a piece of sales strategy. And if he subsequently responds to your refusal by proposing that you, at least, give him the names of some friends he might call on, use your mental maneuver on him again. Define his retreat to this smaller request as what (it is hoped after reading this chapter) you recognize it to be—a compliance tactic. Once done, there would be no pressure to offer the names as a return concession, since his reduced request would not be viewed as a real concession. At this point, unhampered by an inappropriately triggered sense of obligation, you may once again be as compliant or noncompliant as you wish.

Provided you are so inclined, you might even turn his own weapon of influence against him. Recall that the rule for reciprocation entitles a person who has acted in a certain way to a dose of the same thing. If you have determined that the "fire inspector's" gifts were used, not as genuine gifts, but to make a profit from you, then you might want to use them to make a profit of your own. Simply take whatever the inspector is willing to provide—safety information, home extinguisher—thank him politely, and show him out the door. After all, the reciprocity rule asserts that if justice is to be done, exploitation attempts should be exploited.

3

COMMITMENT
AND CONSISTENCY
Hobgoblins of the mind

❋

A study done by a pair of Canadian psychologists uncovered something fascinating about people at the racetrack: Just after placing a bet, they are much more confident of their horse's chances of winning than they are immediately before laying down that bet.[1] Of course, nothing about the horse's chances actually shifts; it's the same horse, on the same track, in the same field; but in the minds of those bettors, its prospects improve significantly once that ticket is purchased. Although a bit puzzling at first glance, the reason for the dramatic change has to do with a common weapon of social influence. Like the other weapons of influence, this one lies deep within us, directing our actions with quiet power. It is, quite simply, our nearly obsessive desire to be (and to appear) consistent with what we have already done. Once we have made a choice or taken a stand, we will encounter personal and interpersonal pressures to behave consistently with that commitment. Those pressures will cause us to respond in ways that justify our earlier decision.

COMMITMENT AND CONSISTENCY

Take the bettors in the racetrack experiment. Thirty seconds before putting down their money, they had been tentative and uncertain; thirty seconds after the deed, they were significantly more optimistic and self-assured. The act of making a final decision—in this case, of buying a ticket—had been the critical factor. Once a stand had been taken, the need for consistency pressured these people to bring what they felt and believed into line with what they had already done. They simply convinced themselves that they had made the right choice and, no doubt, felt better about it all.

Before we see such self-delusion as unique to racetrack habitués, we should examine the story of my neighbor Sara and her live-in boyfriend, Tim. They met at a hospital where he worked as an X-ray technician and she as a nutritionist. They dated for a while, even after Tim lost his job, and eventually they moved in together. Things were never perfect for Sara: She wanted Tim to marry her and to stop his heavy drinking; Tim resisted both ideas. After an especially difficult period of conflict, Sara broke off the relationship and Tim moved out. At the same time, an old boyfriend of Sara's returned to town after years away and called her. They started seeing each other socially and quickly became serious enough to plan a wedding. They had gone so far as to set a date and issue invitations when Tim called. He had repented and wanted to move back in. When Sara told him her marriage plans, he begged her to change her mind; he wanted to be together with her as before. But Sara refused, saying she didn't want to live like that again. Tim even offered to marry her, but she still said she preferred the other boyfriend. Finally, Tim volunteered to quit drinking if she would only relent. Feeling that under those conditions Tim had the edge, Sara decided to break her engagement, cancel the wedding, retract the invitations and let Tim move back in with her.

Within a month, Tim informed Sara that he didn't think he needed to stop his drinking after all; a month later, he had decided that they should "wait and see" before getting married. Two years have since passed; Tim and Sara continue to live together exactly as before. He still drinks, there are still no marriage plans, yet Sara is more devoted to Tim than she ever was. She says that being forced to choose taught her that Tim really is number one in her heart. So, after choosing Tim over her other boyfriend, Sara became happier with him, even though the conditions under which she had made her choice have never been fulfilled. Obviously, horse-race bettors are not alone in their willingness to believe in the correctness of a difficult choice once made. Indeed, we all fool ourselves from time to time in order to keep our thoughts and beliefs consistent with what we have already done or decided.

Psychologists have long understood the power of the consistency principle to direct human action. Prominent theorists such as Leon Festinger, Fritz Hieder, and Theodore Newcomb have viewed the desire for consistency as a central motivator of our behavior. But is this tendency to be consistent really strong enough to compel us to do what we ordinarily would not want to do? There is no question about it. The drive to be (and look) consistent constitutes a highly potent weapon of social influence, often causing us to act in ways that are clearly contrary to our own best interests.

To understand why consistency is so powerful a motive, it is important to recognize that in most circumstances consistency is valued and adaptive. Inconsistency is commonly thought to be an undesirable personality trait. The woman who changes her mind again and again is considered flighty or scatterbrained. The man whose opinions can be easily influenced is viewed as indecisive and weak-willed. The person whose beliefs, words, and deeds don't match may be seen as confused, two-faced, or even mentally ill. On the other side, a high degree of consistency is normally associated with personal and intellectual strength. It is at the heart of logic, rationality, stability, and honesty.

Certainly, then, good personal consistency is highly valued in our culture. And well it should be. It provides us with a reasonable and gainful orientation to the world. Most of the time we will be better off if our approach to things is well laced with consistency. Without it our lives would be difficult, erratic, and disjointed.

But because it is so typically in our best interests to be consistent, we easily fall into the habit of being automatically so,

COMMITMENT AND CONSISTENCY

even in situations where it is not the sensible way to be. When it occurs unthinkingly, consistency can be disastrous. Nonetheless, even blind consistency has its attractions.

First, like most other forms of automatic responding, it offers a shortcut through the density of modern life. Once we have made up our minds about an issue, stubborn consistency allows us a very appealing luxury: We really don't have to think hard about the issue anymore. We don't have to sift through the blizzard of information we encounter every day to identify relevant facts; we don't have to expend the mental energy to weigh the pros and cons; we don't have to make any further tough decisions. Instead, all we have to do when confronted with the issue is to turn on our consistency tape, *whirr,* and we know just what to believe, say, or do. We need only believe, say, or do whatever is consistent with our earlier decision.

The allure of such a luxury is not to be minimized. It allows us a convenient, relatively effortless, and efficient method for dealing with complex daily environments that make severe demands on our mental energies and capacities. It is not hard to understand, then, why automatic consistency is a difficult reaction to curb. It offers us a way to evade the rigors of continuing thought. And as Sir Joshua Reynolds noted, "There is no expedient to which a man will not resort to avoid the real labor of thinking." With our consistency tapes operating, then, we can go about our business happily excused from the toil of having to think too much.

There is a second, more perverse attraction of mechanical consistency as well. Sometimes it is not the effort of hard, cognitive work that makes us shirk thoughtful activity, but the harsh consequences of that activity. Sometimes it is the cursedly clear and unwelcome set of answers provided by straight thinking that makes us mental slackers. There are certain disturbing things we simply would rather not realize. Because it is a preprogrammed and mindless method of responding, automatic consistency can supply a safe hiding place from those troubling realizations. Sealed within the fortress walls of rigid consistency, we can be impervious to the sieges of reason.

One night at an introductory lecture given by the Transcendental Meditation program, I witnessed a nice illustration of how people will hide inside the walls of consistency to protect themselves from the troublesome consequences of thought. The lecture itself was presided over by two earnest young men and was designed to recruit new members into the program. The program claimed it could teach a unique brand of meditation (TM) that would allow us to achieve all manner of desirable things, ranging from simple inner peace to the more spectacular abilities to fly and pass through walls at the program's advanced (and more expensive) stages.

I had decided to attend the meeting to observe the kind of compliance tactics used in recruitment lectures of this sort and had brought along an interested friend, a university professor whose areas of specialization were statistics and symbolic logic. As the meeting progressed and the lecturers explained the theory behind TM, I noticed my logician friend becoming increasingly restless. Looking more and more pained and shifting about constantly in his seat, he was finally unable to resist. When the leaders called for questions at the completion of the lecture, he raised his hand and gently but surely demolished the presentation we had just heard. In less than two minutes, he pointed out precisely where and why the lecturers' complex argument was contradictory, illogical, and unsupportable. The effect on the discussion leaders was devastating. After a confused silence, each attempted a weak reply only to halt midway to confer with his partner and finally to admit that my colleague's points were good ones "requiring further study."

More interesting to me, though, was the effect upon the rest of the audience. At the end of the question period, the two recruiters were faced with a crush of audience members submitting their seventy-five-dollar down payments for admission to the TM program. Nudging, shrugging, and chuckling to one another as they took in the payments, the recruiters betrayed signs of giddy bewilderment. After what appeared to have been an embarrassingly clear collapse of their presentation, the meeting had somehow turned into a great success, generating mystifyingly high levels of compliance from the audience. Although more than a bit puzzled, I chalked up the audience response to a failure to understand the logic of my colleague's arguments. As it turned out, however, just the *reverse* was the case.

Outside the lecture room after the meeting, we were approached by three members of the audience, each of whom had given a down payment immediately after the lecture. They wanted to know why we had come to the session. We explained, and we asked the same question of them. One was an aspiring actor who wanted desperately to succeed at his craft and had come to the meeting to learn if TM would allow him to achieve the necessary self-control to master the art; the recruiters had assured him that it would. The second described herself as a severe insomniac who had hopes that TM would provide her with a way to relax and fall asleep easily at night. The third served as unofficial spokesman. He also had a sleep-related problem. He was failing college because there didn't seem to be enough time to study. He had come to the meeting to find out if TM could help by training him to need fewer hours of sleep each night; the additional time could then be used for study. It is interesting to note that the recruiters informed him as well as the insomniac that Transcendental Meditation techniques could solve their respective, though opposite, problems.

Still thinking that the three must have signed up because they hadn't understood the points made by my logician friend, I began to question them about aspects of his argument. To my surprise, I found that they had understood his comments quite well; in fact, all too well. It was precisely the cogency of his argument that drove them to sign up for the program on the spot. The spokesman put it best: "Well, I wasn't going to put down any money tonight because I'm really quite broke right now; I was going to wait until the next meeting. But when your buddy started talking, I knew I'd better give them my money now, or I'd go home and start thinking about what he said and *never* sign up."

All at once, things began to make sense. These were people with real problems; and they were somewhat desperately searching for a way to solve those problems. They were seekers who, if our discussion leaders were to be believed, had found a potential solution in TM. Driven by their needs, they very much wanted to believe that TM was their answer.

Now, in the form of my colleague, intrudes the voice of

reason, showing the theory underlying their newfound solution to be unsound. Panic! Something must be done at once before logic takes its toll and leaves them without hope again. Quickly, quickly, walls against reason are needed; and it doesn't matter that the fortress to be erected is a foolish one. "Quick, a hiding place from thought! Here, take this money. Whew, safe in the nick of time. No need to think about the issues any longer. The decision has been made, and from now on the consistency tape can be played whenever necessary: 'TM? Certainly I think it will help me; certainly I expect to continue; certainly I believe in TM. I already put my money down for it, didn't I?' Ah, the comforts of mindless consistency. I'll just rest right here for a while. It's so much nicer than the worry and strain of that hard, hard search."

If, as it appears, automatic consistency functions as a shield against thought, it should not be surprising that such consistency can also be exploited by those who would prefer that we not think too much in response to their requests for our compliance. For the exploiters, whose interest will be served by an unthinking, mechanical reaction to their requests, our tendency for automatic consistency is a gold mine. So clever are they at arranging to have us play our consistency tapes when it profits them that we seldom realize we have been taken. In fine jujitsu fashion, they structure their interactions with us so that our *own* need to be consistent will lead directly to their benefit.

Certain large toy manufacturers use just such an approach to reduce a problem caused by seasonal buying patterns. Of course, the boom time for toy sales occurs before and during the Christmas holiday season. The toy companies make fat profits during this period. Their problem is that toy sales then go into a terrible slump for the next couple of months. Their customers have already spent the amount in their toy budgets and are stiffly resistant to their children's pleas for more. Even those children whose birthdays fall soon after the holidays receive fewer toys because of the recent Christmas spree.

So the toy manufacturers are faced with a dilemma: how to keep sales high during the peak season and, at the same time, retain a healthy demand for toys in the immediately following months. Their difficulty certainly doesn't lie in convincing our naturally insatiable offspring to want a continuous flow of new amusements. A series of flashy television commercials placed among the Saturday morning cartoon shows will produce the usual amounts of begging, whining, and wheedling no matter when it appears during the year. No, the problem is not in motivating kids to want more toys after Christmas.

The problem is in motivating postholiday spent-out parents to reach down for the price of yet another plaything for their already toy-glutted children. What could the toy companies possibly do to produce that unlikely behavior? Some have tried a greatly increased advertising campaign, others have reduced prices during the slack period, but neither of those standard sales devices has proved successful. Not only are both tactics costly but both have also been ineffective in increasing sales to desired levels. Parents are simply not in a toy-buying mood, and the influences of advertising or reduced expense are not enough to shake that stony resistance.

Certain large toy manufacturers, however, think they have found a solution. It's an ingenious one, involving no more than a normal advertising expense and an understanding of the powerful pull of the need for consistency. My first hint of how the toy companies' strategy worked came after I fell for it and then, in true patsy form, fell for it again.

It was January, and I was in the town's largest toy store. After purchasing all too many gifts there for my son a month before, I had sworn not to enter that place or any like it for a long, long time. Yet there I was, not only in the diabolic place but also in the process of buying my son another expensive toy—a big, electric road-race set. In front of the road-race display I happened to meet a former neighbor who was buying his son the same toy. The odd thing was that we almost never saw each other anymore. In fact, the last time was a year earlier in that same store where we were both buying our sons an expensive post-Christmas gift—that time a robot that walked, talked, and laid waste. We laughed about our strange pattern of seeing each other only once a year at the same time, in the same place, while doing the same thing. Later that day, I mentioned the coincidence to a friend who, it turned out, had once worked in the toy business.

"No coincidence," he said knowingly.

"What do you mean, 'No coincidence'?"

"Look," he said, "let me ask you a couple of questions about the road-race set you bought this year. First, did you promise your son that he'd get one for Christmas?"

"Well, yes, I did. Christopher had seen a bunch of ads for them on the Saturday morning cartoon shows and said that was what he wanted for Christmas. I saw a couple of the ads myself and it looked like fun; so I said okay."

"Strike one," he announced. "Now for my second question. When you went to buy one, did you find all the stores sold out?"

"That's right, I did! The stores said they'd ordered some but didn't know when they'd get any more in. So I had to buy Christopher some other toys to make up for the road-race set. But how did you know?"

"Strike two," he said. "Just let me ask one more question. Didn't this same sort of thing happen the year before with the robot toy?"

"Wait a minute . . . you're right. That's just what happened. This is incredible. How did you know?"

"No psychic powers; I just happen to know how several of the big toy companies jack up their January and February sales. They start prior to Christmas with attractive TV ads for certain special toys. The kids, naturally, want what they see and extract Christmas promises for these items from their parents. Now here's where the genius of the companies' plan comes in: They *undersupply* the stores with the toys they've gotten the parents to promise. Most parents find those things sold out and are forced to substitute other toys of equal value. The toy manufacturers, of course, make a point of supplying the stores with plenty of these substitutes. Then, after Christmas, the companies start running the ads again for the other, special toys. That juices up the kids to want those toys more than ever. They go running to their parents whining, 'You promised, you promised,' and the adults go trudging off to the store to live up dutifully to their words."

"Where," I said, beginning to seethe now, "they meet other parents they haven't seen for a year, falling for the same trick, right?"

"Right. Uh, where are you going?"

"I'm going to take that road-race set right back to the store." I was so angry I was nearly shouting.

"Wait. Think for a minute first. Why did you buy it this morning?"

"Because I didn't want to let Christopher down and because I wanted to teach him that promises are to be lived up to."

"Well, has any of that changed? Look, if you take his toy away now, he won't understand why. He'll just know that his father broke a promise to him. Is that what you want?"

"No," I said, sighing, "I guess not. So, you're telling me that they doubled their profit on me for the past two years, and I never even knew it; and now that I do, I'm still trapped—by my own words. So, what you're really telling me is, 'Strike three.'"

He nodded, "And you're out."

※

COMMITMENT IS THE KEY

Once we realize that the power of consistency is formidable in directing human action, an important practical question immediately arises: How is that force engaged? What produces the *click* that activates the *whirr* of the powerful consistency tape? Social psychologists think they know the answer: commitment. If I can get you to make a commitment (that is, to take a stand, to go on record), I will have set the stage for your automatic and ill-considered consistency with that earlier commitment. Once a stand is taken, there is a natural tendency to behave in ways that are stubbornly consistent with the stand.

As we've already seen, social psychologists are not the only ones who understand the connection between commitment and consistency. Commitment strategies are aimed at us by compliance professionals of nearly every sort. Each of the strategies is intended to get us to take some action or make some statement that will trap us into later compliance through consistency pressures. Procedures designed to create commitment take various forms. Some are fairly straightforward; others are among the most devious compliance tactics we will encounter.

The question of what makes a commitment effective has a number of answers. A variety of factors affect the ability of a commitment to constrain our future behavior. One large-scale program designed to produce compliance illustrates nicely how several of the factors work. The remarkable thing about this program is that it was systematically employing these factors decades ago, well before scientific research had identified them.

During the Korean War many captured American soldiers found themselves in prisoner-of-war camps run by the Chinese Communists. It became clear early in the conflict that the Chinese treated captives quite differently than did their allies, the North Koreans, who favored savagery and harsh punishment to gain compliance. Specifically avoiding the appearance of brutality, the Red Chinese engaged in what they termed their "lenientpolicy," which was in reality a concerted and sophisticated psychological assault on their captives. After the war, American psychologists questioned the returning prisoners intensively to determine what had occurred. The intensive psychological investigation took place, in part, because of the unsettling success of some aspects of the Chinese program. For example, the Chinese were very effective in getting Americans to inform on one another, in striking contrast to the behavior of American POWs in World War II. For this reason, among others, escape plans were quickly uncovered and the escapes themselves almost always unsuccessful. "When an escape did occur," wrote Dr. Edgar Schein, a principal American investigator of the Chinese indoctrination program in Korea, "the Chinese usually recovered the man easily by offering a bag of rice to anyone turning him in." In fact, nearly all American prisoners in the Chinese camps are said to have collaborated with the enemy in one form or another.[2]

An examination of the Chinese prison-camp program shows that they relied heavily on commitment and consistency pressures to gain the desired compliance from their captives. Of course, the first problem facing the Chinese was how to get any collaboration at all from the Americans. These were men who were trained to provide nothing but name, rank, and serial number. Short of physical brutalization, how could the captors hope to get such men to give military information, turn in fellow prisoners, or publicly denounce their country? The Chinese answer was elementary: Start small and build.

For instance, prisoners were frequently asked to make statements so mildly anti-American or pro-Communist as to seem inconsequential ("The United States is not perfect." "In a Communist country, unemployment is not a problem.") But once these minor requests were complied with, the men found themselves pushed to submit to related yet more substantive requests. A man who had just agreed with his Chinese interrogator that the United States is not perfect might then be asked to indicate some of the ways in which he thought this was the case. Once he had so explained himself, he might be asked to make a list of these "problems with America" and to sign his name to it. Later he might be asked to read his list in a discussion group with other prisoners. "After all, it's what you really believe, isn't it?" Still later he might be asked to write an essay expanding on his list and discussing these problems in greater detail.

The Chinese might then use his name and his essay in an anti-American radio broadcast beamed not only to the entire camp but to other POW camps in North Korea as well as to American forces in South Korea. Suddenly he would find himself a "collaborator," having given aid and comfort to the enemy. Aware that he had written the essay without any strong threats or coercion, many times a man would change his image of himself to be consistent with the deed and with the new "collaborator" label, often resulting in even more extensive acts of collaboration. Thus, while "only a few men were able to avoid collaboration altogether," according to Dr. Schein, "the majority collaborated at one time or another by doing things which seemed to them trivial but which the Chinese were able to turn to their own advantage. . . . This was particularly effective in eliciting confessions, self-criticism, and information during interrogation."[3]

If the Chinese know about the subtle power of this approach, it should not be surprising that another group of people interested in compliance is also aware of its usefulness. Many business organizations employ it regularly.

For the salesperson, the strategy is to obtain a large purchase by starting with a small one. Almost any small sale will do be-

INFLUENCE

FIGURE 3–1

WRITING IS BELIEVING

*This ad invites readers to participate in a sweep-
stakes by providing a handwritten message detailing
the product's favorable features. (Courtesy of
Schieffelin & Co.)*

cause the purpose of that small transaction is not profit. It is
commitment. Further purchases, even much larger ones, are expected to flow naturally from the commitment. An article in the
trade magazine *American Salesman* put it succinctly:

> The general idea is to pave the way for full-line distribution
> by starting with a small order. . . . Look at it this way—when
> a person has signed an order for your merchandise, even

though the profit is so small it hardly compensates for the time and effort of making the call, he is no longer a prospect—he is a customer.[4]

The tactic of starting with a little request in order to gain eventual compliance with related larger requests has a name: the foot-in-the-door technique. Social scientists first became aware of its effectiveness in the mid-1960s when psychologists Jonathan Freedman and Scott Fraser published an astonishing set of data.[5] They reported the results of an experiment in which a researcher, posing as a volunteer worker, had gone door to door in a residential California neighborhood making a preposterous request of homeowners. The homeowners were asked to allow a public-service billboard to be installed on their front lawns. To get an idea of just how the sign would look, they were shown a photograph depicting an attractive house, the view of which was almost completely obscured by a very large, poorly lettered sign reading DRIVE CAREFULLY. Although the request was normally and understandably refused by the great majority (83 percent) of the other residents in the area, this particular group of people reacted quite favorably. A full 76 percent of them offered the use of their front yards.

The prime reason for their startling compliance has to do with something that had happened to them about two weeks earlier: They had made a small commitment to driver safety. A different volunteer worker had come to their doors and asked them to accept and display a little three-inch-square sign that read BE A SAFE DRIVER. It was such a trifling request that nearly all of them had agreed to it. But the effects of that request were enormous. Because they had innocently complied with a trivial safe-driving request a couple of weeks before, these homeowners became remarkably willing to comply with another such request that was massive in size.

Freedman and Fraser didn't stop there. They tried a slightly different procedure on another sample of homeowners. These people first received a request to sign a petition that favored "keeping California beautiful." Of course, nearly everyone signed since state beauty, like efficiency in government or sound prenatal care, is one of those issues almost no one is against.

INFLUENCE

After waiting about two weeks, Freedman and Fraser sent a new "volunteer worker" to these same homes to ask the residents to allow the big DRIVE CAREFULLY sign to be erected on their lawns. In some ways, their response was the most astounding of any of the homeowners in the study. Approximately half of these people consented to the installation of the DRIVE CAREFULLY billboard, even though the small commitment they had made weeks earlier was not to driver safety but to an entirely different public-service topic, state beautification.

At first, even Freedman and Fraser were bewildered by their findings. Why should the little act of signing a petition supporting state beautification cause people to be so willing to perform a different and much larger favor? After considering and discarding other explanations, Freedman and Fraser came upon one that offered a solution to the puzzle: Signing the beautification petition changed the view these people had of themselves. They saw themselves as public-spirited citizens who acted on their civic principles. When, two weeks later, they were asked to perform another public service by displaying the DRIVE CAREFULLY sign, they complied in order to be consistent with their newly formed self-images. According to Freedman and Fraser,

> What may occur is a change in the person's feelings about getting involved or taking action. Once he has agreed to a request, his attitude may change, he may become, in his own eyes, the kind of person who does this sort of thing, who agrees to requests made by strangers, who takes action on things he believes in, who cooperates with good causes.[6]

What the Freedman and Fraser findings tell us, then, is to be very careful about agreeing to trivial requests. Such an agreement can not only increase our compliance with very similar, much larger requests, it can also make us more willing to perform a variety of larger favors that are only remotely connected to the little one we did earlier. It's this second, general kind of influence concealed within small commitments that scares me.

It scares me enough that I am rarely willing to sign a petition anymore, even for a position I support. Such an action has the potential to influence not only my future behavior but also my self-image in ways I may not want. And once a person's self-image is altered, all sorts of subtle advantages become available to someone who wants to exploit that new image.

Who among Freedman and Fraser's homeowners would have thought that the "volunteer worker" who asked them to sign a state beautification petition was really interested in having them display a safe-driving billboard two weeks later? And who among them could have suspected that their decision to display the billboard was largely due to the act of signing the petition? No one, I'd guess. If there were any regrets after the billboard went up, who could they conceivably hold responsible but *themselves* and their own damnably strong civic spirit? They probably never even considered the guy with the "keeping California beautiful" petition and all that knowledge of jujitsu.

Notice that all of the foot-in-the-door experts seem to be excited about the same thing: You can use small commitments to manipulate a person's self-image; you can use them to turn citizens into "public servants," prospects into "customers," prisoners into "collaborators." And once you've got a man's self-image where you want it, he should comply *naturally* with a whole range of your requests that are consistent with this view of himself.

Not all commitments affect self-image, however. There are certain conditions that should be present for a commitment to be effective in this way. To discover what they are, we can once again look to the American experience in the Chinese prison camps of Korea. It is important to understand that the major intent of the Chinese was not simply to extract information from their prisoners. It was to indoctrinate them, to change their attitudes and perceptions of themselves, of their political system, of their country's role in the war, and of communism. And there is evidence that the program often worked alarmingly well.

Dr. Henry Segal, chief of the neuropsychiatric evaluation team that examined returning POWs at the war's end, reported that war-related beliefs had been substantially shifted. The majority of the men believed the Chinese story that the United

States had used germ warfare, and many felt that their own forces had been the initial aggressors in starting the war. Similar inroads had been made in the political attitudes of the men:

> Many expressed antipathy toward the Chinese Communists but at the same time praised them for "the fine job they have done in China." Others stated that "although communism won't work in America, I think it's a good thing for Asia."[7]

It appears that the real goal of the Chinese was to modify, at least for a time, the hearts and minds of their captives. If we measure their achievement in terms of "defection, disloyalty, changed attitudes and beliefs, poor discipline, poor morale, poor *esprit,* and doubts as to America's role," Dr. Segal concluded that "their efforts were highly successful." Because commitment tactics were so much a part of the effective Chinese assault on hearts and minds, it is quite informative to examine the specific features of the tactics they used.

The magic act

Our best evidence of what people truly feel and believe comes less from their words than from their deeds. Observers trying to decide what a man is like look closely at his actions. What the Chinese have discovered is that the man himself uses this same evidence to decide what he is like. His behavior tells him about himself; it is a primary source of information about his beliefs and values and attitudes. Understanding fully this important principle of self-perception, the Chinese set about arranging the prison-camp experience so that their captives would consistently *act* in desired ways. Before long, the Chinese knew, these actions would begin to take their toll, causing the men to change their views of themselves to align with what they had done.

Writing was one sort of confirming action that the Chinese urged incessantly upon the men. It was never enough for the prisoners to listen quietly or even to agree verbally with the Chinese line; they were always pushed to write it down as well. So intent were the Chinese on securing a written statement that if a

COMMITMENT AND CONSISTENCY

prisoner was not willing to write a desired response freely, he was prevailed upon to copy it. The American psychologist Edgar Schein describes a standard indoctrination session tactic of the Chinese in these terms:

> A further technique was to have the man write out the question and then the [pro-Communist] answer. If he refused to write it voluntarily, he was asked to copy it from the notebooks, which must have seemed like a harmless enough concession.

But, oh, those "harmless" concessions. We've already seen how apparently trifling commitments can lead to extraordinary further behavior. And the Chinese knew that, as a commitment device, a written declaration has some great advantages. First, it provides physical evidence that the act occurred. Once a man wrote what the Chinese wanted, it was very difficult for him to believe that he had not done so. The opportunities to forget or to deny to himself what he had done were not available, as they are for purely verbal statements. No; there it was in his own handwriting, an irrevocably documented act driving him to make his beliefs and his self-image consistent with what he had undeniably done.

A second advantage of a written testament is that it can be shown to other people. Of course, that means it can be used to persuade those people. It can persuade them to change their own attitudes in the direction of the statement. But more important for the purpose of commitment, it can persuade them that the author genuinely believes what was written. People have a natural tendency to think that a statement reflects the true attitude of the person who made it. What is surprising is that they continue to think so even when they know that the person did not freely choose to make the statement.

Some scientific evidence that this is the case comes from a study by psychologists Edward Jones and James Harris, who showed people an essay that was favorable to Fidel Castro and asked them to guess the true feelings of its author.[8] Jones and Harris told some of these people that the author had chosen to write a pro-Castro essay; and they told the other people that the author had been required to write in favor of Castro. The strange thing was that even those people who knew that the author had been assigned to do a pro-Castro essay guessed that he liked Castro. It seems that a statement of belief produces a *click, whirr* response in those who view it. Unless there is strong evidence to the contrary, observers automatically assume that someone who makes such a statement means it.

Think of the double-barreled effects on the self-image of a prisoner who wrote a pro-Chinese or anti-American statement. Not only was it a lasting personal reminder of his action, it was also likely to persuade those around him that the statement reflected his actual beliefs. And, as we will see in Chapter 4, what those around us think is true of us is enormously important in determining what we ourself think is true. For example, one study found that after hearing that they were considered charitable people, New Haven, Connecticut, housewives gave much more money to a canvasser from the Multiple Sclerosis Association.[9] Apparently the mere knowledge that someone viewed them as charitable caused these women to make their actions consistent with another's perception of them.

Once an active commitment is made, then, self-image is squeezed from both sides by consistency pressures. From the inside, there is a pressure to bring self-image into line with action. From the outside, there is a sneakier pressure—a tendency to adjust this image according to the way others perceive us. And because others see us as believing what we have written (even when we've had little choice in the matter), we will once again experience a pull to bring self-image into line with the written statement.

In Korea, several subtle devices were used to get the prisoners to write, without direct coercion, what the Chinese wanted. For example, the Chinese knew that many prisoners were anxious to let their families know that they were alive. At the same time, the men knew that their captors were censoring the mails and that only some letters were being allowed out of camp. To ensure that their own letters would be released, some prisoners began including in their messages peace appeals, claims of kind treatment, and statements sympathetic to communism. The hope was that the Chinese would want such letters to sur-

COMMITMENT AND CONSISTENCY

face and would, therefore, allow their delivery. Of course, the Chinese were happy to cooperate because those letters served their interests marvelously. First, their worldwide propaganda effort benefited greatly from the appearance of pro-Communist statements by American servicemen. Second, in the service of prisoner indoctrination, they had, without raising a finger of physical force, gotten many men to go on record as supporting the Chinese cause.

A similar technique involved political essay contests that were regularly held in camp. The prizes for winning were invariably small—a few cigarettes or a bit of fruit—but were sufficiently scarce that they generated a lot of interest from the men. Usually the winning essay was one that took a solidly pro-Communist stand . . . but not always. The Chinese were wise enough to realize that most of the prisoners would not enter a contest that they could win only by writing a Communist tract. And the Chinese were clever enough to know how to plant small commitments to communism in the men that could be nurtured into later bloom. So occasionally the prize was given to an essay that generally supported the United States but that bowed once or twice to the Chinese view. The effects of this strategy were exactly what the Chinese wanted. The men continued to participate voluntarily in the contests because they saw that they could win with an essay highly favorable to their own country. But perhaps without realizing it, they began to shade their essays a bit toward communism in order to have a better chance of winning. The Chinese were ready to pounce on any concession to Communist dogma and to bring consistency pressures to bear upon it. In the case of a written declaration within a voluntary essay, they had a perfect commitment from which to build toward collaboration and conversion.

Other compliance professionals also know about the committing power of written statements. The enormously successful Amway Corporation, for instance, has hit upon a way to spur their sales personnel to greater and greater accomplishments. Members of the staff are asked to set individual sales goals and commit themselves to those goals by personally recording them on paper:

One final tip before you get started: Set a goal and *write it down*. Whatever the goal, the important thing is that you set it, so you've got something for which to aim—and that you write it down. There is something magical about writing things down. So set a goal and write it down. When you reach that goal, set another and write that down. You'll be off and running.[10]

If the Amway people have found "something magical about writing things down," so have other business organizations. Some door-to-door sales companies use the magic of written commitments to battle the "cooling-off" laws recently passed in many states. The laws are designed to allow customers a few days after purchasing an item to cancel the sale and receive a full refund. At first this legislation hurt the hard-sell companies deeply. Because they emphasize high-pressure tactics, their customers often buy, not because they want the product but because they are duped or intimidated into the sale. When the new laws went into effect, these customers began canceling in droves.

The companies have since learned a beautifully simple trick that cuts the number of such cancellations drastically. They merely have the customer, rather than the salesman, fill out the sales agreement. According to the sales-training program of a prominent encyclopedia company, that personal commitment alone has proved to be "a very important psychological aid in preventing customers from backing out of their contracts." Like the Amway Corporation, then, these organizations have found that something special happens when people personally put their commitments on paper: They live up to what they have written down.

Another common way for businesses to cash in on the "magic" of written declarations occurs through the use of an innocent-looking promotional device. Before I began to study weapons of social influence, I used to wonder why big companies such as Procter & Gamble and General Foods are always running those "25-, 50-, or 100 words or less" testimonial contests. They all seem to be alike. The contestant is to compose a short personal statement that begins with the words, "Why I like . . ." and goes on to laud the features of whatever cake mix or floor wax happens to be at issue. The company judges the entries and awards some stunningly large prizes to the winners. What had puzzled me was what the companies got out of the deal. Often the contest requires no purchase; anyone submitting an entry is eligible. Yet, the companies appear to be strangely willing to incur the huge costs of contest after contest.

I am no longer puzzled. The purpose behind the testimonial contests is the same as the purpose behind the political essay contests of the Chinese Communists. In both instances, the aim is to get as many people as possible to go on record as liking the product. In Korea, the product was a brand of Chinese communism; in the United States, it might be a brand of cuticle remover. The type of product doesn't matter; the process is the same. Participants voluntarily write essays for attractive prizes that they have only a small chance to win. But they know that for an essay to have any chance of winning at all, it must include praise for the product. So they find praiseworthy features of the product and describe them in their essays. The result is hundreds of men in Korea or hundreds of thousands of people in America who testify in writing to the product's appeal and who, consequently, experience that "magical" pull to believe what they have written.

The public eye

One reason that written testaments are effective in bringing about genuine personal change is that they can so easily be made public. The prisoner experience in Korea showed the Chinese to be quite aware of an important psychological principle: Public commitments tend to be lasting commitments. The Chinese constantly arranged to have the pro-Communist statements of their captives seen by others. A man who had written a political essay the Chinese liked, for example, might find copies of it posted around camp, or might be asked to read it to a prisoner discussion group, or even to read it on the camp radio broadcast. As far as the Chinese were concerned, the more public the better. Why?

Whenever one takes a stand that is visible to others, there arises a drive to maintain that stand in order to *look* like a consistent person. Remember that earlier in this chapter we described how desirable good personal consistency is as a trait; how someone without it could be judged as fickle, uncertain, pliant, scatterbrained, or unstable; how someone with it is viewed as rational, assured, trustworthy, and sound. Given this context, it is hardly surprising that people try to avoid the look of inconsistency. For appearances' sake, then, the more public a stand, the more reluctant we will be to change it.

An illustration of how public commitments can lead to doggedly consistent further action is provided in a famous experiment performed by a pair of prominent social psychologists, Morton Deutsch and Harold Gerard.[11] The basic procedure was to have college students first estimate in their own minds the length of lines they were shown. At this point, one sample of the students had to commit themselves publicly to their initial judgments by writing them down, signing their names to them, and turning them in to the experimenter. A second sample of students also committed themselves to their first estimates, but they did so privately by putting them on a Magic Writing Pad and then erasing them by lifting the Magic Pad's plastic cover before anyone could see what they had written. A third set of students did not commit themselves to their initial estimates at all; they just kept the estimates in mind privately.

In these ways, Deutsch and Gerard had cleverly arranged for some students to commit themselves publicly, some privately, and some not at all to their initial decisions. What Deutsch and Gerard wanted to find out was which of the three types of students would be most inclined to stick with their first judgments after receiving information that those judgments were incorrect. So all of the students were given new evidence suggesting that their initial estimates were wrong, and they were then given the chance to change their estimates.

The results were quite clear. The students who had never written down their first choices were the least loyal to those choices. When new evidence was presented that questioned the wisdom of decisions that had never left their heads, these students were the most influenced by the new information to change what they had viewed as the "correct" decision. Compared to these uncommitted students, those who had merely

COMMITMENT AND CONSISTENCY

written their decisions for a moment on a Magic Pad were significantly less willing to change their minds when given the chance. Even though they had committed themselves under the most anonymous of circumstances, the act of writing down their first judgments caused them to resist the influence of contradictory new data and to remain consistent with the preliminary choices. But Deutsch and Gerard found that, by far, it was the students who had publicly recorded their initial positions who most resolutely refused to shift from those positions later. Public commitment had hardened them into the most stubborn of all.

The Deutsch and Gerard finding that we are truest to our decisions if we have bound ourselves to them publicly can be put to good use. Consider the organizations dedicated to helping people rid themselves of bad habits. Many weight-reduction clinics, for instance, understand that often a person's private decision to lose weight will be too weak to withstand the blandishments of bakery windows, wafting cooking scents, and late-night Sara Lee commercials. So they see to it that the decision is buttressed by the pillars of public commitment. They require their clients to write down an immediate weight-loss goal and *show* that goal to as many friends, relatives, and neighbors as possible. Clinic operators report that frequently this simple technique works where all else has failed.

Of course, there's no need to pay a special clinic in order to engage a visible commitment as an ally. One San Diego woman described to me how she employed a public promise to help herself finally stop smoking:

> I remember it was after I heard about another scientific study showing that smoking causes cancer. Every time one of those things came out, I used to get determined to quit, but I never could. This time, though, I decided I had to do something. I'm a proud person. It matters to me if other people see me in a bad light. So I thought, "Maybe I can use that pride to help me dump this damn habit." So I made a list of all the people who I really wanted to respect me. Then I went out and got some blank business cards and I wrote on the back of each card, "I promise you that I will never smoke another cigarette."

Within a week, I had given or sent a signed card to everybody on the list—my dad, my brother back East, my boss, my best girlfriend, my ex-husband, everybody but one—the guy I was dating then. I was just crazy about him, and I really wanted him to value me as a person. Believe me, I thought twice about giving him a card because I knew that if I couldn't keep my promise to him I'd die. But one day at the office—he worked in the same building as I did—I just walked up to him, handed him the card, and walked away without saying anything.

Quitting "cold turkey" was the hardest thing I've ever done. There must have been a thousand times when I thought I *had* to have a smoke. But whenever that happened, I'd just picture how all of the people on my list, especially this one guy, would think less of me if I couldn't stick to my guns. And that's all it took. I've never taken another puff.

You know, the interesting thing is the guy turned out to be a real schmuck. I can't figure out what I saw in him back then. But at the time, without knowing it, he helped me get through the toughest part of the toughest thing I've ever had to do. I don't even like him anymore. Still, I do feel grateful in a way because I think he saved my life.

The effort extra

Yet another reason that written commitments are so effective is that they require more work than verbal ones. And the evidence is clear that the more effort that goes into a commitment, the greater is its ability to influence the attitudes of the person who made it. We can find that evidence quite close to home or as far away as the back regions of the primitive world. For example, there is a tribe in southern Africa, the Thonga, that requires each of its boys to go through an elaborate initiation ceremony before he can be counted a man of the tribe. As with many other primitive peoples, a Thonga boy endures a great deal before he is admitted to adult membership in the group. Anthropologists Whiting, Kluckhohn, and Anthony have described this three-month ordeal in brief but vivid terms:

COMMITMENT AND CONSISTENCY

When a boy is somewhere between 10 and 16 years of age, he is sent by his parents to "circumcision school," which is held every 4 or 5 years. Here in company with his age-mates he undergoes severe hazing by the adult males of the society. The initiation begins when each boy runs the gauntlet between two rows of men who beat him with clubs. At the end of this experience he is stripped of his clothes and his hair is cut. He is next met by a man covered with lion manes and is seated upon a stone facing this "lion man." Someone then strikes him from behind and when he turns his head to see who has struck him, his foreskin is seized and in two movements cut off by the "lion man." Afterward he is secluded for three months in the "yard of mysteries," where he can be seen only by the initiated.

During the course of his initiation, the boy undergoes six major trials: beatings, exposure to cold, thirst, eating of un-savory foods, punishment, and the threat of death. On the slightest pretext, he may be beaten by one of the newly initi-ated men, who is assigned to the task by the older men of the tribe. He sleeps without covering and suffers bitterly from the winter cold. He is forbidden to drink a drop of water during the whole three months. Meals are often made nauseating by the half-digested grass from the stomach of an antelope, which is poured over his food. If he is caught breaking any impor-tant rule governing the ceremony, he is severely punished. For example, in one of these punishments, sticks are placed be-tween the fingers of the offender, then a strong man closes his hand around that of the novice, practically crushing his fin-gers. He is frightened into submission by being told that in former times boys who had tried to escape or who had re-vealed the secrets to women or to the uninitiated were hanged and their bodies burned to ashes.[12]

On the face of it, these rites seem extraordinary and bizarre. Yet, at the same time, they can be seen to be remarkably similar in principle and even in detail to the common initiation cere-monies of school fraternities. During the traditional "Hell Week" held yearly on college campuses, fraternity pledges must per-severe through a variety of activities designed by the older mem-bers to test the limits of physical exertion, psychological strain, and social embarrassment. At week's end, the boys who have persisted through the ordeal are accepted for full group membership. Mostly their tribulations have left them no more than greatly tired and a bit shaky, although sometimes the negative effects are more serious.

What is interesting is how closely the particular features of Hell Week tasks match those of the tribal initiation rites. Recall that anthropologists identified six major trials to be endured by a Thonga initiate during his stay in the "yard of mysteries." A scan of newspaper reports shows that each trial also has its place in the hazing rituals of Greek-letter societies:

□ *Beatings.* Fourteen-year-old Michael Kalogris spent three weeks in a Long Island hospital recovering from internal injuries suffered during a Hell Night initiation ceremony of his high-school fraternity, Omega Gamma Delta. He had been administered the "atomic bomb" by his prospective brothers, who told him to hold his hands over his head and keep them there while they gathered around to slam fists into his stomach and back simultaneously and repeatedly.

□ *Exposure to cold.* On a winter night, Frederick Bronner, a California junior-college student, was taken three thousand feet up and ten miles into the hills of a national forest by his prospective fraternity brothers. Left to find his way home wearing only a thin sweat shirt and slacks, Fat Freddy, as he was called, shivered in a frigid wind until he tumbled down a steep ravine, fracturing bones and hurting his head. Prevented by his injuries from going on, he huddled there against the cold until he died of exposure.

□ *Thirst.* Two Ohio State University freshmen found themselves in the "dungeon" of their prospective fraternity house after breaking the rule requiring all pledges to crawl into the dining area prior to Hell Week meals. Once locked in the house storage closet, they were given only salty foods to eat for nearly two days. Nothing was provided for drinking purposes except a pair of plastic cups in which they could catch their own urine.

COMMITMENT AND CONSISTENCY

□ *Eating of unsavory foods.* At Kappa Sigma house on the campus of the University of Southern California, the eyes of eleven pledges bulged when they saw the sickening task before them. Eleven quarter-pound slabs of raw liver lay on a tray. Cut thick and soaked in oil, each was to be swallowed whole, one to a boy. Gagging and choking repeatedly, young Richard Swanson failed three times to down his piece. Determined to succeed, he finally got the oil-soaked meat into his throat where it lodged and, despite all efforts to remove it, killed him.

□ *Punishment.* In Wisconsin, a pledge who forgot one section of a ritual incantation to be memorized by all initiates was punished for his error. He was required to keep his feet under the rear legs of a folding chair while the heaviest of his fraternity brothers sat down and drank a beer. Although the pledge did not cry out during the punishment, a bone in each of his feet was broken.

□ *Threats of death.* A pledge of Zeta Beta Tau fraternity was taken to a beach area of New Jersey and told to dig his "own grave." Seconds after he complied with orders to lie flat in the finished hole, the sides collapsed, suffocating him before his prospective fraternity brothers could dig him out.

There is another striking similarity between the initiation rites of tribal and fraternal societies: They simply will not die. Resisting all attempts to eliminate or suppress them, such hazing practices have been phenomenally resilient. Authorities, in the form of colonial governments or university administrations, have tried threats, social pressures, legal actions, banishments, bribes, and bans to persuade the groups to remove the hazards and humiliations from their initiation ceremonies. None has been successful. Oh, there may be a change while the authority is watching closely. But this is usually more apparent than real, the harsher trials occurring under more secret circumstances until the pressure is off and they can surface again.

INFLUENCE

On some college campuses, officials have tried to eliminate dangerous hazing practices by substituting a "Help Week" of civic service or by taking direct control of the initiation rituals. When such attempts are not slyly circumvented by fraternities, they are met with outright physical resistance. For example, in the aftermath of Richard Swanson's choking death at USC, the university president issued new rules requiring that all pledging activities be reviewed by school authorities before going into effect and that adult advisers be present during initiation ceremonies. According to one national magazine, "The new 'code' set off a riot so violent that city police and fire detachments were afraid to enter campus."

Resigning themselves to the inevitable, other college representatives have given up on the possibility of abolishing the degradations of Hell Week. "If hazing is a universal human activity, and every bit of evidence points to this conclusion, you most likely won't be able to ban it effectively. Refuse to allow it openly and it will go underground. You can't ban sex, you can't prohibit alcohol, and you probably can't eliminate hazing!"[13]

What is it about hazing practices that make them so precious to these societies? What could make the groups want to evade, undermine, or contest any effort to ban the degrading and perilous features of their initiation rights? Some have argued that the groups themselves are composed of psychological or social miscreants whose twisted needs demand that others be harmed and humiliated. But the evidence does not support such a view. Studies done on the personality traits of fraternity members, for instance, show them to be, if anything, slightly healthier than other college students in their psychological adjustment. Similarly, fraternities are known for their willingness to engage in beneficial community projects for the general social good. What they are not willing to do, however, is substitute these projects for their initiation ceremonies. One survey at the University of Washington found that, of the fraternity chapters examined, most had a type of Help Week tradition but that this community service was in addition to Hell Week. In only one case was such service directly related to initiation procedures.[14]

The picture that emerges of the perpetrators of hazing practices is of normal individuals who tend to be psychologically sta-

COMMITMENT AND CONSISTENCY

ble and socially concerned but who become aberrantly harsh as a group at only one time—immediately before the admission of new members to the society. The evidence, then, points to the ceremony as the culprit. There must be something about its rigors that is vital to the group. There must be some function to its harshness that the group will fight relentlessly to maintain. What?

My own view is that the answer appeared in 1959 in the results of a study little known outside of social psychology. A pair of young researchers, Elliot Aronson and Judson Mills, decided to test their observation that "persons who go through a great deal of trouble or pain to attain something tend to value it more highly than persons who attain the same thing with a minimum of effort." The real stroke of inspiration came in their choice of the initiation ceremony as the best place to examine this possibility. They found that college women who had to endure a severely embarrassing initiation ceremony in order to gain access to a sex discussion group convinced themselves that their new group and its discussions were extremely valuable, even though Aronson and Mills had previously rehearsed the other group members to be as "worthless and uninteresting" as possible. Different coeds, who went through a much milder initiation ceremony or went through no initiation at all, were decidedly less positive about the "worthless" new group they had joined. Additional research showed the same results when coeds were required to endure pain rather than embarrassment to get into a group. The more electric shock a woman received as part of the initiation ceremony, the more she later persuaded herself that her new group and its activities were interesting, intelligent, and desirable.[15]

Now the harassments, the exertions, even the beatings of initiation rituals begin to make sense. The Thonga tribesman watching, with tears in his eyes, his ten-year-old son tremble through a night on the cold ground of the "yard of mysteries," the college sophomore punctuating his Hell Night paddling of his fraternity "little brother" with bursts of nervous laughter, these are not acts of sadism. They are acts of group survival. They function, oddly enough, to spur future society members to find the group more attractive and worthwhile. As long as it is the case that people like and believe in what they have struggled to get, these groups will continue to arrange effortful and troublesome initiation rites. The loyalty and dedication of those who emerge will increase to a great degree the chances of group cohesiveness and survival. Indeed, one study of fifty-four tribal cultures found that those with the most dramatic and stringent initiation ceremonies were those with the greatest group solidarity.[16] Given Aronson and Mills' demonstration that the severity of an initiation ceremony significantly heightens the newcomer's *commitment* to the group, it is hardly surprising that groups will oppose all attempts to eliminate this crucial link to their future strength.

The inner choice

Examination of such diverse activities as the indoctrination practices of the Chinese Communists and the initiation rituals of college fraternities has provided some valuable information about commitment. It appears that commitments are most effective in changing a person's self-image and future behavior when they are active, public, and effortful. But there is another property of effective commitment that is more important than the other three combined. To understand what it is, we first need to solve a pair of puzzles in the actions of Communist interrogators and fraternity brothers.

The first puzzle comes from the refusal of fraternity chapters to allow public-service activities to be part of their initiation ceremonies. Recall that one survey showed that community projects, though frequent, were nearly always separated from the membership-induction program. But why? If an effortful commitment is what fraternities are after in their initiation rites, surely they could structure enough distasteful and strenuous civic activities for their pledges; there is plenty of exertion and unpleasantness to be had in the world of old-age-home repairs, mental-health-center yard work, and hospital bedpan duty. Besides, community-spirited endeavors of this sort would do much to improve the highly unfavorable public and media image of

COMMITMENT AND CONSISTENCY

fraternity Hell Week rites; a survey showed that for every positive newspaper story concerning Hell Week, there were five negative stories. If only for public-relations reasons, then, fraternities should want to incorporate community-service efforts into their initiation practice. But they don't.

To examine the second puzzle, we need to return to the Chinese prison camps of Korea and the regular political essay contests held for American captives. The Chinese wanted as many Americans as possible to enter these contests so that, in the process, they might write things favorable to the Communist view. If, however, the idea was to attract large numbers of entrants, why were the prizes so small? A few extra cigarettes or a little fresh fruit were often all that a contest winner could expect. In the setting, even these prizes were valuable, but still there were much larger rewards—warm clothing, special mail privileges, increased freedom of movement in camp—that the Chinese could have used to increase the number of essay writers. Yet they specifically chose to employ the smaller rather than the larger, more motivating rewards.

Although the settings are quite different, the surveyed fraternities refused to allow civic activities into their initiation ceremonies for the same reason that the Chinese withheld large prizes in favor of less powerful inducements: They wanted the men to *own* what they had done. No excuses, no ways out were allowed. A man who suffered through an arduous hazing could not be given the chance to believe he did so for charitable purposes. A prisoner who salted his political essay with a few anti-American comments could not be permitted to shrug it off as motivated by a big reward. No, the fraternity chapters and Chinese Communists were playing for keeps. It was not enough to wring commitments out of their men; those men had to be made to take inner responsibility for their actions.

Social scientists have determined that we accept inner responsibility for a behavior when we think we have chosen to perform it in the absence of strong outside pressures. A large reward is one such external pressure. It may get us to perform a certain action, but it won't get us to accept inner responsibility for the act. Consequently, we won't feel committed to it. The same is true of a strong threat; it may motivate immediate compliance, but it is unlikely to produce long-term commitment.

All this has important implications for rearing children. It suggests that we should never heavily bribe or threaten our children to do the things we want them truly to believe in. Such pressures will probably produce temporary compliance with our wishes. However, if we want more than just that, if we want the children to believe in the correctness of what they have done, if we want them to continue to perform the desired behavior when we are not present to apply those outside pressures, then we must somehow arrange for them to accept inner responsibility for the actions we want them to take. An experiment by Jonathan Freedman gives us some hints about what to do and what not to do in this regard.

Freedman wanted to see if he could prevent second- to fourth-grade boys from playing with a fascinating toy, just because he had said that it was wrong to do so some six weeks earlier. Anyone familiar with seven-to-nine-year-old boys must realize the enormity of the task. But Freedman had a plan. If he could first get the boys to convince themselves that it was wrong to play with the forbidden toy, perhaps that belief would keep them from playing with it thereafter. The difficult thing was making the boys believe that it was wrong to amuse themselves with the toy—an extremely expensive, battery-controlled robot.

Freedman knew it would be easy enough to have a boy obey temporarily. All he had to do was threaten the boy with severe consequences should he be caught playing with the toy. As long as he was nearby to deal out stiff punishment, Freedman figured that few boys would risk operating the robot. He was right. After showing a boy an array of five toys and warning him, "It is wrong to play with the robot. If you play with the robot, I'll be very angry and will have to do something about it," Freedman left the room for a few minutes. During that time, the boy was observed secretly through a one-way mirror. Freedman tried this threat procedure on twenty-two different boys, and twenty-one of them never touched the robot while he was gone.

So a strong threat was successful while the boys thought they might be caught and punished. But Freedman had already guessed that. He was really interested in the effectiveness of the threat in guiding the boys' behavior later on, when he was no longer around. To find out what would happen then, he sent a young woman back to the boys' school about six weeks after he had been there. She took the boys out of the class one at a time to participate in an experiment. Without ever mentioning any connection with Freedman, she escorted each boy back to the room with the five toys and gave him a drawing test. While she was scoring the test, she told the boy that he was free to play with any toy in the room. Of course, almost all the boys played with a toy. The interesting result was that, of the boys playing with a toy, 77 percent chose to play with the robot that had been forbidden to them earlier. Freedman's severe threat, which had been so successful six weeks before, was almost totally unsuccessful when he was no longer able to back it up with punishment.

But Freedman wasn't finished yet. He changed his procedure slightly with a second sample of boys. These boys, too, were initially shown the array of five toys by Freedman and warned not to play with the robot while he was briefly out of the room because "It is wrong to play with the robot." But this time, Freedman provided no strong threat to frighten a boy into obedience. He simply left the room and observed through the one-way mirror to see if his instruction against playing with the forbidden toy was enough. It was. Just as with the other sample, only one of the twenty-two boys touched the robot during the short time Freedman was gone.

The real difference between the two samples of boys came six weeks later, when they had a chance to play with the toys while Freedman was no longer around. An astonishing thing happened with the boys who had earlier been given no strong threat against playing with the robot: When given the freedom to play with any toy they wished, most avoided the robot, even though it was by far the most attractive of the five toys available (the others were a cheap plastic submarine, a child's baseball glove without a ball, an unloaded toy rifle, and a toy tractor). When these boys played with one of the five toys, only 33 percent chose the robot.

Something dramatic had happened to both groups of boys. For the first group, it was the severe threat they heard from Freedman to back up his statement that playing with the robot was "wrong." It had been quite effective at first, while Freedman could catch them should they violate his rule. Later, though, when he was no longer present to observe the boys' behavior, his threat was impotent and his rule was, consequently, ignored. It seems clear that the threat had not taught the boys that operating the robot was wrong, only that it was unwise to do so when the possibility of punishment existed.

For the other boys, the dramatic event had come from the inside, not the outside. Freedman had instructed them, too, that playing with the robot was wrong, but he had added no threat of punishment should they disobey him. There were two important results. First, Freedman's instruction alone was enough to prevent the boys from operating the robot while he was briefly out of the room. Second, the boys took personal responsibility for their choice to stay away from the robot during that time. They decided that they hadn't played with it because *they* didn't want to. After all, there were no strong punishments associated with the toy to explain their behavior otherwise. Thus, weeks later, when Freedman was nowhere around, they still ignored the robot because they had been changed inside to believe that they did not want to play with it.[17]

Adults facing the child-rearing experience can take a cue from the Freedman study. Suppose a couple wants to impress upon their daughter that lying is wrong. A strong, clear threat ("It's bad to lie, honey; so if I catch you at it, I'll cut your tongue out") might well be effective when the parents are present or when the girl thinks she can be discovered. But it will not achieve the larger goal of convincing her that she does not want to lie because *she* thinks it's wrong. To do that, a much subtler approach is required. A reason must be given that is just strong enough to get her to be truthful most of the time but is not so strong that she sees *it* as the obvious reason for her truthfulness. It's a tricky business because exactly what this barely sufficient reason will be changes from child to child. For one little girl, a simple appeal may be enough ("It's bad to lie, honey; so I hope you won't do it"); for another child, it may be necessary to add a somewhat stronger reason (" . . . because if you do, I'll be disappointed in you"); for a third child, a mild form of warning may be required as well (" . . . and I'll probably have to do something I don't want to do"). Wise parents will know which kind of reason will work on their own children. The important thing is to use a reason that will initially produce the desired behavior and will, at the same time, allow a child to take personal responsibility for that behavior. Thus, the less detectable outside pressure such a reason contains, the better. Selecting just the right reason is not an easy task for parents. But the effort should pay off. It is likely to mean the difference between short-lived compliance and long-term commitment.

For a pair of reasons we have already talked about, compliance professionals love commitments that produce inner change. First, that change is not just specific to the situation where it first occurred; it covers a whole range of related situations, too. Second, the effects of the change are lasting. So, once a man has been induced to take action that shifts his self-image to that of, let's say, a public-spirited citizen, he is likely to be public-spirited in a variety of other circumstances where his compliance may also be desired, and he is likely to continue his public-spirited behavior for as long as his new self-image holds.

There is yet another attraction in commitments that lead to inner change—they grow their own legs. There is no need for the compliance professional to undertake a costly and continuing effort to reinforce the change; the pressure for consistency will take care of all that. After our friend comes to view himself as a public-spirited citizen, he will automatically begin to see things differently. He will convince himself that it is the correct way to be. He will begin to pay attention to facts he hadn't noticed before about the value of community service. He will make himself available to hear arguments he hadn't heard before favoring civic action. And he will find such arguments more persuasive than before. In general, because of the need to be consistent within his system of beliefs, he will assure himself that his choice to take public-spirited action was right. What is important about this process of generating additional reasons to justify the commitment is that the reasons are *new*. Thus, even if the original reason for the civic-minded behavior was taken away, these newly discovered reasons might be enough by themselves to support his perception that he had behaved correctly.

The advantage to an unscrupulous compliance professional

INFLUENCE

is tremendous. Because we build new struts to undergird choices we have committed ourselves to, an exploitative individual can offer us an inducement for making such a choice, and after the decision has been made, can remove that inducement, knowing that our decision will probably stand on its own newly created legs. New-car dealers frequently try to benefit from this process through a trick they call "throwing a low-ball." I first encountered the tactic while posing as a sales trainee at a local Chevrolet dealership. After a week of basic instruction, I was allowed to watch the regular salesmen perform. One practice that caught my attention right away was the low-ball.

For certain customers, a very good price is offered on a car, perhaps as much as four hundred dollars below competitors' prices. The good deal, however, is not genuine; the dealer never intends it to go through. Its only purpose is to cause a prospect to *decide* to buy one of the dealership's cars. Once the decision is made, a number of activities develop the customer's sense of personal commitment to the car—a raft of purchase forms are filled out, extensive financing terms are arranged, sometimes the customer is encouraged to drive the car for a day before signing the contract, "so you can get the feel of it and show it around in the neighborhood and at work." During this time, the dealer knows, customers automatically develop a range of new reasons to support the choice they have now made.

Then something happens. Occasionally an "error" in the calculations is discovered—maybe the salesman forgot to add in the cost of the air conditioner, and if the buyer still requires air conditioning, four hundred dollars must be added to the price. To throw suspicion off themselves, some dealers let the bank handling the financing find the mistake. At other times, the deal is disallowed at the last moment when the salesman checks with his boss, who cancels it because "We'd be losing money." For only another four hundred dollars the car can be had, which, in the context of a multithousand-dollar deal, doesn't seem too steep since, as the salesman emphasizes, the cost is equal to competitors' and "This is the car you chose, right?" Another, even more insidious form of low-balling occurs when the salesman makes an inflated trade-in offer on the prospect's old car as part of the buy/trade package. The customer recognizes the offer as overly generous and jumps at the deal. Later, before the contract is signed, the used-car manager says that the salesman's estimate was four hundred dollars too high and reduces the trade-in allowance to its actual, blue-book level. The customer, realizing that the reduced offer is the fair one, accepts it as appropriate and sometimes feels guilty about trying to take advantage of the salesman's high estimate. I once witnessed a woman provide an embarrassed apology to a salesman who had used the last version of low-balling on her—this while she was signing a new-car contract giving him a huge commission. He looked hurt but managed a forgiving smile.

No matter which variety of low-balling is used, the sequence is the same: An advantage is offered that induces a favorable purchase decision; then, sometime after the decision has been made but before the bargain is sealed, the original purchase advantage is deftly removed. It seems almost incredible that a customer would buy a car under these circumstances. Yet it works—not on everybody, of course, but it is effective enough to be a staple compliance procedure in many, many car showrooms. Automobile dealers have come to understand the ability of a personal commitment to build its own support system, a support system of new justifications for the commitment. Often these justifications provide so many strong legs for the decision to stand on that when the dealer pulls away only one leg, the original one, there is no collapse. The loss can be shrugged off by the customer who is consoled, even made happy, by the array of other good reasons favoring the choice. It never occurs to the buyer that those additional reasons might never have existed had the choice not been made in the first place.[18]

The impressive thing about the low-ball tactic is its ability to make a person feel pleased with a poor choice. Those who have only poor choices to offer us, then, are especially fond of the technique. We can find them throwing low-balls in business, social, and personal situations. For instance, there's my neighbor Tim, a true low-ball aficionado. Recall that he's the one who, by promising to change his ways, got his girlfriend, Sara, to cancel her impending marriage to another and to take him back. Since her decision for Tim, Sara has become more devoted to him than ever, even though he has not fulfilled his promises. She explains this by saying that she has allowed herself to see all sorts of positive qualities in Tim she had never recognized before.

I know full well that Sara is a low-ball victim. Just as sure as I had watched buyers fall for the give-it-and-take-it-away-later strategy in the car showroom, I watched her fall for the same trick with Tim. For his part, Tim remains the guy he has always been. But because the new attractions Sara has discovered (or created) in him are quite real for her, she now seems satisfied with the same arrangement that was unacceptable before her enormous commitment. The decision to choose Tim, poor as it may have been objectively, has grown its own supports and appears to have made Sara genuinely happy. I have never mentioned to Sara what I know about low-balling. The reason for my silence is not that I think her better off in the dark on the issue. As a general guiding principle, more information is always better than less information. It's just that, if I said a word, I am confident she would hate me for it.

Depending on the motives of the person wishing to use them, any of the compliance techniques discussed in this book can be employed for good or for ill. It should not be surprising, then, that the low-ball tactic can be used for more socially beneficial purposes than selling new cars or reestablishing relationships with former lovers. One research project done in Iowa, for example, shows how the low-ball procedure can influence homeowners to conserve energy.[19] The project, headed by Dr. Michael Pallak, began at the start of the Iowa winter when residents who heated their homes with natural gas were contacted by an interviewer. The interviewer gave them some energy-conservation tips and asked them to try to save fuel in the future. Although they all agreed to try, when the researchers examined the utility records of these families after a month and again at winter's end, it was clear that no real savings had occurred. The residents who had promised to make a conservation attempt used just as much natural gas as a random sample of their neighbors who had not been contacted by an interviewer. Just good intentions coupled with information about saving fuel, then, were not enough to change habits.

COMMITMENT AND CONSISTENCY

Even before the project began, Pallak and his research team had recognized that something more would be needed to shift long-standing energy patterns. So they tried a slightly different procedure on a comparable sample of Iowa natural-gas users. These people, too, were contacted by an interviewer, who provided energy-saving hints and asked them to conserve. But for these families, the interviewer offered something else: Those residents agreeing to save energy would have their names publicized in newspaper articles as public-spirited, fuel-conserving citizens. The effect was immediate. One month later, when the utility companies checked their meters, the homeowners in this sample had saved an average of 422 cubic feet of natural gas apiece. The chance to have their names in the paper had motivated these residents to substantial conservation efforts for a period of a month.

Then the rug was pulled out. The researchers extracted the reason that had initially caused these people to save fuel. Each family that had been promised publicity received a letter saying it would not be possible to publicize their names after all.

At the end of the winter, the research team examined the effect that letter had had on the natural-gas usage of the families. Did they return to their old, wasteful habits when the chance to be in the newspaper was removed? Hardly. For each of the remaining winter months, they actually conserved *more* fuel than they had during the time they thought they would be publicly celebrated for it! In terms of percentage of energy savings, they had managed a 12.2 percent first-month gas savings because they expected to see themselves lauded in the paper. But after the letter arrived informing them to the contrary, they did not return to their previous energy-use levels; instead, they increased their savings to a 15.5 percent level for the rest of the winter.

Although we can never be completely sure of such things, one explanation for their persistent behavior presents itself immediately. These people had been low-balled into a conservation commitment through a promise of newspaper publicity. Once made, that commitment started generating its own support: The homeowners began acquiring new energy habits, began feeling good about their public-spirited efforts, began convincing themselves of the vital need to reduce American dependence on foreign fuel, began appreciating the monetary savings in their utility bills, began feeling proud of their capacity for self-denial, and, most important, began viewing themselves as conservation-minded. With all these new reasons present to justify the commitment to use less energy, it is no wonder that the commitment remained firm even after the original reason, newspaper publicity, had been kicked away.

But strangely enough, when the publicity factor was no longer a possibility, these families did not merely maintain their fuel-saving effort, they heightened it. Any of a number of interpretations could be offered for that still stronger effort, but I have a favorite. In a way, the opportunity to receive newspaper publicity had prevented the homeowners from fully owning their commitment to conservation. Of all the reasons supporting the decision to try to save fuel, it was the only one that had come from the outside; it was the only one preventing the homeowners from thinking that they were conserving gas because they believed in it. So when the letter arrived canceling the publicity agreement, it removed the only impediment to these residents' images of themselves as fully concerned, energy-conscious citizens. This unqualified, new self-image then pushed them to even greater heights of conservation. Whether or not such an explanation is correct, a repeat study done by Pallak indicates that this hidden benefit of the low-ball tactic is no fluke.

The experiment was done in summer on Iowans whose homes were cooled by central air conditioning. Those homeowners who were promised newspaper publicity decreased their electricity use by 27.8 percent during July, as compared to similar homeowners who were not promised any coverage or who were not contacted at all. At the end of July, a letter was sent canceling the publicity promise. Rather than reverting to their old habits, the low-balled residents increased their August energy savings to a stunning 41.6 percent. Much like Sara, they appeared to have become committed to a choice through an initial inducement and were still more dedicated to it after the inducement had been removed.

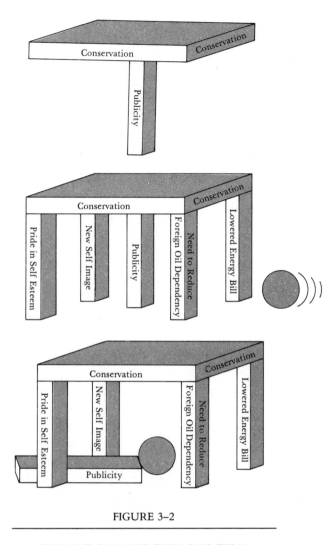

FIGURE 3–2

THE LOW-BALL FOR THE LONG-TERM

In this illustration of the Iowa energy research, we can see how the original conservation effort rested on the promise of publicity (top). Before long, however, this energy commitment led to the sprouting of new, self-generated supports, allowing the research team to throw its low-ball (middle). The consequence was a persisting level of conservation that stood firmly on its own legs after the initial publicity prop had been knocked down (bottom). (Artisti: Maria Picardi; copyright © Robert B. Cialdini.)

❋

HOW TO SAY NO

"Consistency is the hobgoblin of little minds." Or, at least, so goes a frequently heard quotation attributed to Ralph Waldo Emerson. But what a very odd thing to say. Looking around, it is obvious that, quite contrary to what Emerson seems to have suggested, internal consistency is a hallmark of logic and intellectual strength, while its lack characterizes the intellectually scattered and limited among us. What, then, could a thinker of Emerson's caliber have meant when he assigned the trait of consistency to the small-minded? I was sufficiently intrigued to go back to the original source of his statement, the essay "Self-Reliance," where it was clear that the problem lay not in Emerson but in the popular version of what he had said. Actually he wrote, "A *foolish* consistency is the hobgoblin of little minds." For some obscure reason, a central distinction had been lost as the years eroded the accurate version of his statement to mean something entirely different and, upon close inspection, entirely silly.[20]

That distinction should not be lost on us, however, because it is vital to the only effective defense I know against the weapons of influence embodied in the combined principles of commitment and consistency. Although consistency is generally good, even vital, there is a foolish, rigid variety to be shunned. It is this tendency to be automatically and unthinkingly consistent that Emerson referred to. And it is this tendency that we must be wary of, for it lays us open to the maneuvers of those who want to exploit the mechanical commitment⟶ consistency sequence for profit.

But since automatic consistency is so useful in allowing us an economical and appropriate way of behaving most of the time, we can't decide merely to eliminate it from our lives altogether. The results would be disastrous. If, rather than whirring along in accordance with our prior decisions and deeds, we stopped to think through the merits of every new action before performing it, we would never have time to accomplish anything

COMMITMENT AND CONSISTENCY

significant. We need even that dangerous, mechanical brand of consistency. The only way out of the dilemma is to know when such consistency is likely to lead to a poor choice. There are certain signals—two separate kinds of signals, in fact—to tip us off. We register each type in a different part of our bodies.

The first sort of signal is easy to recognize. It occurs right in the pit of our stomachs when we realize we are trapped into complying with a request we *know* we don't want to perform. It has happened to me a hundred times. An especially memorable instance, though, took place on a summer evening well before I began to study compliance tactics. I answered my doorbell to find a stunning young woman dressed in shorts and a revealing halter top. I noticed, nonetheless, that she was carrying a clipboard and was asking me to participate in a survey. Wanting to make a favorable impression, I agreed and, I do admit, stretched the truth in my interview answers so as to present myself in the most positive light. Our conversation went as follows:

STUNNING YOUNG WOMAN: Hello, I'm doing a survey on the entertainment habits of city residents, and I wonder if you could answer a few questions for me.

CIALDINI: Do come in.

SYW: Thank you. I'll just sit right here and begin. How many times per week would you say that you go out to dinner?

C: Oh, probably three, maybe four times a week. Whenever I can, really; I love fine restaurants.

SYW: How nice. And do you usually order wine with your dinner?

C: Only if it's imported.

SYW: I see. What about movies? Do you go to the movies much?

C: The cinema? I can't get enough of good films. I especially like the sophisticated kind with the words on the bottom of the screen. How about you? Do you like to see films?

SYW: Uh . . . yes, I do. But let's get back to the interview. Do you go to many concerts?

C: Definitely. The symphonic stuff mostly, of course; but I do enjoy a quality pop group as well.

SYW *(writing rapidly)*: Great! Just one more question. What about touring performances by theatrical or ballet companies? Do you see them when they're in town?

C: Ah, the ballet—the movement, the grace, the form—I love it. Mark me down as *loving* the ballet. See it every chance I get.

SYW: Fine. Just let me recheck my figures here for a moment, Mr. Cialdini.

C: Actually, it's Dr. Cialdini. But that sounds so formal; why don't you call me Bob?

SYW: All right, *Bob*. From the information you've already given me, I'm pleased to say that you could save up to twelve hundred dollars a year by joining Clubamerica! A small membership fee entitles you to discounts on most of the activities you've mentioned. Surely someone as socially vigorous as yourself would want to take advantage of the tremendous savings our company can offer on all the things you've already told me you do.

C *(trapped like a rat)*: Well . . . uh . . . I . . . uh . . . I guess so.

I remember quite well feeling my stomach tighten as I stammered my agreement. It was a clear call to my brain, "Hey, you're being taken here!" But I couldn't see a way out. I had been cornered by my own words. To decline her offer at that point would have meant facing a pair of distasteful alternatives: If I tried to back out by protesting that I was not actually the man-about-town I had claimed to be during the interview, I would come off a liar; but trying to refuse without that protest would make me come off a fool for not wanting to save twelve hundred dollars. So I bought the entertainment package, even though I knew I had been set up so that the need to be consistent with what I had already said would snare me.

No more, though. I listen to my stomach these days. And I have discovered a way to handle people who try to use the consistency principle on me. I just tell them exactly what they are doing. It works beautifully. Most of the time, they don't understand me; they just become sufficiently confused to want to leave me alone. I think they suspect lunacy in anyone who responds to their requests by explaining what Ralph Waldo Emerson meant in distinguishing between consistency and foolish consistency. Usually they have already begun edging away by the time I have mentioned "hobgoblins of the mind" and are gone long before I have described the *click, whirr* character of commitment and consistency. Occasionally, though, they realize that I am on to their game. I always know when that happens—it's as clear as the egg on their faces. They invariably become flustered, bumble through a hasty exit line, and go for the door.

This tactic has become the perfect counterattack for me. Whenever my stomach tells me I would be a sucker to comply with a request merely because doing so would be consistent with some prior commitment I was tricked into, I relay that message to the requester. I don't try to deny the importance of consistency; I just point out the absurdity of foolish consistency. Whether, in response, the requester shrinks away guiltily or retreats in bewilderment, I am content. I have won; an exploiter has lost.

I sometimes think about how it would be if that stunning young woman of years ago were to try to sell me an entertainment-club membership now. I have it all worked out. The entire interaction would be the same, except for the end:

SYW: . . . Surely someone as socially vigorous as yourself would want to take advantage of the tremendous savings our company can offer on all the things you've already told me you do.

C *(with great self-assurance):* Quite wrong. You see, I recognize what has gone on here. I know that your story about doing a survey was just a pretext for getting people to tell you how often they go out and that, under those circumstances, there is a natural tendency to exaggerate. I also realize that your bosses selected you for this job because of your physical attractiveness and told you to wear clothes showing a lot of your resilient body tissue because a pretty, scantily clad woman is likely to get men to brag about what swingers they are in order to impress her. So I'm not interested in your entertainment club because of what Emerson said about foolish consistency and hobgoblins of the mind.

INFLUENCE

SYW *(staring blankly)*: Huh?

C: Look. What I told you during your fake survey doesn't matter. I refuse to allow myself to be locked into a mechanical sequence of commitment and consistency when I know it's wrongheaded. No *click, whirr* for me.

SYW: Huh?

C: Okay, let me put it this way: (1) It would be stupid of me to spend money on something I don't want. (2) I have it on excellent authority, direct from my stomach, that I don't want your entertainment plan. (3) Therefore, if you still believe that I will buy it, you probably also still believe in the Tooth Fairy. Surely, someone as intelligent as yourself would be able to understand that.

SYW *(trapped like a stunning young rat)*: Well . . . uh . . . I . . . uh . . . I guess so.

Stomachs are not especially perceptive or subtle organs. Only when it is obvious that we are about to be conned are they likely to register and transmit that message. At other times, when it is not clear that we are being taken, our stomachs may never catch on. Under those circumstances we have to look elsewhere for a clue. The situation of my neighbor Sara provides a good illustration. She made an important commitment to Tim by canceling her prior marriage plans. That commitment has grown its own supports, so that even though the original reasons for the commitment are gone, she remains in harmony with it. She has convinced herself with newly formed reasons that she did the right thing, so she stays with Tim. It is not difficult to see why there would be no tightening in Sara's stomach as a result. Stomachs tell us when we are doing something we think is wrong for us. Sara *thinks* no such thing. To her mind, she has chosen correctly and is behaving consistently with that choice.

Yet, unless I badly miss my guess, there is a part of Sara that recognizes her choice as a mistake and her current living arrangement as a brand of foolish consistency. Where, exactly, that part of Sara is located we can't be sure. But our language does give it a name: heart of hearts. It is, by definition, the one place where we cannot fool ourselves. It is the place where none of our justi-

COMMITMENT AND CONSISTENCY

fications, none of our rationalizations penetrate. Sara has the truth there, although, right now, she can't hear its signal clearly through the noise and static of the new support apparatus she has erected.

If Sara has erred in her choice of Tim, how long could she go without clearly recognizing it, without having a massive heart of hearts attack? There is no telling. One thing is certain, however: As time passes, the various alternatives to Tim are disappearing. She had better determine soon whether she is making a mistake.

Easier said than done, of course. She must answer an extremely intricate question: "Knowing what I now know, if I could go back in time, would I make the same choice?" The problem lies in the "Knowing what I now know" part of the question. Just what does she now know, accurately, about Tim? How much of what she thinks of him is the result of a desperate attempt to justify the commitment she made? She claims that, since her decision to take him back, he cares for her more, is trying hard to stop his excessive drinking, has learned to make a wonderful omelet, etc. Having tasted a couple of his omelets, I have my doubts. The important issue, though, is whether *she* believes these things, not just intellectually—we can play such mind games on ourselves—but in her heart of hearts.

There may be a little device Sara can use to find out how much of her current satisfaction with Tim is real and how much is foolish consistency. Accumulating psychological evidence indicates that we experience our feelings toward something a split second before we can intellectualize about it.[21] My suspicion is that the message sent by the heart of hearts is a pure, basic feeling. Therefore, if we train ourselves to be attentive, we should register it ever so slightly before our cognitive apparatus engages. According to this approach, were Sara to ask herself the crucial "Would I make the same choice again?" question, she would be well advised to look for and trust the first flash of feeling she experienced in response. It would likely be the signal from her heart of hearts, slipping through undistorted just before the means by which she could kid herself flooded in.[22]

I have begun using the same device myself whenever I even suspect I might be acting in a foolishly consistent manner. One

INFLUENCE

time, for instance, I had stopped at the self-service pump of a filling station advertising a price per gallon a couple of cents below the rate of other stations in the area. But with pump nozzle in hand, I noticed that the price listed on the pump was two cents higher than the display sign price. When I mentioned the difference to a passing attendant, who I later learned was the owner, he mumbled unconvincingly that the rates had changed a few days ago but there hadn't been time to correct the display. I tried to decide what to do. Some reasons for staying came to mind— "I really do need gasoline badly." "This pump is available, and I am in sort of a hurry." "I think I remember that my car runs better on this brand of gas."

I needed to determine whether those reasons were genuine or mere justifications for my decision to stop there. So I asked myself the crucial question, "Knowing what I know about the real price of this gasoline, if I could go back in time, would I make the same choice again?" Concentrating on the first burst of impression I sensed, the answer was clear and unqualified. I would have driven right past. I wouldn't even have slowed down. I knew then that without the price advantage, those other reasons would not have brought me there. They hadn't created the decision; the decision had created them.

That settled, there was another decision to be faced, though. Since I was already there holding the hose, wouldn't it be better to use it than to suffer the inconvenience of going elsewhere to pay the same price? Fortunately, the station attendant-owner came over and helped me make up my mind. He asked why I wasn't pumping any gas. I told him I didn't like the price discrepancy and he said with a snarl, "Listen, nobody's gonna tell me how to run my business. If you think I'm cheating you, just put that hose down *right now* and get off my property as fast as you can do it, bud." Already certain he was a cheat, I was happy to act consistently with my belief and his wishes. I dropped the hose on the spot . . . and drove over it on my way to the closest exit. Sometimes consistency can be a marvelously rewarding thing.

4

SOCIAL PROOF
Truths are us

❊

I don't know anyone who likes canned laughter. In fact, when I surveyed the people who came into my office one day—several students, two telephone repairmen, a number of university professors, and the janitor—the reaction was invariably critical. Television, with its incessant system of laugh tracks and technically augmented mirth, received the most heat. The people I questioned hated canned laughter. They called it stupid, phony, and obvious. Although my sample was small, I would bet that it closely reflects the negative feelings of most of the American public toward laugh tracks.

Why, then, is canned laughter so popular with television executives? They have won their exalted positions and splendid salaries by knowing how to give the public what it wants. Yet they religiously employ the laugh tracks that their audiences find distasteful. And they do so over the objections of many of their most talented artists. It is not uncommon for acclaimed directors, writers, or actors to demand the elimination of canned responses

INFLUENCE

from the television projects they undertake. These demands are only sometimes successful, and when they are, it is not without a battle.

What could it be about canned laughter that is so attractive to television executives? Why would these shrewd and tested businessmen champion a practice that their potential watchers find disagreeable and their most creative talents find personally insulting? The answer is at once simple and intriguing: They know what the research says. Experiments have found that the use of canned merriment causes an audience to laugh longer and more often when humorous material is presented and to rate the material as funnier. In addition, some evidence indicates that canned laughter is most effective for poor jokes.[1]

In the light of these data, the actions of television executives make perfect sense. The introduction of laugh tracks into their comic programming will increase the humorous and appreciative responses of an audience, even—and especially—when the material is of poor quality. Is it any surprise, then, that television, glutted as it is with artless situation-comedy attempts, should be saturated with canned laughter? Those executives know precisely what they are doing.

But with the mystery of the widespread use of laugh tracks solved, we are left with a more perplexing question: Why does canned laughter work on us the way it does? It is no longer the television executives who appear peculiar; they are acting logically and in their own interests. Instead, it is the behavior of the audience, of you and me, that seems strange. Why should we laugh more at comedy material afloat in a sea of mechanically fabricated merriment? And why should we think that comic flotsam funnier? The executives aren't really fooling us. Anyone can recognize dubbed laughter. It is so blatant, so clearly counterfeit, that there could be no confusing it with the real thing. We know full well that the hilarity we hear is irrelevant to the humorous quality of the joke it follows, is created not spontaneously by a genuine audience but artificially by a technician at a control board. Yet, transparent forgery that it is, it works on us!

To discover why canned laughter is so effective, we first need to understand the nature of yet another potent weapon of influence: the principle of social proof. It states that one means we use to determine what is correct is to find out what other people think is correct. The principle applies especially to the way we decide what constitutes correct behavior. We view a behavior as more correct in a given situation to the degree that we see others performing it. Whether the question is what to do with an empty popcorn box in a movie theater, how fast to drive on a certain stretch of highway, or how to eat the chicken at a dinner party, the actions of those around us will be important in defining the answer.

The tendency to see an action as more appropriate when others are doing it normally works quite well. As a rule, we will make fewer mistakes by acting in accord with social evidence than contrary to it. Usually, when a lot of people are doing something, it is the right thing to do. This feature of the principle of social proof is simultaneously its major strength and its major weakness. Like the other weapons of influence, it provides a convenient shortcut for determining how to behave but, at the same time, makes one who uses the shortcut vulnerable to the attacks of profiteers who lie in wait along its path.

In the case of canned laughter, the problem comes when we begin responding to social proof in such a mindless and reflexive fashion that we can be fooled by partial or fake evidence. Our folly is not that we use others' laughter to help decide what is humorous and when mirth is appropriate; that is in keeping with the well-founded principle of social proof. The folly is that we do so in response to patently fraudulent laughter. Somehow, one disembodied feature of humor—a sound—works like the essence of humor. The example from Chapter 1 of the turkey and the polecat is instructive here. Remember that because the particular "cheep-cheep" of turkey chicks is normally associated with newborn turkeys, their mothers will display or withhold maternal care solely on the basis of that sound? And remember how, consequently, it was possible to trick a female turkey into mothering a stuffed polecat as long as the replica played the recorded "cheep-cheep" of a baby turkey? The simulated chick sound was enough to start the female's mothering tape whirring.

The lesson of the turkey and the polecat illustrates uncomfortably well the relationship between the average viewer and the laugh-track-playing television executive. We have become so accustomed to taking the humorous reactions of others as evidence of what deserves laughter that we too can be made to respond to the sound and none of the substance of the real thing. Much as a "cheep-cheep" noise removed from the reality of a chick can stimulate a female turkey to mother, so can a recorded "ha-ha" removed from the reality of a genuine audience stimulate us to laugh. The television executives are exploiting our preference for shortcuts, our tendency to react automatically on the basis of partial evidence. They know that their tapes will cue our tapes. *Click, whirr.*

Television executives are hardly alone in their use of social evidence for profit. Our tendency to assume that an action is more correct if others are doing it is exploited in a variety of settings. Bartenders often "salt" their tip jars with a few dollar bills at the beginning of the evening to simulate tips left by prior customers and thereby to give the impression that tipping with folding money is proper barroom behavior. Church ushers sometimes salt collection baskets for the same reason and with the same positive effect on proceeds. Evangelical preachers are known to seed their audience with "ringers," who are rehearsed to come forward at a specified time to give witness and donations. For example, an Arizona State University research team that infiltrated the Billy Graham organization reported on such advance preparations prior to one of his Crusade visits. "By the time Graham arrives in town and makes his altar call, an army of six thousand wait with instructions on when to come forth at varying intervals to create the impression of a spontaneous mass outpouring."[2]

Advertisers love to inform us when a product is the "fastest-growing" or "largest-selling" because they don't have to convince us directly that the product is good, they need only say that many others think so, which seems proof enough. The producers of charity telethons devote inordinate amounts of time to the incessant listing of viewers who have already pledged contributions. The message being communicated to the holdouts is clear: "Look at all the people who have decided to give. It *must* be the correct thing to do." At the height of the disco craze, certain discotheque owners manufactured a brand of visible social proof for their clubs' quality by creating long waiting lines outside when there was plenty of room inside. Salesmen are taught to spice their pitches with numerous accounts of individuals who have purchased the product. The most-sought-after sales and motivation consultant working today, Cavett Robert, captures the principle nicely in his advice to sales trainees: "Since 95 percent of the people are imitators and only 5 percent initiators, people are persuaded more by the actions of others than by any proof we can offer."

Researchers, too, have employed procedures based on the principle of social proof—sometimes with astounding results. One psychologist in particular, Albert Bandura, has led the way in developing such procedures for the elimination of undesirable behavior. Bandura and his colleagues have shown how people suffering from phobias can be rid of these extreme fears in an amazingly simple fashion. For instance, in an early study nursery-school-age children chosen because they were terrified of dogs merely watched a little boy playing happily with a dog for twenty minutes a day. This exhibition produced such marked changes in the reactions of the fearful children that after only four days, 67 percent of them were willing to climb into a playpen with a dog and remain confined there petting and scratching it while everyone else left the room. Moreover, when the researchers tested the children's fear levels again one month later, they found that the improvement had not evaporated during that time; in fact, the children were more willing than ever to interact with dogs.

An important practical discovery was made in a second study of children who were exceptionally afraid of dogs: To reduce their fears, it was not necessary to provide live demonstrations of another child playing with a dog, film clips had the same effect. And the most effective type of clips were those depicting not one but a variety of other children interacting with their dogs; apparently the principle of social proof works best when the proof is provided by the actions of a lot of other people.[3]

The powerful influence of filmed examples in changing the behavior of children can be used as therapy for various problems. Some striking evidence is available in the research of psychologist Robert O'Connor on socially withdrawn preschool children. We have all seen children of this sort, terribly shy, standing alone at the fringes of the games and groupings of their peers. O'Connor worried that a long-term pattern of isolation was forming, even at an early age, that would create persistent difficulties in social comfort and adjustment through adulthood. In an attempt to reverse the pattern, O'Connor made a film containing eleven different scenes in a nursery-school setting. Each scene began by showing a different solitary child watching some ongoing social activity and then actively joining the activity, to everyone's enjoyment. O'Connor selected a group of the most severely withdrawn children from four preschools and showed them his film. The impact was impressive. The isolates immediately began to interact with their peers at a level equal to that of the normal children in the schools. Even more astonishing was what O'Connor found when he returned to observe six weeks later. While the withdrawn children who had not seen O'Connor's film remained as isolated as ever, those who *had* viewed it were now leading their schools in amount of social activity. It seems that this twenty-three-minute movie, viewed just once, was enough to reverse a potential pattern of lifelong maladaptive behavior. Such is the potency of the principle of social proof.[4]

When it comes to illustrations of the strength of social proof, there is one that is far and away my favorite. Several features account for its appeal: It offers a superb example of the much underused method of participant observation, in which a scientist studies a process by becoming immersed in its natural occurrence; it provides information of interest to such diverse groups as historians, psychologists, and theologians; and, most important, it shows how social evidence can be used on us—not by others, but by ourselves—to assure us that what we prefer to be true will seem to be true.

The story is an old one, requiring an examination of ancient data, for the past is dotted with millennial religious movements. Various sects and cults have prophesied that on one or another particular date there would arrive a period of redemption and great happiness for those who believed in the group's teachings. In each instance it has been predicted that the beginning of the

time of salvation would be marked by an important and undeniable event, usually the cataclysmic end of the world. Of course,
these predictions have invariably proved false. To the acute dis-
may of the members of such groups, the end has never appeared
as scheduled.

But immediately following the obvious failure of the prophecy, history records an enigmatic pattern. Rather than disbanding
in disillusion, the cultists often become strengthened in their convictions. Risking the ridicule of the populace, they take to the
streets, publicly asserting their dogma and seeking converts with
a fervor that is intensified, not diminished, by the clear disconfirmation of a central belief. So it was with the Montanists of sec-
ond-century Turkey, with the Anabaptists of sixteenth-century
Holland, with the Sabbataists of seventeenth-century Izmir, with
the Millerites of nineteenth-century America. And, thought a
trio of interested social scientists, so it might be with a doomsday
cult based in modern-day Chicago. The scientists—Leon Festinger, Henry Riecken, and Stanley Schachter—who were then
colleagues at the University of Minnesota, heard about the Chicago group and felt it worthy of close study. Their decision to
investigate by joining the group, incognito, as new believers and
by placing additional paid observers among its ranks resulted in a
remarkably rich firsthand account of the goings-on before and
after the day of predicted catastrophe.[5]

The cult of believers was small, never numbering more than
thirty members. Its leaders were a middle-aged man and woman,
whom the researchers renamed, for purposes of publication, Dr.
Thomas Armstrong and Mrs. Marian Keech. Dr. Armstrong, a
physician on the staff of a college student health service, had a
long-held interest in mysticism, the occult, and flying saucers; as
such he served as a respected authority on these subjects for the
group. Mrs. Keech, though, was the center of attention and activity. Earlier in the year she had begun to receive messages from
spiritual beings, whom she called the Guardians, located on other
planets. It was these messages, flowing through Marian Keech's
hand via the device of "automatic writing," that were to form
the bulk of the cult's religious belief system. The teachings of the
Guardians were loosely linked to traditional Christian thought.
No wonder that one of the Guardians, Sananda, eventually "re-

vealed" himself as the current embodiment of Jesus.

The transmissions from the Guardians, always the subjects of much discussion and interpretation among the group, gained new significance when they began to foretell a great impending disaster—a flood that would begin in the Western Hemisphere and eventually engulf the world. Although the cultists were understandably alarmed at first, further messages assured them that they and all those who believed in the Lessons sent through Mrs. Keech would survive. Before the calamity, spacemen were to arrive and carry off the believers in flying saucers to a place of safety, presumably on another planet. Very little detail was provided about the rescue except that the believers were to make themselves ready for pickup by rehearsing certain passwords to be exchanged ("I left my hat at home." "What is your question?" "I am my own porter.") and by removing all metal from their clothes—because the wearing or carrying of metal made saucer travel "extremely dangerous."

As Festinger, Riecken, and Schachter observed the preparations during the weeks prior to the flood date, they noted with special interest two significant aspects of the members' behavior. First, the level of commitment to the cult's belief system was very high. In anticipation of their departure from doomed Earth, irrevocable steps were taken by the group members. Most had incurred the opposition of family and friends to their beliefs but had persisted nonetheless in their convictions, often when it meant losing the affections of these others. In fact, several of the members were threatened by neighbors or family with legal actions designed to have them declared insane. In Dr. Armstrong's case, a motion was filed by his sister to have his two younger children taken away. Many believers quit their jobs or neglected their studies to devote full time to the movement. Some even gave or threw away their personal belongings, expecting them shortly to be of no use. These were people whose certainty that they had the truth allowed them to withstand enormous social, economic, and legal pressures and whose commitment to their dogma grew as each pressure was resisted.

The second significant aspect of the believers' preflood actions was a curious form of inaction. For individuals so clearly convinced of the validity of their creed, they did surprisingly little to spread the word. Although they did initially make public the news of the coming disaster, there was no attempt to seek converts, to proselyte actively. They were willing to sound the alarm and to counsel those who voluntarily responded to it, but that was all.

The group's distaste for recruitment efforts was evident in various ways besides the lack of personal persuasion attempts. Secrecy was maintained in many matters—extra copies of the Lessons were burned, passwords and secret signs were instituted, the contents of certain private tape recordings were not to be discussed with outsiders (so secret were the tapes that even long-time believers were prohibited from taking notes of them). Publicity was avoided. As the day of disaster approached, increasing numbers of newspaper, television, and radio reporters converged on the group's headquarters in the Keech house. For the most part, these people were turned away or ignored. The most frequent answer to their questions was, "No comment." Although discouraged for a time, the media representatives returned with a vengeance when Dr. Armstrong's religious activities caused him to be fired from his post on the college health service staff; one especially persistent newsman had to be threatened with a lawsuit. A similar siege was repelled on the eve of the flood when a swarm of reporters pushed and pestered the believers for information. Afterward, the researchers summarized the group's pre-flood stance on public exposure and recruitment in respectful tones: "Exposed to a tremendous burst of publicity, they had made every attempt to dodge fame; given dozens of opportunities to proselyte, they had remained evasive and secretive and behaved with an almost superior indifference."

Eventually, when all the reporters and would-be converts had been cleared from the house, the believers began making their final preparations for the arrival of the spaceship scheduled for midnight that night. The scene as viewed by Festinger, Riecken, and Schachter must have seemed like absurdist theater. Otherwise ordinary people—housewives, college students, a high-school boy, a publisher, an M.D., a hardware-store clerk and his mother—were participating earnestly in tragic comedy. They took direction from a pair of members who were periodically in touch with the Guardians; Marian Keech's written messages from Sananda were being supplemented that evening by "the Bertha," a former beautician through whose tongue the "Creator" gave instruction. They rehearsed their lines diligently, calling out in chorus the responses to be made before entering the rescue saucer, "I am my own porter." "I am my own pointer." They discussed seriously whether the message from a caller identifying himself as Captain Video—a TV space character of the time—was properly interpreted as a prank or a coded communication from their rescuers. And they performed in costume. In keeping with the admonition to carry nothing metallic aboard the saucer, the believers wore clothing that had been cut open to allow the metal pieces to be torn out. The metal eyelets in their shoes had been ripped away. The women were braless or wore brassieres whose metal stays had been removed. The men had yanked the zippers out of their pants, which were supported by lengths of rope in place of belts.

The group's fanaticism concerning the removal of all metal was vividly experienced by one of the researchers who remarked, twenty-five minutes before midnight, that he had forgotten to extract the zipper from his trousers. As the observers tell it, "this knowledge produced a near panic reaction. He was rushed into the bedroom where Dr. Armstrong, his hands trembling and his eyes darting to the clock every few seconds, slashed out the zipper with a razor blade and wrenched its clasps free with wire-cutters." The hurried operation finished, the researcher was returned to the living room a slightly less metallic but, one supposes, much paler man.

As the time appointed for their departure grew very close, the believers settled into a lull of soundless anticipation. With trained scientists on site, we are afforded a detailed account of the events that transpired during this momentous period in the life of the group:

> The last ten minutes were tense ones for the group in the living room. They had nothing to do but sit and wait, their coats in their laps. In the tense silence two clocks tickled loudly, one about ten minutes faster than the other. When the faster of the two pointed to twelve-five, one of the observers remarked aloud on the fact. A chorus of people replied that midnight

had not yet come. Bob Eastman affirmed that the slower clock was correct; he had set it himself only that afternoon. It showed only four minutes before midnight.

These four minutes passed in complete silence except for a single utterance. When the [slower] clock on the mantel showed only one minute remaining before the guide to the saucer was due, Marian exclaimed in a strained, high-pitched voice: "And not a plan has gone astray!" The clock chimed twelve, each stroke painfully clear in the expectant hush. The believers sat motionless.

One might have expected some visible reaction. Midnight had passed and nothing had happened. The cataclysm itself was less than seven hours away. But there was little to see in the reactions of the people in that room. There was no talking, no sound. People sat stock-still, their faces seemingly frozen and expressionless. Mark Post was the only person who even moved. He lay down on the sofa and closed his eyes but did not sleep. Later, when spoken to, he answered monosyllabically but otherwise lay immobile. The others showed nothing on the surface, although it became clear later that they had been hit hard.

Gradually, painfully, an atmosphere of despair and confusion settled over the group. They reexamined the prediction and the accompanying messages. Dr. Armstrong and Mrs. Keech reiterated their faith. The believers mulled over their predicament and discarded explanation after explanation as unsatisfactory. At one point, toward 4 A.M., Mrs. Keech broke down and cried bitterly. She knew, she sobbed, that there were some who were beginning to doubt but that the group must beam light to those who needed it most and that the group must hold together. The rest of the believers were losing their composure, too. They were all visibly shaken and many were close to tears. It was now almost 4:30 A.M. and still no way of handling the disconfirmation had been found. By now, too, most of the group were talking openly about the failure of the escort to come at midnight. The group seemed near dissolution.

In the midst of this gathering doubt, as cracks crawled through the believers' confidence, the researchers witnessed a pair of remarkable incidents, one after another. The first occurred at about 4:45 A.M., when Marian Keech's hand suddenly leapt to the task of transcribing through "automatic writing" the text of a holy message from above. When read aloud, the communication proved to be an elegant explanation for the events of that night. "The little group, sitting alone all night long, had spread so much light that God had saved the world from destruction." Although neat and efficient, this explanation was not wholly satisfying by itself; for example, after hearing it, one member simply rose, put on his hat and coat, and left. Something additional was needed to restore the believers to their previous levels of faith.

It was at this point that the second notable incident occurred to meet that need. Once again, the words of those who were present offer a vivid description:

> The atmosphere in the group changed abruptly and so did their behavior. Within minutes after she had read the message explaining the disconfirmation, Mrs. Keech received another message instructing her to publicize the explanation. She reached for the telephone and began dialing the number of a newspaper. While she was waiting to be connected, someone asked: "Marian, is this the first time you have called the newspaper yourself?" Her reply was immediate: "Oh, yes, this is the first time I have ever called them. I have never had anything to tell them before, but now I feel it is urgent." The whole group could have echoed her feelings, for they all felt a sense of urgency. As soon as Marian had finished her call, the other members took turns telephoning newspapers, wire services, radio stations, and national magazines to spread the explanation of the failure of the flood. In their desire to spread the word quickly and resoundingly, the believers now opened for public attention matters that had been thus far utterly secret. Where only hours earlier they had shunned newspaper reporters and felt that the attention they were getting in the press was painful, they now became avid seekers for publicity.

Not only had the long-standing policies concerning secrecy and publicity done an about-face, so too had the group's attitude toward potential converts. Whereas likely recruits who previously visited the house had been mostly ignored, turned away,

SOCIAL PROOF

or treated with casual attention, the day following the disconfirmation saw a different story. All callers were admitted, all questions were answered, attempts were made to proselyte all such
visitors. The members' unprecedented willingness to accommo-
date possible new recruits was perhaps best demonstrated when
nine high-school students arrived on the following night to speak
with Mrs. Keech.

> They found her at the telephone deep in a discussion of flying
> saucers with a caller whom, it later turned out, she believed to
> be a spaceman. Eager to continue talking to him and at the
> same time anxious to keep her new guests, Marian simply in-
> cluded them in the conversation and, for more than an hour,
> chatted alternately with her guests in the living room and the
> "spaceman" on the other end of the telephone. So intent was
> she on proselyting that she seemed unable to let any oppor-
> tunity go by.

To what can we attribute the believers' radical turnabout? In
the space of a few hours, they went from clannish and taciturn
hoarders of the Word to expansive and eager disseminators of it.
And what could have possessed them to choose such an ill-timed
instant—when the failure of the flood was likely to cause nonbelievers to view the group and its dogma as laughable?

The crucial event occurred sometime during "the night of
the flood" when it became increasingly clear that the prophecy
would not be fulfilled. Oddly, it was not their prior certainty
that drove the members to propagate the faith, it was an en-
croaching sense of uncertainty. It was the dawning realization
that if the spaceship and flood predictions were wrong, so might
be the entire belief system on which they rested. For those huddled in the Keech living room, that growing possibility must
have seemed hideous.

The group members had gone too far, given up too much
for their beliefs to see them destroyed; the shame, the economic
cost, the mockery would be too great to bear. The overarching
need of the cultists to cling to those beliefs seeps poignantly from
their own words: From a young woman with a three-year-old
child:

I have to believe the flood is coming on the twenty-first because I've spent all my money. I quit my job, I quit computer school. . . . I have to believe.

And from Dr. Armstrong to one of the researchers four hours after the failure of the saucermen to arrive:

I've had to go a long way. I've given up just about everything. I've cut every tie. I've burned every bridge. I've turned my back on the world. I can't afford to doubt. I have to believe. And there isn't any other truth.

Imagine the corner in which Dr. Armstrong and his followers found themselves as morning approached. So massive was the commitment to their beliefs that no other truth was tolerable. Yet that set of beliefs had just taken a merciless pounding from physical reality: No saucer had landed, no spacemen had knocked, no flood had come, nothing had happened as prophesied. Since the only acceptable form of truth had been undercut by physical proof, there was but one way out of the corner for the group. They had to establish another type of proof for the validity of their beliefs: social proof.

This, then, explains their sudden shift from secretive conspirators to zealous missionaries. And it explains the curious timing of the shift—precisely when a direct disconfirmation of their beliefs had rendered them least convincing to outsiders. It was necessary to risk the scorn and derision of the nonbelievers because publicity and recruitment efforts provided the only remaining hope. If they could spread the Word, if they could inform the uninformed, if they could persuade the skeptics, and if, by so doing, they could win new converts, their threatened but treasured beliefs would become *truer*. The principle of social proof says so: The greater the number of people who find any idea correct, the more the idea will be correct. The group's assignment was clear; since the physical evidence could not be changed, the social evidence had to be. Convince and ye shall be convinced![6]

SOCIAL PROOF

✳

CAUSE OF DEATH: UNCERTAIN(TY)

All the weapons of influence discussed in this book work better under some conditions than under others. If we are to defend ourselves adequately against any such weapon, it is vital that we know its optimal operating conditions in order to recognize when we are most vulnerable to its influence. In the case of the principle of social proof, we have already had a hint of one time when it works best. Among the Chicago believers, it was a sense of shaken confidence that triggered their craving for converts. In general, when we are unsure of ourselves, when the situation is unclear or ambiguous, when uncertainty reigns, we are most likely to look to and accept the actions of others as correct.

In the process of examining the reactions of other people to resolve our uncertainty, however, we are likely to overlook a subtle but important fact. Those people are probably examining the social evidence, too. Especially in an ambiguous situation, the tendency for everyone to be looking to see what everyone else is doing can lead to a fascinating phenomenon called "pluralistic ignorance." A thorough understanding of the pluralistic ignorance phenomenon helps immeasurably to explain a regular occurrence in our country that has been termed both a riddle and a national disgrace: the failure of entire groups of bystanders to aid victims in agonizing need of help.

The classic example of such bystander inaction and the one that has produced the most debate in journalistic, political, and scientific circles began as an ordinary homicide case in the borough of Queens in New York City. A woman in her late twenties, Catherine Genovese, was killed in a late-night attack on her home street as she returned from work. Murder is never an act to be passed off lightly, but in a city the size and tenor of New York, the Genovese incident warranted no more space than a fraction of a column in *The New York Times*. Catherine Genovese's story would have died with her on that day in March 1964 if it hadn't been for a mistake.

INFLUENCE

The metropolitan editor of the *Times,* A. M. Rosenthal, happened to be having lunch with the city police commissioner a week later. Rosenthal asked the commissioner about a different Queens-based homicide and the commissioner, thinking he was being questioned about the Genovese case, revealed something staggering that had been uncovered by the police investigation. It was something that left everyone who heard it, the commissioner included, aghast and grasping for explanations. Catherine Genovese had not experienced a quick, muffled death. It had been a long, loud, tortured, *public* event. Her assailant had chased and attacked her in the street three times over a period of thirty-five minutes before his knife finally silenced her cries for help. Incredibly, thirty-eight of her neighbors watched the events of her death unfold from the safety of their apartment windows without so much as lifting a finger to call the police.

Rosenthal, a former Pulitzer Prize-winning reporter, knew a story when he heard one. On the day of his lunch with the commissioner, he assigned a reporter to investigate the "bystander angle" of the Genovese incident. Within a week, the *Times* published a long, page 1 article that was to create a swirl of controversy and speculation. The first few paragraphs of that report provide the tone and focus of the burgeoning story:

> For more than half an hour thirty-eight respectable, law-abiding citizens in Queens watched a killer stalk and stab a woman in three separate attacks in Kew Gardens.
>
> Twice the sound of their voices and the sudden glow of their bedroom lights interrupted him and frightened him off. Each time he returned, sought her out, and stabbed her again. Not one person telephoned the police during the assault; one witness called after the woman was dead.
>
> That was two weeks ago today. But Assistant Chief Inspector Frederick M. Lussen, in charge of the borough's detectives and a veteran of twenty-five years of homicide investigations, is still shocked.
>
> He can give a matter-of-fact recitation of many murders. But the Kew Gardens slaying baffles him—not because it is a murder, but because "good people" failed to call the police.

SOCIAL PROOF

As with Assistant Chief Inspector Lussen, shock and bafflement were the standard reactions of almost everyone who learned the story's details. The shock struck first, leaving the police, the newspeople, and the reading public stunned. The bafflement followed quickly. How could thirty-eight "good people" fail to act under those circumstances? No one could understand it. Even the murder witnesses themselves were bewildered. "I don't know," they answered one after another. "I just don't know." A few offered weak reasons for their inaction. For example, two or three people explained that they were "afraid" or "did not want to get involved." But these reasons do not stand up to close scrutiny: A simple anonymous call to the police could have saved Catherine Genovese without threatening the witness's future safety or free time. No, it wasn't the observers' fear or reluctance to complicate their lives that explained their lack of action; something else was going on there that even they could not fathom.

Confusion, though, does not make for good news copy. So the press as well as the other media—several papers, TV stations, and magazines were pursuing follow-up stories by now—emphasized the only explanation available at the time: The witnesses, no different from the rest of us, hadn't cared enough to get involved. We were becoming a nation of selfish, insensitive people. The rigors of modern life, especially city life, were hardening us. We were becoming "The Cold Society," unfeeling and indifferent to the plight of our fellow citizens.

In support of this interpretation, news stories began appearing regularly in which various kinds of public apathy were detailed. The *Times* actually appears to have developed an apathy "beat" for a period following the Genovese revelations. Also supporting such an interpretation were the remarks of a range of armchair social commentators, who, as a breed, seem never to admit to bafflement when speaking to the press. They, too, saw the Genovese case as having large-scale social significance. All used the word "apathy," which, it is interesting to note, had been in the headline of the *Times*'s front-page story, although they accounted for the apathy differently. One attributed it to the effects of TV violence, another to repressed aggressiveness, but most implicated the "depersonalization" of urban life with its "megalopolitan societies" and its "alienation of the individual from the group." Even Rosenthal, the newsman who first broke the story and who ultimately made it the subject of a book, subscribed to the city-caused apathy theory.

> Nobody can say why the thirty-eight did not lift the phone while Miss Genovese was being attacked, since they cannot say themselves. It can be assumed, however, that their apathy was indeed one of the big-city variety. It is almost a matter of psychological survival, if one is surrounded and pressed by millions of people, to prevent them from constantly imping-ing on you, and the only way to do this is to ignore them as often as possible. Indifference to one's neighbor and his trou-bles is a conditioned reflex in life in New York as it is in other big cities.[7]

As the Genovese story grew—aside from Rosenthal's book, it became the focus of numerous newspaper and magazine pieces, several television news documentaries, and an off-Broadway play—it attracted the professional attention of a pair of New York-based psychology professors, Bibb Latané and John Darley. They examined the reports of the Genovese incident and on the basis of their knowledge of social psychology, hit on what had seemed the most unlikely explanation of all—it was that thirty-eight witnesses were present. Previous accounts of the story had invariably emphasized that no action was taken, *even though* thirty-eight individuals had looked on. Latané and Darley suggested that no one had helped precisely because there were so many observers. The psychologists speculated that, for at least two reasons, a bystander to an emergency would be unlikely to help when there were a number of other bystanders present. The first reason is fairly straightforward. With several potential help-ers around, the personal responsibility of each individual is re-duced: "Perhaps someone else will give or call for aid, perhaps someone else already has." So with everyone thinking that some-one else will help or has helped, no one does.

The second reason is the more psychologically intriguing one; it is founded on the principle of social proof and involves

SOCIAL PROOF

the pluralistic ignorance effect. Very often an emergency is not obviously an emergency. Is the man lying in the alley a heart-attack victim or a drunk sleeping one off? Are the sharp sounds from the street gunshots or truck backfires? Is the commotion next door an assault requiring the police or an especially loud marital spat where intervention would be inappropriate and un-welcome? What is going on? In times of such uncertainty, the natural tendency is to look around at the actions of others for clues. We can learn, from the way the other witnesses are react-ing, whether the event is or is not an emergency.

What is easy to forget, though, is that everybody else ob-serving the event is likely to be looking for social evidence, too. And because we all prefer to appear poised and unflustered among others, we are likely to search for that evidence placidly, with brief, camouflaged glances at those around us. Therefore everyone is likely to see everyone else looking unruffled and fail-ing to act. As a result, and by the principle of social proof, the event will be roundly interpreted as a nonemergency. This, ac-cording to Latané and Darley, is the state of pluralistic ignorance "in which each person decides that since nobody is concerned, nothing is wrong. Meanwhile, the danger may be mounting to the point where a single individual, uninfluenced by the seeming calm of others, *would* react."[8]

The fascinating upshot of Latané and Darley's reasoning is that, for the emergency victim, the idea of "safety in numbers" may often be completely wrong. It might be that someone in need of emergency aid would have a better chance of survival if a single bystander, rather than a crowd, was present. To test this unusual thesis, Darley, Latané, their students and colleagues per-formed a systematic and impressive program of research that produced a clear set of findings. Their basic procedure was to stage emergency events that were observed either by a single in-dividual or by a group of people. They then recorded the num-ber of times the emergency victim received help under those circumstances. In their first experiment, a New York college stu-dent who appeared to be having an epileptic seizure received help 85 percent of the time when there was a single bystander present but only 31' percent of the time with five bystanders present. With almost all the single bystanders helping, it becomes difficult

FIGURE 4–1

VICTIM?

At times like this one, when the need for emergency aid is unclear, even genuine victims are unlikely to be helped in a crowd. Think how, if you were the second passerby in this picture, you might be influenced by the first passerby to believe that no aid was called for. (Source: Jan Halaska/Photo Research-ers, Inc.)

to argue that ours is "The Cold Society" where no one cares for suffering others. Obviously it was something about the presence of other bystanders that reduced helping to shameful levels.

Other studies have examined the importance of social proof in causing widespread witness "apathy." They have done so by planting within a group of witnesses to a possible emergency people who are rehearsed to act as if no emergency were occurring. For instance, in another New York-based experiment, 75 percent of lone individuals who observed smoke seeping from under a door reported the leak; however, when similar leaks were observed by three-person groups, the smoke was reported only 38 percent of the time. The smallest number of bystanders took action, though, when the three-person groups included two individuals who had been coached to ignore the smoke; under those conditions, the leaks were reported only 10 percent of the time. In a similar study conducted in Toronto, single bystanders provided emergency aid 90 percent of the time, whereas such aid occurred in only 16 percent of the cases when a bystander was in the presence of two other bystanders who remained passive.

After more than a decade of such research, social scientists now have a good idea of when a bystander will offer emergency aid. First, and contrary to the view that we have become a society of callous, uncaring people, once witnesses are convinced that an emergency situation exists, aid is very likely. Under these conditions, the numbers of bystanders who either intervene themselves or summon help is quite comforting. For example, in four separate experiments done in Florida, accident scenes involving a maintenance man were staged. When it was clear that the man was hurt and required assistance, he was helped 100 percent of the time in two of the experiments. In the other two experiments, where helping involved contact with potentially dangerous electrical wires, the victim still received bystander aid in 90 percent of the instances. In addition, these extremely high levels of assistance occurred whether the witnesses observed the event singly or in groups.[9]

The situation becomes very different when, as in many cases, bystanders cannot be sure that the event they are witnessing is an emergency. Then a victim is much more likely to be helped by a lone bystander than by a group, especially if the people in the group are strangers to one another. It seems that the pluralistic ignorance effect is strongest among strangers: Because we like to look poised and sophisticated in public and because we are unfamiliar with the reactions of those we do not know, we are unlikely to give off or correctly read expressions of concern when in a grouping of strangers. Therefore, a possible emergency becomes viewed as a nonemergency and the victim suffers.[10]

A close look at this set of research findings reveals an enlightening pattern. All the conditions that decrease an emergency victim's chances for bystander aid exist normally and innocently in the city: (1) In contrast to rural areas, cities are more clamorous, distracting, rapidly changing places where it is difficult to be certain of the nature of the events one encounters. (2) Urban environments are more populous, by their nature; consequently, people are more likely to be with others when witnessing a potential emergency situation. (3) City dwellers know a much smaller percentage of fellow residents than do people who live in small towns; therefore, city dwellers are more likely to find themselves in a group of strangers when observing an emergency.

These three natural characteristics of urban environments—their confusion, their populousness, and their low levels of acquaintanceship—fit in very well with the factors shown by research to decrease bystander aid. Without ever having to resort to such sinister concepts as "urban depersonalization" and "megalopolitan alienation," then, we can explain why so many instances of bystander inaction occur in our cities.

Devictimizing yourself

But explaining the dangers of modern urban life in less ominous terms does not dispel them. And as the world's populations move increasingly to the cities—half of all humanity will be city dwellers within fifteen years—there will be a growing need to reduce those dangers. Fortunately, our newfound understanding of the bystander "apathy" process offers real hope. Armed with this scientific knowledge, an emergency victim can increase enormously the chances of receiving aid from others. The key is the realization that groups of bystanders fail to help because the bystanders are unsure rather than unkind. They don't help because they are unsure of whether an emergency actually exists and whether they are responsible for taking action. When they are sure of their responsibilities for intervening in a clear emergency, people are exceedingly responsive!

Once it is understood that the enemy is not some unmanageable societal condition like urban depersonalization but is, instead, the simple state of uncertainty, it becomes possible for emergency victims to take specific steps to protect themselves by reducing the bystanders' uncertainty. Imagine, for example, you are spending a summer afternoon at a music concert in the park. As the concert ends and people begin leaving, you notice a slight numbness in one arm but dismiss it as nothing to be alarmed about. Yet, while moving with the crowd to the distant parking areas, you feel the numbness spreading down to your hand and up one side of your face. Feeling disoriented, you decide to sit against a tree for a moment to rest. Soon you realize that something is drastically wrong. Sitting down has not helped; in fact, the control and coordination of your muscles has worsened to the point that you are starting to have difficulty moving your mouth and tongue to speak. You try to get up but can't. A terrifying thought slashes to mind: "Oh, God, I'm having a stroke!" Groups of people are passing by and most are paying you no attention. The few who notice the odd way you are slumped against the tree or the strange look on your face check the social evidence around them and, seeing that no one else is reacting with concern, walk on past convinced that nothing is wrong.

Were you to find yourself in such a predicament, what could you do to overcome the odds against receiving help? Because your physical abilities would be deteriorating, time would be crucial. If, before you could summon aid, you lost your speech or mobility or consciousness, your chances for assistance and for recovery would plunge drastically. It would be essential to try to request help quickly. But what would the most effective form of that request be? Moans, groans, or outcries probably would not do. They might bring you some attention, but they would not provide enough information to assure passersby that a true emergency existed.

If mere outcries are unlikely to produce help from the passing crowd, perhaps you should be more specific. Indeed, you need to do more than try to gain attention; you should call out clearly your need for assistance. You must not allow bystanders to define your situation as a nonemergency. Use the word "Help" to cry out your need for emergency aid. And don't worry about being wrong. Embarrassment is a villain to be crushed here. In the context of a possible stroke, you cannot afford to be worried about the awkwardness of overestimating your problem. The difference in cost is that between a moment of embarrassment and possible death or lifelong paralysis.

But even a resounding call for help is not your most effective tactic. Although it may reduce bystanders' doubts about whether a real emergency exists, it will not remove several other important uncertainties within each onlooker's mind: What kind of aid is required here? Should I be the one to provide the aid, or should someone more qualified do it? Has someone else already gone to get professional help, or is it my responsibility? While the bystanders stand gawking at you and grappling with these questions, time vital to your survival could be slipping away.

Clearly, then, as a victim you must do more than alert bystanders to your need for emergency assistance; you must also remove their uncertainties about how that assistance should be provided and who should provide it. But what would be the most efficient and reliable way to do so?

Based on the research findings we have seen, my advice would be to isolate one individual from the crowd: Stare, speak, and point directly at that person and no one else: "You, sir, in the blue jacket, I need help. Call an ambulance." With that one utterance you should dispel all the uncertainties that might prevent or delay help. With that one statement you will have put the man in the blue jacket in the role of "rescuer." He should now understand that emergency aid is needed; he should understand that he, not someone else, is responsible for providing the aid; and, finally, he should understand exactly how to provide it. All the scientific evidence indicates that the result should be quick, effective assistance.

In general, then, your best strategy when in need of emergency help is to reduce the uncertainties of those around you concerning your condition and their responsibilities. Be as precise as possible about your need for aid. Do not allow bystanders to come to their own conclusions because, especially in a crowd, the principle of social proof and the consequent pluralistic ignorance effect might well cause them to view your situation as a nonemergency.

And request assistance of a single individual from the group of onlookers. Fight the natural tendency to make a general request for help. Pick out one person and *assign* the task to that individual. Otherwise, it is too easy for everyone in the crowd to assume that someone else should help, will help, or has helped. Of all the techniques in this book designed to produce compliance with a request, this one may be the most important to remember. After all, the failure of your request for emergency aid could have severe personal consequences.

Not long ago, I received some firsthand evidence on this point. I was involved in a rather serious automobile collision. Both I and the other driver were plainly hurt: He was slumped, unconscious, over his steering wheel while I managed to stagger, bloody, from behind mine. The accident had occurred in the center of an intersection in full view of several individuals stopped in their cars at the traffic light. As I knelt in the road beside my door, trying to clear my head, the light changed and the waiting cars began to roll slowly through the intersection; their drivers gawked but did not stop.

I remember thinking, "Oh no, it's happening just like the research says. They're all passing by!" I consider it fortunate that, as a social psychologist, I knew enough about the bystander studies to have that particular thought. By thinking of my predicament in terms of the research findings, I knew exactly what to do. Pulling myself up so I could be seen clearly, I pointed at the driver of one car: "Call the police." To a second and a third driver, pointing directly each time: "Pull over, we need help." The responses of these people were instantaneous. They summoned a police car and ambulance immediately, they used their handkerchiefs to blot the blood from my face, they put a jacket under my head, they volunteered to serve as witnesses to the accident; one even offered to ride with me to the hospital.

Not only was this help rapid and solicitous, it was infectious. After drivers entering the intersection from the other direction saw cars stopping for me, they stopped and began tending to the other victim. The principle of social proof was working *for* us now. The trick had been to get the ball rolling in the direction of aid. Once that was accomplished, I was able to relax and let the bystanders' genuine concern and social proof's natural momentum do the rest.

※

MONKEY ME, MONKEY DO

A bit earlier we stated that the principle of social proof, like all other weapons of influence, works better under some conditions than under others. We have already explored one of those conditions: uncertainty. Without question, when people are uncertain, they are more likely to use others' actions to decide how they themselves should act. But, in addition, there is another important working condition: similarity. The principle of social proof operates most powerfully when we are observing the behavior of people just like us. It is the conduct of such people that gives us the greatest insight into what constitutes correct behavior for ourselves. Therefore we are more inclined to follow the lead of a similar individual than a dissimilar one.

That is why I believe we are seeing an increasing number of average-man-on-the-street testimonials on TV these days. Advertisers now know that one successful way to sell a product to ordinary viewers (who compose the largest potential market) is to demonstrate that other "ordinary" people like and use it. So whether the product is a brand of soft drink, or a pain reliever, or a laundry detergent, we hear volleys of praise from John or Mary Everyperson.

More compelling evidence for the importance of similarity in determining whether we will imitate another's behavior comes from scientific research. An especially apt illustration can be found in a study done several years ago by Columbia University psychologists. The researchers placed wallets on the ground in various locations around midtown Manhattan to observe what would happen when they were found. The wallets all contained $2.00 in cash, a $26.30 check, and various information providing

SOCIAL PROOF

the name and address of the wallet's "owner." In addition to this material, the wallet also contained a letter that made it evident that the wallet had been lost not once, but twice. The letter was written to the wallet's owner from a man who had found it earlier and whose intention was to return it. The finder indicated in his letter that he was happy to help and that the chance to be of service in this way had made him feel good.

It was evident to anyone who found one of these wallets that this well-intentioned individual had then lost the wallet himself on the way to the mailbox—the wallet was wrapped in an envelope addressed to the owner. The researchers wanted to know

FIGURE 4–2

FREE-THINKING YOUTH

We frequently think of teenagers as rebellious and independent-minded. It is important to recognize, however, that typically that is true only with respect to their parents. Among similar others, they conform massively to what social proof tells them is proper. (Source: Eric Knoll/Taurus)

how many people finding such a wallet would follow the lead of the first finder and mail it, intact, to the original owner. Before they dropped the wallets, however, the researchers varied one feature of the letter it contained. Some of the letters were written in standard English by what seemed to be an average American, while the other letters were written in broken English by the first finder, who identified himself as a recently arrived foreigner. In other words, the person who had initially found the wallet and had tried to return it was depicted by the letter as being either similar or dissimilar to most Americans.

The interesting question was whether the Manhattanites who found the wallet and letter would be more influenced to mail the wallet if the first man who had tried to do so was similar to them. The answer was plain: Only 33 percent of the wallets were returned when the first finder was seen as dissimilar, but fully 70 percent were returned when he was thought to be a similar other. These results suggest an important qualification of the principle of social proof. We will use the actions of others to decide on proper behavior for ourselves, *especially when we view those others as similar to ourselves.*[11]

Any factor that can spur 70 percent of New Yorkers to return a wallet, with all its contents included, must be considered impressive. Yet the outcome of the lost-wallet study offers just a hint of the immense impact that the conduct of similar others has on human behavior. Other, more powerful examples exist. To my mind, the most telling illustration of this impact starts with a seemingly nonsensical statistic: After a suicide has made front-page news, airplanes—private planes, corporate jets, airliners—begin falling out of the sky at an alarming rate.

For example, it has been shown that immediately following certain kinds of highly publicized suicide stories, the number of people who die in commercial-airline crashes increases by 1,000 percent! Even more alarming: The increase is not limited to airplane deaths. The number of automobile fatalities shoots up as well.[12] What could possibly be responsible?

One explanation suggests itself immediately: The same social conditions that cause some people to commit suicide cause others to die accidentally. For instance, certain individuals, the

SOCIAL PROOF

suicide-prone, may react to stressful societal events (economic downturns, rising crime rates, international tensions) by ending it all. But others will react differently to these same events; they might become angry or impatient or nervous or distracted. To the degree that such people operate (or service) the cars and planes of our society, the vehicles will be less safe, and consequently, we will see a sharp increase in the number of automobile and air fatalities.

According to this "social conditions" interpretation, then, some of the same societal factors that cause intentional deaths also cause accidental ones, and that is why we find so strong a connection between suicide stories and fatal crashes. But another fascinating statistic indicates that this is not the correct explanation: Fatal crashes increase dramatically only in those regions where the suicide has been highly publicized. Other places, existing under similar social conditions, whose newspapers have not publicized the story, have shown no comparable jump in such fatalities. Furthermore, within those areas where newspaper space has been allotted, the wider the publicity given the suicide, the greater has been the rise in subsequent crashes. Thus it is not some set of common societal events that stimulates suicides on the one hand and fatal accidents on the other. Instead it is the publicized suicide story itself that produces the car and plane wrecks.

To explain the strong association between suicide-story publicity and subsequent crashes, a "bereavement" account has been suggested. Because, it has been argued, front-page suicides often involve well-known and respected public figures, perhaps their highly publicized deaths throw many people into states of shocked sadness. Stunned and preoccupied, these individuals become careless around cars and planes. The consequence is the sharp increase in deadly accidents involving such vehicles that we see after front-page suicide stories. Although the bereavement theory can account for the connection between the degree of publicity given a story and subsequent crash fatalities—the more people who learn of the suicide, the larger number of bereaved and careless individuals there will be—it cannot explain yet another startling fact: Newspaper stories reporting on suicide victims who died alone produce an increase in the frequency of

INFLUENCE

single-fatality wrecks only, whereas stories reporting on suicide-plus-murder incidents produce an increase in multiple-fatality wrecks only. Simple bereavement could not cause such a pattern.

The influence of suicide stories on car and plane crashes, then, is fantastically specific. Stories of pure suicides, in which only one person dies, generate wrecks in which only one person dies; stories of suicide-murder combinations, in which there are multiple deaths, generate wrecks in which there are multiple deaths. If neither "social conditions" nor "bereavement" can make sense of this bewildering array of facts, what can? There is a sociologist at the University of California at San Diego who thinks he has found the answer. His name is David Phillips, and he points a convincing finger at something called the "Werther effect."

The story of the Werther effect is both chilling and intriguing. More than two centuries ago, the great man of German literature, Johann von Goethe, published a novel entitled *Die Leiden des jungen Werthers (The Sorrows of Young Werther)*. The book, in which the hero, named Werther, commits suicide, had a remarkable impact. Not only did it provide Goethe with immediate fame, but it also sparked a wave of emulative suicides across Europe. So powerful was this effect that authorities in several countries banned the novel.

Professor Phillips's own work has traced the Werther effect to modern times. His research has demonstrated that immediately following a front-page suicide story the suicide rate increases dramatically in those geographical areas where the story has been highly publicized. It is Phillips's argument that certain troubled people who read of another's self-inflicted death kill themselves in imitation. In a morbid illustration of the principle of social proof, these people decide how they should act on the basis of how some other troubled person has acted.

Phillips got his evidence for the modern-day Werther effect by examining the suicide statistics in the United States between 1947 and 1968. He found that within two months after every front-page suicide story, an average of fifty-eight more people than usual killed themselves. In a sense, each suicide story killed fifty-eight people who otherwise would have gone on living. Phillips also found that this tendency for suicides to beget suicides occurred principally in those parts of the country where the first suicide was highly publicized and that the wider the publicity given the first suicide, the greater the number of later suicides.

If the facts surrounding the Werther effect seem to you suspiciously like those surrounding the influence of suicide stories on air and traffic fatalities, the similarities have not been lost on Professor Phillips either. In fact, he contends that all the excess deaths following a front-page suicide incident can be explained as the same thing: copycat suicides. Upon learning of another's suicide, an uncomfortably large number of people decide that suicide is an appropriate action for themselves as well. Some of these individuals then proceed to commit the act in a straightforward, no-bones-about-it fashion, causing the suicide rate to jump.

Others, however, are less direct. For any of several reasons—to protect their reputations, to spare their families the shame and hurt, to allow their dependents to collect on insurance policies—they do not want to appear to have killed themselves. They would rather seem to have died accidentally. So, purposively but furtively, they cause the wreck of a car or a plane they are operating or are simply riding in. This could be accomplished in a variety of all-too-familiar-sounding ways. A commercial airline pilot could dip the nose of the aircraft at a crucial point of takeoff or could inexplicably land on an already occupied runway against instructions from the control tower; the driver of a car could suddenly swerve into a tree or into oncoming traffic; a passenger in an automobile or corporate jet could incapacitate the operator, causing a deadly crash; the pilot of a private plane could, despite all radio warnings, plow into another aircraft. Thus the alarming climb in crash fatalities we find following front-page suicides is, according to Dr. Phillips, most likely due to the Werther effect secretly applied.

I consider this insight brilliant. First, it explains all of the data beautifully. If these wrecks really are hidden instances of imitative suicide, it makes sense that we should see an increase in the wrecks after suicide stories appear. And it makes sense that the greatest rise in wrecks should occur after the suicide stories that have been most widely publicized and have, consequently,

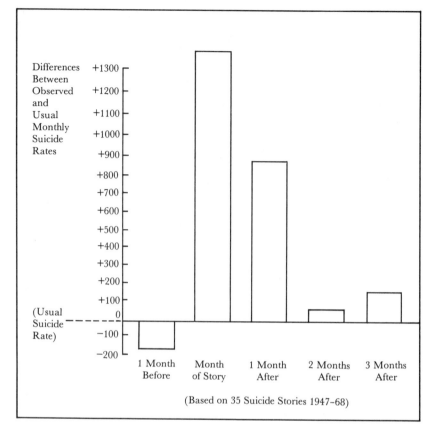

Differences Between Observed and Usual Monthly Suicide Rates

+1300
+1200
+1100
+1000
+900
+800
+700
+600
+500
+400
+300
+200
+100

(Usual Suicide Rate) 0

−100
−200

1 Month Before   Month of Story   1 Month After   2 Months After   3 Months After

(Based on 35 Suicide Stories 1947–68)

CHART 1

FLUCTUATION IN NUMBER OF SUICIDES BEFORE, DURING, AND AFTER
MONTH OF SUICIDE STORY

This evidence raises an important ethical issue. The suicides that follow these stories are excess *deaths. After the initial spurt, the suicide rates do not drop below traditional levels but only return to those levels. Such a statistic might well give pause to newspaper editors who are inclined to give front-page space to sensational suicide accounts. If Phillips's findings still hold, and there is no reason to believe that they do not, those accounts are likely to lead to the deaths of scores of people. More recent data indicate that in addition to newspaper editors, television news broadcasters have cause for concern about the way they present suicide stories. Phillips and Kenneth Bollen recently reported that between 1972 and 1976 each highly publicized suicide story on network evening news programs was followed by an average increase of thirty-five suicides over what would have been expected in the next week.*[13]

reached the most people. And it makes sense that the number of crashes should jump appreciably only in those geographical areas where the suicide stories were publicized. And it even makes sense that single-victim suicides should lead only to single-victim crashes, whereas multiple-victim suicide incidents should lead only to multiple-victim crashes. Imitation is the key.

But there is a second valuable feature of Phillips's insight. Not only does it allow us to explain the existing facts, it also allows us to predict new facts that had never been uncovered before. For example, if the abnormally frequent crashes following publicized suicides are genuinely due to imitative rather than accidental actions, they should be more deadly as a result. That is, people trying to kill themselves will likely arrange (with a foot on the accelerator instead of the brake, with the nose of the plane down instead of up) for the impact to be as lethal as possible. The consequence should be quick and sure death. When Phillips examined the records to check on this prediction, he found that the average number of people killed in a fatal crash of a commercial airliner is more than three times greater if the crash happened one week after a front-page suicide story than if it happened one week before. A similar phenomenon can be found in traffic statistics where there is evidence for the deadly efficiency of postsuicide-story auto crashes. Victims of fatal car wrecks that follow front-page suicide stories die four times more quickly than normal.

Still another fascinating prediction flows from Phillips's idea. If the increase in wrecks following suicide stories truly represents a set of copycat deaths, then the imitators should be most likely to copy the suicides of people who are similar to them. The principle of social proof states that we use information about how others have behaved to help us determine proper conduct for ourselves. But as the dropped-wallet experiment showed, we are most influenced in this fashion by the actions of others like us.

Therefore, Phillips reasoned, if the principle of social proof is behind the phenomenon, there should be some clear similarity between the victim of the highly publicized suicide and those who cause subsequent wrecks. Realizing that the clearest test of this possibility would come from the records of automobile

INFLUENCE

crashes involving a single car and a lone driver, Phillips compared the age of the suicide-story victim with the ages of the lone drivers killed in single-car crashes immediately after the story appeared in print. Once again the predictions were strikingly accurate: When the newspaper detailed the suicide of a young person, it was young drivers who then piled their cars into trees, poles, and embankments with fatal results; but when the news story concerned an older person's suicide, older drivers died in such crashes.

This last statistic is the crusher for me. I am left wholly convinced and, simultaneously, wholly amazed by it. Evidently, the principle of social proof is so wide-ranging and powerful that its domain extends to the fundamental decision for life or death. Professor Phillips's findings have persuaded me of a distressing tendency for suicide publicity to motivate certain people who are similar to the victim to kill themselves—because they now find the idea of suicide more legitimate. Truly frightening are the data indicating that many innocent people die in the bargain. A glance at the graphs documenting the undeniable increase in traffic and air fatalities following publicized suicides, especially those involving murder, is enough to cause concern for one's own safety. I have been sufficiently affected by these statistics to begin

CHART 2

DAILY FLUCTUATION IN NUMBER OF ACCIDENT FATALITIES BEFORE, ON, AND AFTER SUICIDE STORY DATE

As is apparent from these graphs, the greatest danger exists three to four days following the news story's publication. After a brief dropoff, there comes another peak approximately one week after the story. By the eleventh day, there is no hint of an effect left. This pattern across various types of data indicates something noteworthy about secret suicides. Those who try to disguise their imitative self-destruction as accidents wait a few days before committing the act—perhaps to build their courage, to plan the incident, or to put their affairs in order. Whatever the reason for the remarkable regularity of this pattern, we know that travelers' safety is most severely jeopardized three to four days after a suicide-murder story and then again, but to a lesser degree, a few days later. We would be well advised, then, to take special care in our travels at these times.

SOCIAL PROOF

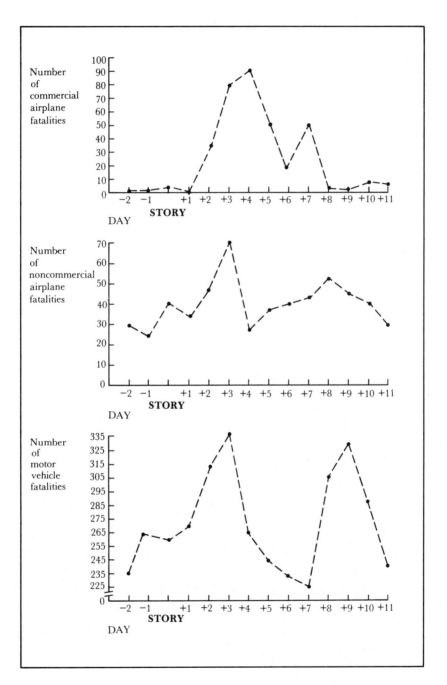

to take note of front-page suicide stories and to change my behavior in the period after their appearance. I try to be especially cautious behind the wheel of my car. I am reluctant to take extended trips requiring a lot of air travel. If I must fly during such a period, I purchase substantially more flight insurance than I normally would. Dr. Phillips has done us a service by demonstrating that the odds for survival when we travel change measurably for a time following the publication of certain kinds of front-page suicide stories. It would seem only prudent to play those odds.

As if the frightening features of Phillips's suicide data weren't enough, his newest research brings more cause for alarm: Homicides in this country have a stimulated, copycat character after highly publicized acts of violence. Heavyweight championship prize fights that receive coverage on network evening news appear to produce measurable increases in the U.S. homicide rate. This analysis of heavyweight championship fights (between 1973–1978) is perhaps most compelling in its demonstration of the remarkably specific nature of the imitative aggression that is generated. When such a match was lost by a black fighter, the homicide rate during the following ten days rose significantly for young black male victims but not young white males. On the other hand, when a white fighter lost a match, it was young white men but not young black men who were killed more frequently in the next ten days.[14] When these results are combined with the parallel findings in Phillips's suicide data, it is clear that widely publicized aggression has the nasty tendency to spread to similar victims, no matter whether the aggression is inflicted on the self or on another.

Work like Dr. Phillips's helps us appreciate the awesome influence of the behavior of similar others. Once the enormity of that force is recognized, it becomes possible to understand perhaps the most spectacular act of compliance of our time—the mass suicide at Jonestown, Guyana. Certain crucial features of that event deserve review.

The People's Temple was a cultlike organization that began in San Francisco and drew its recruits from the poor of that city. In 1977, the Reverend Jim Jones—who was the group's undisputed political, social, and spiritual leader—moved the bulk of the membership with him to a jungle settlement in Guyana, South America. There, the People's Temple existed in relative obscurity until November 18, 1978, when four men of a fact-finding party led by Congressman Leo J. Ryan were murdered as they tried to leave Jonestown by plane. Convinced that he would be arrested and implicated in the killings and that the demise of the People's Temple would result, Jones sought to control the end of the Temple in his own way. He gathered the entire community around him and issued a call for each person's death in a unified act of self-destruction.

The first response was that of a young woman who calmly approached the now famous vat of strawberry-flavored poison, administered one dose to her baby, one to herself, and then sat down in a field, where she and her child died in convulsions within four minutes. Others followed steadily in turn. Although a handful of Jonestowners escaped rather than comply and a few others are reported to have resisted, the survivors claim that the great majority of the 910 people who died did so in an orderly, willful fashion.

News of the event shocked us. The broadcast media and the papers provided a barrage of reports, updates, and analyses. For days, our conversations were full of the topic, "How many have they found dead now?" "A guy who escaped says they were drinking the poison like they were hypnotized or something." "What were they doing down in South America, anyway?" "It's so hard to believe. What caused it?"

Yes, "What caused it?"—the critical question. How are we to account for this most astounding of compliant acts? Various explanations have been offered. Some have focused on the charisma of Jim Jones, a man whose style allowed him to be loved like a savior, trusted like a father, and treated like an emperor. Other explanations have pointed to the kind of people who were attracted to the People's Temple. They were mostly poor and uneducated individuals who were willing to give up their freedoms of thought and action for the safety of a place where all decisions would be made for them. Still other explanations have emphasized the quasireligious nature of the People's Temple, in which unquestioned faith in the cult's leader was assigned highest priority.

No doubt each of these features of Jonestown has merit in

explaining what happened there. But I do not find them sufficient. After all, the world abounds with cults populated by dependent people who are led by a charismatic figure. What's more, there has never been a shortage of this combination of circumstances in the past. Yet virtually nowhere do we find evidence of an event even approximating the Jonestown incident among such groups. There must be something else that was critical.

One especially revealing question gives us a clue: "If the community had remained in San Francisco, would Reverend Jones's suicide command have been obeyed?" A highly speculative question to be sure, but the expert most familiar with the People's Temple has no doubt about the answer. Dr. Louis Jolyon West, chairman of psychiatry and biobehavioral sciences at UCLA and director of its neuropsychiatric unit, is an authority on cults who had observed the People's Temple for eight years prior to the Jonestown deaths. When interviewed in the immediate aftermath, he made what strikes me as an inordinately instructive statement: "This wouldn't have happened in California. But they lived in total alienation from the rest of the world in a jungle situation in a hostile country."

Although lost in the welter of commentary following the tragedy, Dr. West's observation, together with what we know about the principle of social proof, seems to me quite important to a satisfactory understanding of the compliant suicides. To my mind, the single act in the history of the People's Temple that most contributed to the members' mindless compliance that day occurred a year earlier with the relocation of the Temple to a jungled country of unfamiliar customs and strange people. If we are to believe the stories of Jim Jones's malevolent genius, he realized fully the massive psychological impact such a move would have on his followers. All at once, they found themselves in a place they knew nothing about. South America, and the rain forests of Guyana, especially, were unlike anything they had experienced in San Francisco. The country—both physical and social—into which they were dropped must have seemed dreadfully uncertain.

Ah, uncertainty—the right-hand man of the principal of social proof. We have already seen that when people are uncertain, they look to the actions of others to guide their own actions. In the alien, Guyanese environment, then, Temple members were very ready to follow the lead of others. But as we have also seen, it is others of a special kind whose behavior will be most unquestioningly followed—similar others. And therein lies the awful beauty of Reverend Jones's relocation strategy. In a country like Guyana, there were no similar others for a Jonestown resident but the people of Jonestown itself.

What was right for a member of the community was determined to a disproportionate degree by what other community members—influenced heavily by Jones—did and believed. When viewed in this light, the terrible orderliness, the lack of panic, the sense of calm with which these people moved to the vat of poison and to their deaths seems more comprehensible. They hadn't been hypnotized by Jones; they had been convinced—partly by him but, more important, by the principle of social proof—that suicide was correct conduct. The uncertainty they surely felt upon first hearing the death command must have caused them to look to those around them for a definition of the appropriate response. It is worth particular note that they found two impressive pieces of social evidence, each pointing in the same direction.

The first was the initial set of their compatriots, who quickly and willingly took the poison drafts. There will always be a few such fanatically obedient individuals in any strong-leader-dominated group. Whether, in this instance, they had been specially instructed beforehand to serve as examples or whether they were just naturally the most compliant with Jones's wishes is difficult to know. No matter; the psychological effect of the actions of those individuals must have been potent. If the suicides of similar others in news stories can influence total strangers to kill themselves, imagine how enormously more compelling such an act would be when performed without hesitation by one's neighbors in a place like Jonestown.

The second source of social evidence came from the reactions of the crowd itself. Given the conditions, I suspect that what occurred was a large-scale instance of the pluralistic ignorance phenomenon that frequently infects onlookers at emergencies. Each Jonestowner looked to the actions of surrounding individuals to assess the situation and—finding seeming calm because everyone else, too, was surreptitiously assessing rather than

FIGURE 4–3

TIDY ROWS OF BUSINESSLIKE DEATH

An aerial photo gives evidence of the orderliness
with which Jonestowners went to their deaths.
(Source: UPI)

reacting—"learned" that patient turn taking was the correct behavior. Such misinterpreted but nonetheless convincing social
evidence would be expected to result precisely in the ghastly
composure of the assemblage that waited in the tropics of
Guyana for businesslike death.

From my own perspective, most attempts to analyze the
Jonestown incident have focused too much on the personal
qualities of Jim Jones. Although he was without question a man
of rare dynamism, the power he wielded strikes me as coming
less from his remarkable personal style than from his understanding of fundamental psychological principles. His real genius as a
leader was his realization of the limitations of individual leadership. No leader can hope to persuade, regularly and single-hand-
edly, all the members of the group. A forceful leader can
reasonably expect, however, to persuade some sizable proportion
of group members. Then the raw information that a substantial
number of group members has been convinced can, by itself,
convince the rest. Thus the most influential leaders are those who

know how to arrange group conditions to allow the principle of social proof to work maximally in their favor.

It is in this that Jones appears to have been inspired. His masterstroke was the decision to move the People's Temple community from its roots in urban San Francisco to the remoteness of equatorial South America, where the conditions of uncertainty and exclusive similarity would make the principle of social proof operate for him as perhaps nowhere else. There a settlement of a thousand people, much too large to be held in persistent sway by the force of one man's personality, could be changed from a following into a *herd*. As slaughterhouse operators have long known, the mentality of a herd makes it easy to manage. Simply get some members moving in the desired direction and the others—responding not so much to the lead animal as to those immediately surrounding them—will peacefully and mechanically go along. The powers of the amazing Reverend Jones, then, are probably best understood not in terms of his dramatic personal style but in his profound knowledge of the art of social jujitsu.

✳

HOW TO SAY NO

This chapter began with an account of the relatively harmless practice of laugh tracking, and has moved on to stories of murder and suicide—all explained by the principle of social proof. How can we expect to defend ourselves against a weapon of influence that pervades such a vast range of behavior? The difficulty is compounded by the realization that, most of the time, we don't want to guard against the information that social proof provides. The evidence it offers about how we should act is usually valid and valuable. With it we can cruise confidently through a myriad of decisions without personally having to investigate the detailed pros and cons of each.

In this sense, the principle of social proof equips us with a wonderful kind of automatic-pilot device not unlike that aboard most aircraft.

Yet there are occasional but real problems with automatic pilots. Those problems appear whenever the flight information locked into the control mechanism is wrong. In these instances, we will be taken off course. Depending on the size of the error, the consequences can be severe. But, because the automatic pilot afforded by the principle of social proof is more often an ally than an enemy, we can't be expected to want simply to disconnect it. Thus we are faced with a classic problem: how to make use of a piece of equipment that simultaneously benefits and imperils our welfare.

Fortunately, there is a way out of the dilemma. Because the disadvantages of automatic pilots arise principally when incorrect data have been put into the control system, our best defense against these disadvantages is to recognize when the data are in error. If we can become sensitive to situations where the social-proof automatic pilot is working with inaccurate information, we can disengage the mechanism and grasp the controls when we need to.

There are two types of situation in which incorrect data cause the principle of social proof to give us poor counsel. The first occurs when the social evidence has been purposely falsified. Invariably these situations are manufactured by exploiters intent on creating the *impression*—reality be damned—that a multitude is performing the way the exploiters want us to perform. The canned laughter of TV comedy shows, which we have already discussed, is one variety of faked data of this sort. But there is a great deal more; and much of the fakery is strikingly obvious.

For instance, canned responses are not unique to the electronic media or even to the electronic age. In fact, the heavy-handed exploitation of the principle of social proof can be traced through the history of one of our most venerable art forms: grand opera. This is the phenomenon called claquing, said to have been begun in 1820 by a pair of Paris opera-house habitués named Sauton and Porcher. The men were more than opera-goers, though. They were businessmen whose product was applause.

Organizing under the title L'Assurance des Succès Dramatiques, they leased themselves and their employees to singers and opera managers who wished to be assured of an appreciative audience response. So effective were they in stimulating genuine audience reaction with their rigged reactions that before long claques (usually consisting of a leader—*chef de claque*—and several individual *claqueurs*) had become an established and persistent tradition throughout the world of opera. As music historian Robert Sabin notes, "By 1830 the claque was a full-bloom institution, collecting by day, applauding by night, all in the honest open. . . . But it is altogether probable that neither Sauton, nor his ally Porcher, had a notion of the extent to which their scheme of paid applause would be adopted and applied wherever opera is sung."[15]

As claquing grew and developed, its practitioners offered an array of styles and strengths. In the same way that laugh-track producers can hire individuals who excel in titters, chuckles, or belly laughs, the claques spawned their own specialists—the *pleureuse,* chosen for her ability to weep on cue; the *bisseur,* who called *"bis"* (repeat) and "encore" in ecstatic tones; and in direct kinship with today's laugh-track performer, the *rieur,* selected for the infectious quality of his laugh.

For our purposes, though, the most instructive parallel to modern forms of canned response is the conspicuous character of the fakery. No special need was seen to disguise or vary the claque, who often sat in the same seats, performance after performance, year after year, led by a *chef de claque* two decades into his position. Even the monetary transactions were not hidden from the public. Indeed, one hundred years after the birth of claquing, a reader of the London *Musical Times* could scan the advertised rates of the Italian *claqueurs.* Whether in the world of *Rigoletto* or *Gilligan's Island,* then, audiences have been successfully manipulated by those who use social evidence, even when that evidence has been openly falsified.

What Sauton and Porcher realized about the mechanical way that we abide by the principle of social proof is understood as well by a variety of today's exploiters. They see no need to hide the manufactured nature of the social evidence they provide—witness the amateurish quality of the average TV laugh track. They seem almost smug in the recognition of our predicament: Either we must allow them to fool us or we must abandon the precious automatic pilots that make us so vulnerable to their tricks. But in their certainty that they have us trapped, such exploiters have made a crucial mistake. The laxity with which they construct phony social evidence gives us a way to fight back.

INFLUENCE

For applause on entrance, if a gentleman 25 lire
For applause on entrance, if a lady 15 lire
Ordinary applause during performance, each 10 lire
Insistent applause during performance, each 15 lire
Still more insistent applause 17 lire
For interruptions with "Bene!" or "Bravo!" 5 lire
For a "Bis" *at any cost* 50 lire
Wild enthusiasm—A special sum to be arranged

FIGURE 4-4

ADVERTISED RATES OF THE ITALIAN CLAQUE

From "ordinary applause" to "wild enthusiasm,"
claqueurs offered their services in an audaciously
public fashion—in this case, in a newspaper read by
many of the audience members they fully expected
to influence. Claque, whirr.

Because automatic pilots can be engaged and disengaged at will, we can cruise along trusting in the course steered by the principle of social proof *until* we recognize that a piece of inaccurate data is being used. Then we can take the controls, make the necessary correction for the misinformation, and reset the automatic pilot. The transparency of the rigged social proof we get these days provides us with exactly the cue we need for knowing when to perform this simple maneuver. With no more cost than a bit of vigilance for plainly counterfeit social evidence, then, we can protect ourselves nicely.

Let's take an example. A bit earlier, we noted the proliferation of average-man-on-the-street ads, in which a number of ordinary people speak glowingly of a product, often without knowing that their words are being recorded. As would be expected according to the principle of social proof, these testimonials from "average people like you and me" make for quite effective advertising campaigns. They have always included one relatively subtle kind of distortion: We hear only from those who like the product; as a result, we get an understandably biased picture of the amount of social support for it. More recently, though, a cruder and more unethical sort of falsification has been introduced. Commercial producers often don't bother to get genuine testimonials. They merely hire actors to play the roles of average people testifying in an unrehearsed fashion to an interviewer. It is amazing how bald-faced these "unrehearsed interview" commercials can be. The situations are obviously staged, the participants are clearly actors, and the dialogue is unmistakably prewritten.

I know that whenever I encounter an influence attempt of this sort, it sets off in me a kind of alarm with a clear directive: *Attention! Attention! Bad social proof in this situation. Temporarily disconnect automatic pilot.* It's so easy to do. We need only make a conscious decision to be alert to counterfeit social evidence, and the smug overconfidence of the exploiters will play directly into our hands. We can relax until their manifest fakery is spotted, at which time we can pounce.

And we should pounce with a vengeance. I am speaking here of more than simply ignoring the misinformation, although this defensive tactic is certainly called for. I am speaking of aggressive counterattack. Whenever possible we ought to sting those responsible for the rigging of social evidence. We should purchase no products featured in phony "unrehearsed interview" commercials. Moreover, each manufacturer of the items should receive a letter explaining our response and recommending that they discontinue use of the advertising agency that produced so deceptive a presentation of their product.

Of course, we don't always want to trust the actions of others to direct our conduct—especially in a situation important enough to warrant our personal investigation of the pros and cons, or in which we are experts—but we do want to be able to count on others' behavior as a source of valid information in a large array of settings. If, in such settings, we find that we cannot trust the information to be valid because someone has tampered with the evidence, we ought to be ready to strike back. In such instances, I personally feel driven by more than the aversion to being duped. I bristle at the tought of being pushed into an unacceptable corner by those who would undermine one of my hedges against the decisional overload of modern life. And I get a genuine sense of righteousness by lashing out when they try. If you are like me, so should you.

In addition to the times when social evidence is deliberately faked, there is another time when the principle of social proof will regularly steer us wrong. In such an instance, an innocent, natural error will produce snowballing social proof that pushes us to the incorrect decision. The pluralist ignorance phenomenon, in which everyone at an emergency sees no cause for alarm, is one example of this process. The best illustration I know, however, comes from a story of one of my students, who was a highway patrolman.

After a class session in which the subject of discussion was the principle of social proof, he stayed to talk with me. He said that he now understood the cause of a type of traffic accident that had always puzzled him before. The accident typically occurred on the city freeway during rush hour, when cars in all lanes were moving steadily but slowly. Events leading to the accident would start when a pair of cars, one behind the other, would simultaneously begin signaling an intention to get out of the lane they were in and into the next. Within seconds, a long line of drivers to the rear of the first two would follow suit, thinking that something—a stalled car or a construction barrier—was blocking the lane ahead. It would be in this crush to cram into the available spaces of the next lane that a collision frequently happened.

The odd thing about it all, according to the patrolman, was that very often there had been no obstruction to be avoided in the first place and by the time of the accident, this should have been obvious to anyone who looked. He said he had more than once witnessed such accidents when there was a visibly clear road in front of the ill-fated lane switchers.

The patrolman's account provides certain insights into the way we respond to social proof. First, we seem to assume that if a lot of people are doing the same thing, they must know something we don't. Especially when we are uncertain, we are willing to place an enormous amount of trust in the collective knowledge of the crowd. Second, quite frequently the crowd is mis-

SOCIAL PROOF

taken because they are not acting on the basis of any superior information but are reacting, themselves, to the principle of social proof.

So if a pair of freeway drivers decided by coincidence to change lanes at the identical moment, the next two drivers might well do the same, assuming that the forward drivers had spotted an obstruction. The resulting social evidence confronting drivers behind this group would be potent—four successive cars, all with their turn signals flashing, trying to angle into the next lane. More signal lights would go on. The social proof would be undeniable by then. For drivers to the rear, there could be no question about the correctness of switching lanes: "All those guys ahead *must* know something." So intent would they be upon working themselves into the next lane that without even checking the true condition of the road before them, the drivers would begin a line-long flank assault. Crash.

There is a lesson here: An automatic-pilot device, like social proof, should never be trusted fully; even when no saboteur has fed bad information into the mechanism, it can sometimes go haywire by itself. We need to check the machine from time to time to be sure that it hasn't worked itself out of synch with the other sources of evidence in the situation—the objective facts, our prior experiences, our own judgments. Fortunately, this precaution requires neither much effort nor much time. A quick glance around is all that is needed. And this little precaution is well worth it. The consequences of single-minded reliance on social evidence can be frightening.

This aspect of the social proof phenomenon always reminds me of the way certain Indian tribes—the Blackfeet, Cree, Snakes, and Crows—used to hunt the North American buffalo. There are two features of buffalo that make them especially susceptible to erroneous social evidence. First, their eyes are set in their heads so that it is easier for them to see to the side than to the front. Second, when they run, as in a stampede, it is with their heads down low so they cannot see above the herd. As a result, the Indians realized, it was possible to kill tremendous numbers of buffalo by starting a herd running toward a cliff. The animals, responding to the thundering social proof around them—and never looking up to see what lay ahead—did the rest. One astonished observer to such a hunt described the deadly outcome of the buffalo's obsessive trust in collective knowledge.

> In this way, it was possible to decoy a herd toward a precipice, and cause it to plunge over en masse, the leaders being thrust over by their followers and all the rest following of their own free will.[16]

Certainly, a flier whose plane is locked onto automatic pilot would be wise to glance occasionally at the instrument panel and out the window. In the same way, we need to look up and around periodically whenever we are locked onto the evidence of the crowd. Without this simple safeguard against misguided social proof, our prospects might well run parallel to those of the freeway lane switchers and the North American buffalo: Crash.

5

LIKING

The friendly thief

※

few people would be surprised to learn that, as a rule, we most prefer to say yes to the requests of someone we know and like. What might be startling to note, however, is that this simple rule is used in hundreds of ways by total strangers to get us to comply with *their* requests.

The clearest illustration I know of the professional exploitation of the liking rule is the Tupperware party, which I consider the quintessential American compliance setting. Anybody familiar with the workings of a Tupperware party will recognize the use of the various weapons of influence we have examined so far: reciprocity (to start, games are played and prizes won by the partygoers; anyone who doesn't win a prize gets to reach into a grab bag for hers so that everyone has received a gift from the Tupperware Lady before the buying begins), commitment (each participant is urged to describe publicly the uses and benefits she has found in the Tupperware she already owns), social proof (once the buying begins, each purchase builds the idea that other, similar people want the product; therefore, it must be good).

All the major weapons of influence are present to help things along, but the real power of the Tupperware party comes from a particular arrangement that trades on the liking rule. Despite the entertaining and persuasive salesmanship of the Tupperware Lady, the true request to purchase the product does not come from this stranger; it comes from a friend to every woman in the room. Oh, the Tupperware Lady may physically ask for each partygoer's order, all right, but the more psychologically compelling requester is a housewife sitting off to the side, smiling, chatting, and serving refreshments. She is the party hostess, who has called her friends together for the demonstration in her home and who, everyone knows, makes a profit from each piece sold at her party.

Simple. By providing the hostess with a percentage of the take, the Tupperware Home Parties Corporation arranges for its customers to buy from and for a friend rather than an unknown salesperson. In this way, the attraction, the warmth, the security, and the obligation of friendship are brought to bear on the sales setting. The results have been remarkable. It was recently estimated that Tupperware sales exceed a million dollars a day!

What is interesting is that the customers appear to be fully aware of the liking and friendship pressures embodied in the Tupperware party. Some don't seem to mind; others do, but don't seem to know how to avoid them. One woman I spoke with described her reactions with more than a bit of frustration in her voice,

> It's gotten to the point now where I hate to be invited to Tupperware parties. I've got all the containers I need; and if I wanted any more, I could buy another brand cheaper in the store. But when a friend calls up, I feel like I have to go. And when I get there, I feel like I have to buy something. What can I do? It's for one of my friends.

With so irresistible an ally as the friendship operating, it is little wonder that the company has abandoned retail sales outlets and has pushed the home party concept until a Tupperware party now starts somewhere every ten seconds. But, of course, all sorts of other compliance professionals recognize the pressure to say yes to someone we know and like. Take, for instance, the growing number of charity organizations who recruit volunteers to canvass for donations close to their own homes. They understand perfectly how much more difficult it is for us to turn down a charity request when it comes from a friend or a neighbor.

Other compliance professionals have found that the friend doesn't even have to be present to be effective; often, just the mention of the friend's name is enough. The Shaklee Corporation, which specializes in door-to-door sales of various home-related products, advises its salespeople to use the "endless chain" method for finding new customers. Once a customer admits to liking a product, he or she can be pressed for the names of friends who would also appreciate learning about it. The individuals on that list can then be approached for sales *and* a list of their friends, who can serve as sources for still other potential customers, and so on in an endless chain.

The key to the success of this method is that each new prospect is visited by a salesperson armed with the name of a friend "who suggested I call on you." Turning the salesperson away under those circumstances is difficult; it's almost like rejecting the friend. The Shaklee sales manual insists that employees use this system without fail: "It would be impossible to overestimate its value. Phoning or calling on a prospect and being able to say that Mr. So-and-so, a friend of his, felt he would benefit by giving you a few moments of his time is virtually as good as a sale 50 percent made before you enter."

The widespread use by compliance practitioners of the liking bond between friends tells us much about the power of the liking rule to produce assent. In fact, we find that such professionals seek to benefit from the rule even when already formed friendships are not present for them to employ. Under these circumstances, the professionals' compliance strategy is quite direct: They first get us to like *them*.

There is a man in Detroit, Joe Girard, who specialized in using the liking rule to sell Chevrolets. He became wealthy in the process, making over two hundred thousand dollars a year. With such a salary, we might guess that he was a high-level GM executive or perhaps the owner of a Chevrolet dealership. But no. He made his money as a salesman on the showroom floor. At what he did, he was phenomenal. Every year from 1966 to 1977, he won the title as the "number one car salesman"; he averaged more than five cars and trucks sold every day he worked; and he has been called the world's "greatest car salesman" by the *Guinness Book of World Records.*

For all his success, the formula he employed was surprisingly simple. It consisted of offering people just two things: a fair price and someone they liked to buy from. "And that's it," he claimed in an interview. "Finding the salesman they like, plus the price; put them both together, and you get a deal."

Fine. The Joe Girard formula tells us how vital the liking rule is to his business, but it doesn't tell us nearly enough. For one thing, it doesn't tell us why customers liked him more than some other salesperson who offered a fair price. There is a crucial—and fascinating—general question that Joe's formula leaves unanswered: What are the factors that cause one person to like another person? If we knew *that* answer, we would be a long way toward understanding how people such as Joe can so successfully arrange to have us like them and, conversely, how we might successfully arrange to have others like us. Fortunately, social scientists have been asking the question for decades. Their accumulated evidence has allowed them to identify a number of factors that reliably cause liking. And, as we will see, each is cleverly used by compliance professionals to urge us along the road to "yes."

Physical attractiveness

Although it is generally acknowledged that good-looking people have an advantage in social interaction, recent findings indicate that we may have sorely underestimated the size and reach of that advantage. There seems to be a *click, whirr* response to attractive people. Like all *click, whirr* reactions, it happens automatically, without forethought. The response itself falls into a category that social scientists call "halo effects." A halo effect

LIKING

occurs when one positive characteristic of a person dominates the way that person is viewed by others. And the evidence is now clear that physical attractiveness is often such a characteristic.

Research has shown that we automatically assign to good-looking individuals such favorable traits as talent, kindness, honesty, and intelligence. Furthermore, we make these judgments without being aware that physical attractiveness plays a role in the process. Certain of the consequences of this unconscious assumption that "good-looking equals good" scare me. For example, a study of the 1974 Canadian federal elections found that attractive candidates received more than two and a half times as many votes as unattractive candidates.[1] Despite such evidence of favoritism toward handsome politicians, follow-up research demonstrated that voters do not realize their bias. In fact, 73 percent of Canadian voters surveyed denied in the strongest possible terms that their votes had been influenced by physical appearance; only 14 percent even allowed for the possibility of such influence.

Equally unsettling research indicates that our judicial process is similarly susceptible to the influences of body dimensions and bone structure. Criminologists have long suspected as much. One expert on crimes committed by women observed that experienced legal-system professionals are frequently taken in by a pretty face.

> Even social workers accustomed to dealing with all types often find it difficult to think of a normal, pretty girl as being guilty of a crime. Most people, for some inexplicable reason, think of crime in terms of abnormality in appearance, and I must say that beautiful women are often not convicted.[2]

Controlled research has not only supported this observation but has extended it to handsome men as well. It now appears that unless they have used their attractiveness to commit a crime (for example, a swindle), good-looking people are likely to receive highly favorable treatment in the legal system. For example, in a Pennsylvania study, researchers rated the physical attractiveness of seventy-four separate male defendants at the start of their criminal trials. When, much later, the researchers checked court records for the results of these cases, they found that the handsome men had received significantly lighter sentences. In fact, the attractive defendants were twice as likely to avoid jail as the unattractive ones.[3] In another study—this one on the damages awarded in a staged negligence trial—a defendant who was better-looking than his victim was assessed an average amount of $5,623; but when the victim was the more attractive of the two, the average compensation was $10,051. What's more, both male and female jurors exhibited the attractiveness-based favoritism.

Other experiments have demonstrated that attractive people are more likely to obtain help when in need and are more persuasive in changing the opinions of an audience. Here, too, both sexes respond in the same way. In the helping study, for instance, the better-looking men and women received aid more often, even from members of their own sex.[4] A major exception to this rule might be expected to occur, of course, if the attractive person is viewed as a direct competitor, especially a romantic rival. Short of this qualification, though, it is apparent that good-looking people enjoy an enormous social advantage in our culture. They are better liked, more persuasive, more frequently helped, and seen as possessing better personality traits and intellectual capacities. And it appears that the social benefits of good looks begin to accumulate quite early. Research on elementary-school children shows that adults view aggressive acts as less naughty when performed by an attractive child and that teachers presume good-looking children to be more intelligent than their less-attractive classmates.[5]

It is hardly any wonder, then, that the halo of physical attractiveness is regularly exploited by compliance professionals. Because we like attractive people and because we tend to comply with those we like, it makes sense that sales training programs include grooming hints, that fashionable clothiers select their floor staffs from among the good-looking candidates, and that con men are handsome and con women pretty.

One industry has begun to take advantage of the halo effect provided by attractiveness in an especially clever way—by publicizing it. The Washington-based Cosmetic, Toiletry, and Fragrance Association now seems to be in the business of sponsoring research projects and symposia designed to inform us of the hidden benefits of personal beauty. One recent New York symposium, to which media representatives were specifically invited, announced the results of "a major research study" confirming that in the eye of the beholder at least, beauty is far more than skin deep. Researchers at the conference trumpeted to the media the news that attractive individuals are: less likely to be convicted of crimes, more likely to be hired for a job, more likely to get a higher salary for the job, and more likely to be viewed as kind, interesting, and competent. Although the scientific community has been aware of these facts for some time, the information is likely to become much more widely disseminated now that the cosmetics industry is aware, too. It is in their interests to let the rest of us in on the secret.

Similarity

But what if physical appearance is not much at issue? After all, most people possess average looks. Are there other factors that can be used to produce liking? As both researchers and compliance professionals know, there are several, and one of the most influential is similarity.

We like people who are similar to us. This fact seems to hold true whether the similarity is in the area of opinions, personality traits, background, or life-style. Consequently, those who wish to be liked in order to increase our compliance can accomplish that purpose by appearing similar to us in any of a wide variety of ways.

Dress is a good example. Several studies have demonstrated that we are more likely to help those who dress like us. In one study, done in the early 1970s when young people tended to dress either in "hippie" or "straight" fashion, experimenters donned hippie or straight attire and asked college students on campus for a dime to make a phone call. When the experimenter was dressed in the same way as the student, the request was granted in more than two thirds of the instances; but when the student and requester were dissimilarly dressed, the dime was provided less than half the time. Another experiment shows how automatic our positive response to similar others can be.

Marchers in an antiwar demonstration were found to be not only more likely to sign the petition of a similarly dressed requester but also to do so without bothering to read it first. *Click, whirr.*[6]

Another way requesters can manipulate similarity to increase liking and compliance is to claim that they have backgrounds and interests similar to ours. Car salesmen, for example, are trained to look for evidence of such things while examining the customer's trade-in. If there is camping gear in the trunk, the salesman might mention, later on, how he loves to get away from the city whenever he can; if there are golf balls on the back seat, he might remark that he hopes the rain will hold off until he can play the eighteen holes he has scheduled for later in the day; if he notices that the car was purchased out of state, he might ask where the customer is from and report—with surprise—that he (or his wife) was born there, too.

As trivial as these similarities may seem, they appear to work. One researcher who examined the sales records of insurance companies found that customers were more likely to buy insurance when the salesperson was like them in such areas as age, religion, politics, and cigarette-smoking habits. Because even small similarities can be effective in producing a positive response to another and because a veneer of similarity can be so easily manufactured, I would advise special caution in the presence of requesters who claim to be "just like you."[7]

Compliments

Actor McLean Stevenson once described how his wife tricked him into marriage: "She said she liked me." Although designed for a laugh, the remark is as much instructive as humorous. The information that someone fancies us can be a bewitchingly effective device for producing return liking and willing compliance. So, often in terms of flattery or simple claims of affinity, we hear positive estimation from people who want something from us.

Remember Joe Girard, the world's "greatest car salesman," who says the secret of his success was getting customers to like him? He did something that, on the face of it, seems foolish and costly. Each month he sent every one of his more than thirteen

LIKING

FIGURE 5–1

CHEEP REAL ESTATE

The potent influence of similarity on sales is some-thing compliance professionals have long under-stood. (Source: Leunig)

thousand former customers a holiday greeting card containing a personal message. The holiday greeting changed from month to month (Happy New Year or Happy Thanksgiving, etc.), but the message printed on the face of the card never varied. It read, "I like you." As Joe explained it, "There's nothing else on the card. Nothin' but my name. I'm just telling 'em that I like 'em."

"I like you." It came in the mail every year twelve times a

year like clockwork. "I like you," on a printed card that went off to thirteen thousand other people, too. Could a statement of liking so impersonal, so obviously designed to sell cars really work? Joe Girard thinks so; and a man as successful as he was at what he did deserves our attention. Joe understands an important fact about human nature: We are phenomenal suckers for flattery. Although there are limits to our gullibility—especially when we can be sure that the flatterer is trying to manipulate us—we tend, as a rule, to believe praise and to like those who provide it, oftentimes when it is clearly false.

An experiment done on men in North Carolina shows how helpless we can be in the face of praise. The men in the study received comments about themselves from another person who needed a favor from them. Some of the men got only positive comments, some got only negative comments, and some got a mixture of good and bad. There were three interesting findings. First, the evaluator who provided only praise was liked best by the men. Second, this was the case even though the men fully realized that the flatterer stood to gain from their liking him. Finally, unlike the other types of comments, pure praise did not have to be accurate to work. Positive comments produced just as much liking for the flatterer when they were untrue as when they were true.[8]

Apparently we have such an automatically positive reaction to compliments that we can fall victim to someone who uses them in an obvious attempt to win our favor. *Click, whirr.* When seen in this light, the expense of printing and mailing well over 150,000 "I like you" cards each year seems neither as foolish nor as costly as before.

Social psychologists have discovered something else about the way praise affects liking—something even Joe Girard probably doesn't realize because it involves a tactic that would be inappropriate in sales. In certain personal interactions, it may pay to be slightly critical. Suppose you have just met a woman you want to like you. Although steadily complimenting her would be one way to accomplish your goal, research conducted at the University of Minnesota indicates that your most effective tactic might be to arrange for the woman to overhear you stating a reservation or two about her that progressively shifts into a crescendo of praise. The research showed that women who overheard themselves being evaluated in initially negative terms and then increasingly glowing ones actually liked their evaluator more than women who overheard themselves described in a wholly positive way.

Anyone who wishes to be successful with this strategy of mixing positive and negative remarks to increase liking needs to understand the secret of the procedure: The criticism should come first and the praise last. According to the Minnesota study, starting with compliments and then moving to disapproval is to invite reduced liking. Thus it is not the mixture of favorable and unfavorable comments that is crucial; it is their proper sequencing. Apparently, when overhearing ourselves discussed, we are fondest of evaluators who allow us to walk away experiencing the aftertaste of flattery's butter and the echo of its music.[9]

Contact and cooperation

For the most part, we like things that are familiar to us. To prove the point to yourself, try a little experiment. Get the negative of an old photograph that shows a front view of your face and have it developed into a pair of pictures—one that shows you as you actually look and one that shows a reverse image (so that the right and left sides of your face are interchanged). Now decide which version of your face you like better and ask a good friend to make the choice, too. If you are at all like a group of Milwaukee women on whom this procedure was tried, you should notice something odd: Your friend will prefer the true print, but you will prefer the reverse image. Why? Because you *both* will be responding favorably to the more familiar face—your friend to the one the world sees, and you to the transposed one you find in the mirror every day.[10]

Because of its effect on liking, familiarity plays a role in decisions about all sorts of things, including the politicians we elect. It appears that in an election booth voters often choose a candidate merely because the name seems familiar. In one controversial Ohio election a few years ago, a man given little chance of winning the state attorney-general race swept to victory when, shortly before the election, he changed his name to Brown—a family name of much Ohio political tradition.[11]

How could such a thing happen? The answer lies partially in the unconscious way that familiarity affects liking. Often we don't realize that our attitude toward something has been influenced by the number of times we have been exposed to it in the past. For example, in one experiment, college students concentrated on performing a task while certain melodies were played in the background. So intent were the students on the task that, later on, they couldn't recognize any of the melodies they had heard. Yet when rated against other melodies, those that had been played earlier were liked best.[12]

On the basis of evidence that we are more favorable toward the things we have had contact with, some people have recommended a "contact" approach to improving race relations. They argue that simply by providing individuals of different ethnic background with more exposure to one another as equals, those individuals will naturally come to like each other better. However, when scientists have examined school integration—the area offering the single best test of the contact approach—they have discovered quite the opposite pattern. School desegregation is more likely to increase prejudice between blacks and whites than to decrease it.[13]

Let's stay with the issue of school desegregation for a while. However well intentioned the proponents of interracial harmony through simple contact, their approach is unlikely to bear fruit because the argument on which it is based is terribly misinformed. First of all, the school setting is no melting pot where children interact as readily with members of other ethnic groups as they do with their own. Years after formal school integration, there is little social integration. The students clot together ethnically, separating themselves for the most part from other groups. Second, even if there were much more interethnic interaction, research shows that becoming familiar with something through repeated contact doesn't necessarily cause greater liking. In fact, continued exposure to a person or object under unpleasant conditions such as frustration, conflict, or competition leads to less liking.[14] And the typical American classroom fosters precisely these unpleasant conditions.

LIKING

Consider the illuminating report of a psychologist, Elliot Aronson, called in to consult with school authorities on problems in the Austin, Texas, schools. His description of how he found education proceeding in the standard classroom could apply to nearly any public school in the United States:

> In general, here is how it works: The teacher stands in front of the class and asks a question. Six to ten children strain in their seats and wave their hands in the teacher's face, eager to be called on and show how smart they are. Several others sit quietly with eyes averted, trying to become invisible. When the teacher calls on one child, you see looks of disappointment and dismay on the faces of the eager students, who missed a chance to get the teacher's approval; and you will see relief on the faces of the others who didn't know the answer. . . . This game is fiercely competitive and the stakes are high, because the kids are competing for the love and approval of one of the two or three most important people in their world.
>
> Further, this teaching process guarantees that the children will not learn to like and understand each other. Conjure up your own experience. If you knew the right answer and the teacher called on someone else, you probably hoped that he or she would make a mistake so that you would have a chance to display your knowledge. If you were called on and failed, or if you didn't even raise your hand to compete, you probably envied and resented your classmates who knew the answer. Children who fail in this system become jealous and resentful of the successes, putting them down as teacher's pets or even resorting to violence against them in the school yard. The successful students, for their part, often hold the unsuccessful children in contempt, calling them "dumb" or "stupid."
>
> This competitive process does not encourage anyone to look benevolently and happily upon his fellow students.[15]

Should we wonder, then, why raw school desegregation—whether by enforced busing, district rezoning, or school closures—so frequently produces increased rather than decreased prejudice? When our own children find their pleasant social and friendship contacts within their own ethnic boundaries and get repeated exposure to other groups only in the competitive cauldron of the classroom, we might expect as much.

Are there available solutions to this problem? One possibility might be to end our attempts at school integration. But that hardly seems workable. Even were we to ignore the inevitable legal and constitutional challenges and the disruptive societal wrangle such a retreat would provoke, there are solid reasons for pursuing classroom integration. For instance, although white students' achievement levels remain steady, it is ten times more likely that the academic performance of minority students will significantly increase rather than significantly decline after desegregation. We must be cautious in our approach to school desegregation not to throw out the baby because it is sitting in some dirty bath water.

The idea, of course, is to jettison just the water, leaving the baby shining from the bath. Right now, though, our baby is soaking in the *schmutzwasser* of increased racial hostility. Fortunately, real hope for draining away that hostility is emerging from the recent research of education specialists into the concept of "cooperative learning." Because much of the heightened prejudice from classroom desegregation seems to stem from increased exposure to outside group members as rivals, these educators have experimented with forms of learning in which cooperation rather than competition with classmates is central.

Off to camp. To understand the logic of the cooperative approach, it helps to reexamine the fascinating, three-decades-old research program of Turkish-born social scientist Muzafer Sherif. Intrigued with the issue of intergroup conflict, Sherif decided to investigate the process as it developed in boys' summer camps. Although the boys never realized that they were participants in an experiment, Sherif and his associates consistently engaged in artful manipulations of the camp's social environment to observe the effects on group relations.

It didn't take much to bring on certain kinds of ill will. Simply separating the boys into two residence cabins was enough to stimulate a "we vs. they" feeling between the groups; and assigning names to the two groups (the Eagles and the Rattlers) accelerated the sense of rivalry. The boys soon began to demean the qualities and accomplishments of the other group. But these forms of hostility were minor compared to what occurred when the experimenters purposely introduced competitive activities into the factions' meetings with one another. Cabin against cabin treasure hunts, tugs-of-war, and athletic contests produced name-calling and physical friction. During the competitions, members of the opposing team were labeled "cheaters," "sneaks," and "stinkers." Afterward, cabins were raided, rival banners were stolen and burned, threatening signs were posted, and lunchroom scuffles were commonplace.

At this point, it was evident to Sherif that the recipe for disharmony was quick and easy: Just separate the participants into groups and let sit for a while in their own juices. Then mix together over the flame of continued competition. And there you have it: Cross-group hatred at a rolling boil.

A more challenging issue then faced the experimenters: how to remove the entrenched hostility they had created. They first tried the contact approach of bringing the bands together more often. But even when the joint activities were pleasant ones such as movies and social events, the results were disastrous. Picnics produced food fights, entertainment programs gave way to shouting contests, dining-hall lines degenerated into shoving matches. Sherif and his research team began to worry that, in Dr. Frankenstein fashion, they might have created a monster they could no longer control. Then, at the height of the strife, they hit on a resolution that was at once simple and effective.

They constructed a series of situations in which competition between the groups would have harmed everyone's interests, in which cooperation was necessary for mutual benefit. On a day-long outing, the single truck available to go into town for food was "found" to be stuck. The boys were assembled and all pulled and pushed together until the vehicle was on its way. In another instance, the researchers arranged for an interruption of the camp's water supply, which came through pipes from a distant tank. Presented with the common crisis and realizing the need for unified action, the boys organized themselves harmoniously to find and fix the problem before day's end. In yet another circumstance requiring cooperation, the campers were informed that a desirable movie was available for rental but that the camp could not afford it. Aware that the only solution was to combine resources, the boys rented the film with pooled money and spent an unusually congenial evening enjoying it together.

The consequences, though not instantaneous, were nonetheless striking. Conjoint efforts toward common goals steadily bridged the rancorous rift between the groups. Before long, the verbal baiting had died, the jostling in lines had ended, and the boys had begun to intermix at the meal tables. Further, when asked to list their best friends, significant numbers changed from an earlier exclusive naming of in-group chums to a listing that included boys in the other group. Some even thanked the researchers for the opportunity to rate their friends again because they realized they had changed their minds since the old days. In one revealing episode, the boys were returning from a campfire on a single bus—something that would have produced bedlam before but was now specifically requested by the boys. When the bus stopped at a refreshment stand, the boys of one group, with five dollars left in its treasury, decided to treat their former bitter adversaries to milkshakes!

We can trace the roots of this surprising turnabout to those times when the boys had to view one another as allies instead of opponents. The crucial procedure was the experimenters' imposition of common goals on the groups. It was the cooperation required to achieve these goals that finally allowed the rival group members to experience one another as reasonable fellows, valued helpers, and friends. And when success resulted from the mutual efforts, it became especially difficult to maintain feelings of hostility toward those who had been teammates in the triumph.[16]

Back to school. In the welter of racial tensions that followed school desegregation, certain educational psychologists began to see the relevance to the classroom in Sherif's findings. If only the learning experience there could be modified to include at least occasional interethnic cooperation toward mutual successes, perhaps cross-group friendships would have a place to grow. Although similar projects have been under way in various states, an especially interesting approach in this direction—termed the jigsaw classroom—was developed by Elliot Aronson and his colleagues in Texas and California.

The essence of the jigsaw route to learning is to require that students work together to master the material scheduled for an upcoming examination. This is accomplished by forming students into cooperating teams and giving each student only one part of the information—one piece of the puzzle—necessary to pass the test. Under this system the students must take turns teaching and helping one another. Everyone needs everyone else to do well. Like Sherif's campers working on tasks that could be successfully accomplished only conjointly, the students became allies rather than enemies.

When tried in recently desegregated classrooms, the jigsaw approach has generated impressive results. Studies have shown that, compared to other classrooms in the same school using the traditional competitive method, jigsaw learning stimulated significantly more friendship and less prejudice between ethnic groups. Besides this vital reduction in hostility, there were other advantages: self-esteem, liking for school, and test scores improved for minority students. And the white students benefited, too. Their self-esteem and liking for school went up, and their test performance was at least as high as that of whites in the traditional classes.

Gains such as these cry out for more detailed explanation. What exactly goes on in the jigsaw classroom to account for effects we had long ago lost hope of attaining in the public schools? A case study provided by Aronson helps us to understand better. It relates the experience of Carlos, a young Mexican-American boy, who found himself in a jigsaw group for the first time. Carlos's job was to learn and then convey to his team information on the middle years of Joseph Pulitzer. A test on the famous newspaperman's life would soon face each group member. Aronson tells what happened:

> Carlos was not very articulate in English, his second language, and because he was often ridiculed when he had spoken up in the past, he had learned over the years to keep quiet in class. We might even say that Carlos and the teacher had entered into a conspiracy of silence. He would become anonymous, buried in the bustle of classroom activity, and not be embarrassed by having to stumble over answers; she, in turn, would not call on him. Her decision probably came from the purest of motives; she didn't want to humiliate him, or watch

INFLUENCE

the other kids make fun of him. But by ignoring Carlos, the teacher had, in effect, written him off. She was implying that he was not worth bothering with; at least that was the message the other kids got. If the teacher wasn't calling on Carlos, it must be because Carlos is stupid. It is likely that Carlos himself came to the same conclusion.

Naturally, Carlos was quite uncomfortable with the new system, which required him to talk to his groupmates; he had a great deal of trouble communicating his paragraph. He stammered, hesitated, and fidgeted. The other kids were not helpful at all; they reacted out of their old, overlearned habit. When a kid stumbles, especially one they think is stupid, they resort to ridicule and teasing. "Aw, you don't know it," accused Mary. "You're dumb; you're stupid. You don't know what you're doing."

One of us, assigned to observe the group process, would intervene with a bit of advice when she overheard such comments: "Okay, you can tease him if you want to," she said, "and that might be fun for you, but it's not going to help you learn about Joseph Pulitzer's middle years. The exam will take place in about an hour." Notice how she changed the reinforcement contingencies. Now Mary doesn't gain much from putting Carlos down, and she stands to lose a great deal. After a few days and several such experiences, it began to dawn on these kids that the only chance they had to learn about Carlos's segment was by paying attention to what Carlos had to say.

And with that realization, the kids began to develop into pretty good interviewers, sort of junior Dick Cavetts. Instead of teasing Carlos or ignoring him, they learned to draw him out, to ask the questions that made it easier for him to explain out loud what was in his head. Carlos, in turn, relaxed more, and this improved his ability to communicate. After a couple of weeks, the children concluded that Carlos wasn't nearly as dumb as they thought he was. They saw things in him they hadn't seen before. They began to like him more, and Carlos began to enjoy school more and think of his Anglo classmates not as tormentors but as friends.[17]

There is a tendency when faced with positive results like those from the jigsaw classroom to become overly enthusiastic about a single, simple solution to a tenacious problem. Experience should tell us that such problems rarely yield to a simple remedy. That is no doubt true in this case, as well. Even within the boundaries of cooperative learning procedures the issues are complex. Before we can feel truly comfortable with the jigsaw, or any similar approach to learning and liking, much more research is needed to determine how frequently, in what size doses, at which ages, and in which sorts of groups cooperative strategies will work. We also need to know the best way for teachers to institute new methods—provided they will institute them at all. After all, not only are cooperative learning techniques a radical departure from the traditional, familiar routine of most teachers, they may also threaten the teacher's sense of importance in the classroom by turning over much of the instruction to the students. Finally, we must realize that competition has its place, too. It can serve as a valuable motivator of desirable action and an important builder of self-concept. The task, then, is not to eliminate academic competition but to break its monopoly in the classroom by introducing regular cooperative successes that include members of all ethnic groups.[18]

Despite these qualifications, I cannot help but be encouraged by the evidence to date. When I talk to my students, or even my neighbors and friends, about the prospects for cooperative learning approaches, I can feel optimism rise in me. The public schools have for so long been the source of discouraging news— sinking test scores, teacher burnout, increasing crime, and, of course, racial conflict. Now there is at least one crack in the gloom, and I find myself genuinely excited about it.

What's the point of this digression into the effects of school desegregation on race relations? The point is to make two points. First, although the familiarity produced by contact usually leads to greater liking, the opposite occurs if the contact carries distasteful experiences with it. Therefore, when children of different racial groups are thrown into the incessant, harsh competition of the standard American classroom, we ought to see—and we do see—the worsening of hostilities. Second, the evidence that team-oriented learning is an antidote to this disorder may tell us about the heavy impact of cooperation on the liking process.

INFLUENCE

But before we assume that cooperation is a powerful cause of liking, we should first pass it through what, to my mind, is the acid test: Do compliance practitioners systematically use cooperation to get us to like them so we will say yes to their requests? Do they point it out when it exists naturally in a situation? Do they try to amplify it when it exists only weakly? And, most instructive of all, do they manufacture it when it is absent?

As it turns out, cooperation passes the test with colors flying. Compliance professionals are forever attempting to establish that we and they are working for the same goals, that we must "pull together" for mutual benefit, that they are, in essence, our *teammates*. A host of examples is possible. Most are familiar, like the new-car salesman who takes our side and "does battle" with his boss to secure us a good deal.[19] But one rather spectacular illustration occurs in a setting few of us would recognize firsthand, because the professionals are police interrogators whose job is to induce suspects to confess to crime.

In recent years, the courts have imposed a variety of restrictions on the way police must behave in handling suspected criminals, especially in seeking confessions. Many procedures that in the past led to admissions of guilt can no longer be employed for fear that they will result in a judge's dismissal of the case. As yet, however, the courts have found nothing illegal in the use by the police of subtle psychology. For this reason, criminal interrogations have taken increasingly to the use of such ploys as the one they call Good Cop/Bad Cop.

Good Cop/Bad Cop works as follows: A young robbery suspect, let's say, who has been advised of his rights and is maintaining his innocence, is brought to a room to be questioned by a pair of officers. One of the officers, either because the part suits him or because it is merely his turn, plays the role of Bad Cop. Before the suspect even sits down, Bad Cop curses "the son-of-a-bitch" for the robbery. For the rest of the session his words come only with snarls and growls. He kicks the prisoner's chair to emphasize his points. When he looks at the man, he seems to see a mound of garbage. If the suspect challenges Bad Cop's accusations or just refuses to answer them, Bad Cop becomes livid. His rage soars. He swears he will do everything possible to assure a maximum sentence. He says he has friends in the district attorney's office who will hear from him of the suspect's non-cooperative attitude and will prosecute the case hard.

At the outset of Bad Cop's performance, his partner, Good Cop, sits in the background. Then, slowly, he starts to chip in. First he speaks only to Bad Cop, trying to temper the burgeoning anger. "Calm down, Frank, calm down." But Bad Cop shouts back, "Don't tell me to calm down when he's lying right to my face! I hate these lying bastards!" A bit later, Good Cop actually says something in the suspect's behalf. "Take it easy, Frank, he's only a kid." Not much in the way of support, but compared to the rantings of Bad Cop, the words fall like music on the prisoner's ears. Still, Bad Cop is unconvinced. "Kid? He's no kid. He's a punk. That's what he is, a punk. And I'll tell you something else. He's over eighteen, and that's all I need to get his ass sent so far behind bars they'll need a flashlight to find him."

Now Good Cop begins to speak directly to the young man, calling him by his first name and pointing out any positive details of the case. "I'll tell you, Kenny, you're lucky that nobody was hurt and you weren't armed. When you come up for sentencing, that'll look good." If the suspect persists in claiming innocence, Bad Cop launches into another tirade of curses and threats. But this time Good Cop stops him, "Okay, Frank," handing Bad Cop some money, "I think we could all use some coffee. How about getting us three cups?" When Bad Cop is gone, it's time for Good Cop's big scene: "Look, man, I don't know why, but my partner doesn't like you, and he's gonna try to get you. And he's gonna be able to do it because we've got enough evidence right now. And he's right about the D.A.'s office going hard on guys who don't cooperate. You're looking at five years, man, five years! Now, I don't want to see that happen to you. So if you admit you robbed that place right now, before he gets back, I'll take charge of your case and put in a good word for you to the D.A. If we work together on this, we can cut that five years down to two, maybe one. Do us both a favor, Kenny. Just tell me how you did it, and then let's start working on getting you through this." A full confession frequently follows.

Good Cop/Bad Cop works as well as it does for several reasons: The fear of long incarceration is quickly instilled by Bad

Cop's threats; the perceptual contrast principle (see pp. 24–27) ensures that compared to the raving, venomous Bad Cop, the interrogator playing Good Cop will seem like an *especially* reasonable and kind man; and because Good Cop has intervened repeatedly on the suspect's behalf—has even spent his own money for a cup of coffee—the reciprocity rule pressures for a return favor. The big reason that the technique is effective, though, is that it gives the suspect the idea that there is someone on his side, someone with his welfare in mind, someone working together with him, for him. In most situations, such a person would be viewed very favorably, but in the deep trouble our robbery suspect finds himself, that person takes on the character of a savior. And from savior, it is but a short step to trusted father confessor.

Conditioning and association

"Why do they blame *me*, Doc?" It was the shaky telephone voice of a local TV weatherman. He had been given my number when he called the psychology department at my university to find someone who could answer his question—a question that had always puzzled him but had recently begun to bother and depress him.

"I mean, it's crazy, isn't it? Everybody knows that I just report the weather, that I don't order it, right? So how come I get so much flak when the weather's bad? During the floods last year, I got hate mail! One guy threatened to shoot me if it didn't stop raining. Christ, I'm still looking over my shoulder from that one. And the people I work with at the station do it, too! Sometimes, right on the air, they'll zing me about a heat wave or something. They have to know that I'm not responsible, but that doesn't seem to stop them. Can you help me understand this, Doc? It's really getting me down."

We made an appointment to talk in my office, where I tried to explain that he was the victim of an ages-old *click, whirr* response that people have to things they perceive as merely connected to one another. Instances of this response abound in modern life. But I felt that the example most likely to help the

LIKING

distressed weatherman would require a bit of ancient history. I asked him to consider the precarious fate of the imperial messengers of old Persia. Any such messenger assigned the role of military courier had special cause to hope mightily for Persian battlefield successes. With news of victory in his pouch, he would be treated as a hero upon his arrival at the palace. The food, drink, and women of his choice were provided gladly and sumptuously. Should his message tell of military disaster, though, the reception would be quite different: He was summarily slain.

I hoped that the point of this story would not be lost on the weatherman. I wanted him to be aware of a fact that is as true today as it was in the time of ancient Persia, or, for that matter, in the time of Shakespeare, who captured the essence of it with one vivid line. "The nature of bad news," he said, "infects the teller." There is a natural human tendency to dislike a person who brings us unpleasant information, even when that person did not cause the bad news. The simple association with it is enough to stimulate our dislike.[20]

But there was something else I hoped the weatherman would get from the historical examples. Not only was he joined in his predicament by centuries of other "tellers," but also, compared to some, such as the Persian messengers, he was very well off. At the end of our session, he said something to convince me that he appreciated this point quite clearly. "Doc," he said on his way out, "I feel a lot better about my job now. I mean, I'm in Phoenix where the sun shines three hundred days a year, right? Thank God I don't do the weather in Buffalo."

The weatherman's parting comment reveals that he understood more than I had told him about the principle that was influencing his viewer's liking for him. Being connected with bad weather does have a negative effect. But on the other side of the coin, being connected with sunshine should do wonders for his popularity. And he was right. The principle of association is a general one, governing both negative and positive connections. An innocent association with either bad things or good things will influence how people feel about us.[21]

Our instruction in how the negative association works seems to have been primarily undertaken by the mothers of our society. Remember how they were always warning us against

Weathermen pay price
for nature's curve balls

By David L. Langford
Associated Press

Television weather forecasters make a good living talking about the weather, but when Mother Nature throws a curve ball, they duck for cover.

Conversations with several veteran prognosticators across the country this week turned up stories of them being whacked by old ladies with umbrellas, accosted by drunks in bars, pelted with snowballs and galoshes, threatened with death, and accused of trying to play God.

"I had one guy call and tell me that if it snowed over Christmas, I wouldn't live to see New Year's," said Bob Gregory, who has been the forecaster at WTHR-TV in Indianapolis for nine years.

Most of the forecasters claimed they are accurate 80 percent to 90 percent of the time on one-day forecasts, but longer-range predictions get tricky. And most conceded they are simply reporting information supplied by computers and anonymous meteorologists from the National Weather Service or a private agency.

But it's the face on the television screen that people go after.

Tom Bonner, 35, who has been with KARK-TV in Little Rock, Ark., for 11 years, remembers the time a burly farmer from Lonoke, with too much to drink, walked up to him in a bar, poked a finger in his chest and said: "You're the one that sent that tor-nado and tore my house up . . . I'm going to take your head off."

Bonner said he looked for the bouncer, couldn't spot him, and replied, "That's right about the tornado, and I'll tell you something else, I'll send another one if you don't back off."

Several years ago, when a major flood left water 10 feet deep in San Diego's Mission Valley, Mike Ambrose of KGTV recalls that a woman walked up to his car, whacked the windshield with an umbrella and said, "This rain is your fault."

Chuck Whitaker of WSBT-TV in South Bend, Ind., says, "One little old lady called the police department and wanted the weatherman arrested for bringing all the snow."

A woman upset that it had rained for her daughter's wedding called Tom Jolls of WKBW-TV in Buffalo, N.Y., to give him a piece of her mind. "She held me responsible and said if she ever met me she would probably hit me," he said.

Sonny Eliot of WJBK-TV, a forecaster in the Detroit area for 30 years, recalls predicting 2 to 4 inches of snow in the city several years ago and more than 8 came down. To retaliate, his colleagues at the station set up a contraption that rained about 200 galoshes on him while he was giving the forecast the next day.

"I've still got the lumps to prove it," he says.

FIGURE 5–2

WEATHERBEATEN

Note the similarities between the account of the weatherman who came to my office and those of other TV weather reporters. (Source: David L. Langford and Associated Press)

playing with the bad kids down the street? Remember how they said it didn't matter if we did nothing bad ourselves because, in the eyes of the neighborhood, we would be "known by the company we kept." Our mothers were teaching us about guilt by association. They were giving us a lesson in the negative side of the principle of association. And they were right. People do assume that we have the same personality traits as our friends.[22]

As for the positive associations, it is the compliance professionals who teach the lesson. They are incessantly trying to connect themselves or their products with the things we like. Did you ever wonder what all those good-looking models are doing standing around in the autmobile ads? What the advertiser hopes they are doing is lending their positive traits—beauty and desirability—to the cars. The advertiser is betting that we will respond to the product in the same ways we respond to the attractive models merely associated with it.

And they are right. In one study, men who saw a new-car ad that included a seductive young woman model rated the *car* as faster, more appealing, more expensive-looking, and better-designed than did men who viewed the same ad without the model. Yet when asked later, the men refused to believe that the presence of the young woman had influenced their judgments.[23]

Because the association principle works so well—and so unconsciously—manufacturers regularly rush to connect their products with the current cultural rage. During the days of the first American moon shot, everything from breakfast drink to deodorant was sold with allusions to the U.S. space program. In Olympiad years, we are told precisely which is the "official" hair spray and facial tissue of our Olympic teams. During the 1970s, when the magic cultural concept appeared to be "naturalness," the "natural" bandwagon was crowded to capacity. Sometimes the connections to naturalness didn't even make sense: "Change your hair color naturally" urged one popular TV commercial.

The linking of celebrities to products is another way advertisers cash in on the association principle. Professional athletes are paid to connect themselves to things that can be directly relevant to their roles (sport shoes, tennis racquets, golf balls) or wholly irrelevant (soft drinks, popcorn poppers, panty hose). The important thing for the advertiser is to establish the connection; it doesn't have to be a logical one, just a positive one.

INFLUENCE

FIGURE 5–3

SEXY SICKBEDS?

Research has shown that an attractive model posing with an automobile will make the car appear more desirable. Some advertisers apparently believe that the same holds true for all sorts of items.

Of course, popular entertainers provide another form of desirability that manufacturers have always paid dearly to tie to their goods. But recently, politicians have caught on to the ability of a celebrity linkage to sway voters. Presidential candidates assemble stables of well-known nonpolitical figures who either actively participate in the campaign or merely lend their names to it. Even at the state and local level, a similar game is played. Take as evidence the comment of a Los Angeles woman I overheard expressing her conflicting feelings over a California referendum to limit smoking in public places. "It's a real tough decision. They've got big stars speaking for it, and big stars speaking against it. You don't know how to vote."

If politicians are relative newcomers to the use of celebrity endorsements, they are old hands at exploiting the association principle in other ways. For example, congressional representatives traditionally announce to the press the start of federal proj-

LIKING

ects that will bring new jobs or benefits to their home states; this is true even when a representative has had nothing to do with advancing the project or has, in some cases, voted against it.

While politicians have long strained to associate themselves with the values of motherhood, country, and apple pie, it may be in the last of these connections—to food—that they have been most clever. For instance, it is White House tradition to try to sway the votes of balking legislators over a meal. It can be a picnic lunch, a sumptuous breakfast, or an elegant dinner; but when an important bill is up for grabs, out comes the silverware. And political fund raising these days regularly involves the presentation of food. Notice, too, that at the typical fund-raising dinner the speeches, the appeals for further contributions and heightened effort never come before the meal is served, only during or after. The advantages to this pairing of the affairs of the table with those of the state are several: For example, time is saved and the reciprocity rule is engaged. The least recognized benefit, however, may be the one uncovered in research conducted in the 1930s by the distinguished psychologist Gregory Razran.

Using what he termed the "luncheon technique," he found that his subjects became fonder of the people and things they experienced while they were eating. In the example most relevant for our purposes, Razran's subjects were presented with some political statements they had rated once before. At the end of the experiment, after all the political statements had been presented, Razran found that only certain of them had gained in approval—those that had been shown while food was being eaten. And these changes in liking seem to have occurred unconsciously, since the subjects could not remember which of the statements they had seen during the food service.[24]

How did Razran come up with the luncheon technique? What made him think it would work? The answer may lie in the dual scholarly roles he played during his career. Not only was he a respected independent researcher, he was also one of the earliest translators into English of the pioneering psychological literature of Russia. It was a literature dedicated to the study of the association principle and dominated by the thinking of a brilliant man, Ivan Pavlov.

INFLUENCE

Although a scientist of varied and elaborated talent—he had, for instance, won a Nobel Prize years earlier for his work on the digestive system—Pavlov's most important experimental demonstration was simplicity itself. He showed that he could get an animal's typical response to food (salivation) to be directed toward something irrelevant to food (a bell) merely by connecting the two things in the animal's mind. If the presentation of food to a dog was always accompanied by the sound of a bell, soon the dog would salivate to the bell alone, even when there was no food to be had.

It is not a long step from Pavlov's classic demonstration to Razran's luncheon technique. Obviously, a normal reaction to food can be transferred to some other thing through the process of raw association. Razran's insight was that there are many normal responses to food besides salivation, one of them being a good and favorable feeling. Therefore, it is possible to attach this pleasant feeling, this positive attitude, to anything (political statements being only an example) that is closely associated with good food.

Nor is there a long step from the luncheon technique to the compliance professionals' realization that all kinds of desirable things can substitute for food in lending their likable qualities to the ideas, products, and people artificially linked to them. In the final analysis, then, that is why those good-looking models are standing around in the magazine ads. And that is why radio programmers are instructed to insert the station's call-letters jingle immediately before a big hit song is played. And that is even why the women playing Barnyard Bingo at a Tupperware party must yell the word "Tupperware" rather than "Bingo" before they can rush to the center of the floor for a prize. It may be "Tupperware" for the women, but it's "Bingo" for the company.

Just because we are often the unaware victims of compliance practitioners' use of the association principle doesn't mean that we don't understand how it works or don't use it ourselves. There is ample evidence, for instance, that we understand fully the predicament of a Persian imperial messenger or modern-day weatherman announcing bad news. In fact, we can be counted on to take steps to avoid putting ourselves in any similar positions.

LIKING

Research done at the University of Georgia shows just how we operate when faced with the task of communicating good or bad news. Students waiting for an experiment to begin were given the job of informing a fellow student that an important phone call had come in for him. Half the time the call was supposed to bring good news and half the time, bad news. The researchers found that the students conveyed the information very differently depending on its quality. When the news was positive, the tellers were sure to mention that feature: "You just got a phone call with *great* news. Better see the experimenter for the details." But when the news was unfavorable, they kept themselves apart from it: "You just got a phone call. Better see the experimenter for the details." Obviously, the students had previously learned that, to be liked, they should connect themselves to good news but not bad news.[25]

A lot of strange behavior can be explained by the fact that people understand the association principle well enough to strive to link themselves to positive events and separate themselves from negative events—even when they have not caused the events. Some of the strangest of such behavior takes place in the great arena of sports. The actions of the athletes are not the issue here, though. After all, in the heated contact of the game, they are entitled to an occasional eccentric outburst. Instead, it is the often raging, irrational, boundless fervor of the sports fan that seems, on its face, so puzzling. How can we account for wild sports riots in Europe, or the murder of players and referees by South American soccer crowds gone berserk, or the unnecessary lavishness of the gifts provided by local fans to already wealthy American ballplayers on the special "day" set aside to honor them? Rationally, none of this makes sense. It's just a game! Isn't it?

Hardly. The relationship between sport and the earnest fan is anything but gamelike. It is serious, intense, and highly personal. An apt illustration comes from one of my favorite anecdotes. It concerns a World War II soldier who returned to his home in the Balkans after the war and shortly thereafter stopped speaking. Medical examinations could find no physical cause for the problem. There was no wound, no brain damage, no vocal impairment. He could read, write, understand a conversation, and follow orders. Yet he would not talk—not for his doctors, not for his friends, not even for his pleading family.

Perplexed and exasperated, his doctors moved him to another city and placed him in a veterans' hospital where he remained for thirty years, never breaking his self-imposed silence and sinking into a life of social isolation. Then one day, a radio in his ward happened to be tuned to a soccer match between his hometown team and a traditional rival. When at a crucial point of play the referee called a foul against a player from the man's home team, the mute veteran jumped from his chair, glared at the radio, and spoke his first words in more than three decades: "You dumb ass!" he cried. "Are you trying to *give* them the match?" With that, he returned to his chair and to a silence he never again violated.

There are two important lessons to be derived from this true story. The first concerns the sheer power of the phenomenon. The veteran's desire to have his hometown team succeed was so strong that it alone produced a deviation from his solidly entrenched way of life. Similar effects of sports events on the long-standing habits of fans are far from unique to the back wards of veterans' hospitals. During the 1980 Winter Olympics, after the U.S. hockey team had upset the vastly favored Soviet team, the teetotaling father of the American goaltender, Jim Craig, was offered a flask. "I've never had a drink in my life," he reported later, "but someone behind me handed me cognac. I drank it. Yes, I did." Nor was such unusual behavior unique to parents of the players. Fans outside the hockey arena were described in news accounts as delirious: "They hugged, sang, and turned somersaults in the snow." Even those fans not present at Lake Placid exulted in the victory and displayed their pride with bizarre behavior. In Raleigh, North Carolina, a swim meet had to be halted when, after the hockey score was announced, the competitors and audience alike chanted "U.S.A.! U.S.A.!" until they were hoarse. In Cambridge, Massachusetts, a quiet supermarket erupted at the news into a riot of flying toilet tissue and paper towel streamers. The customers were joined in their spree—and soon led—by the market employees and manager.

LIKING

FIGURE 5–4

FATAL SPORTS FANATICISM

This newsphoto depicts part of a stadium riot that occurred in Peru after a soccer referee's decision awarded victory to an Argentinian team. Rioting was so violent that 318 persons died while another 400 were injured, mostly from trampling and asphyxiation. (Source: UPI)

Without question, the force is deep and sweeping. But if we return to the account of the silent veteran, we can see that something else is revealed about the nature of the union of sports and sports fan, something crucial to its basic character: It is a personal thing. Whatever fragment of an identity that ravaged, mute man still possessed was engaged by soccer play. No matter how weakened his ego may have become after thirty years of wordless stagnation in a hospital ward, it was involved in the outcome of the match. Why? Because he, personally, would be diminished by a hometown defeat, and he, personally, would be enhanced by a hometown victory. How? Through the principle of association. The mere connection of birthplace hooked him, wrapped him, tied him to the approaching triumph or failure. As distinguished author Isaac Asimov put it in describing our reactions to the contests we view, "All things being equal, you root for your own sex, your own culture, your own locality . . . and what you want to prove is that *you* are better than the other person. Whomever you root for represents *you;* and when he wins, *you* win."[26]

When viewed in this light, the passion of the sports fan begins to make sense. The game is no light diversion to be enjoyed for its inherent form and artistry. The self is at stake. That is why hometown crowds are so adoring and, more tellingly, so grateful toward those regularly responsible for home-team victories. That is also why the same crowds are often ferocious in their treatment of players, coaches, and officials implicated in athletic failures.

So we want our affiliated sports teams to win to prove our own superiority. But to whom are we trying to prove it? Ourselves, certainly; but to everyone else, too. According to the association principle, if we can surround ourselves with success that we are connected with in even a superficial way (for example, place of residence), our public prestige will rise.

Are sports fans right to think that without ever throwing a block, catching a ball, scoring a goal, or perhaps even attending a game, they will receive some of the glory from a hometown championship? I believe so. The evidence is in their favor. Recall that Persia's messengers did not have to cause the news, my weatherman did not have to cause the weather, and Pavlov's bell did not have to cause the food for powerful effects to occur. The association was enough.

It is for this reason that, were the University of Southern California to win the Rose Bowl, we could expect people with a Southern Cal connection to try to increase the visibility of that connection in any of a variety of ways. In one experiment showing how wearing apparel can serve to proclaim such an association, researchers counted the number of school sweat shirts worn on Monday mornings by students on the campuses of seven prominent football universities: Arizona State, Louisiana State, Notre Dame, Michigan, Ohio State, Pittsburgh, and Southern California. The results showed that many more home school shirts were worn if the football team had won its game on the prior Saturday. What's more, the larger the margin of victory, the more such shirts appeared. It wasn't a close, hard-fought game that caused the students to dress themselves, literally, in success; instead, it was a clear, crushing conquest smacking of indisputable superiority.

This tendency to try to bask in reflected glory by publicly trumpeting our connections to successful others has its mirror image in our attempt to avoid being darkened by the shadow of others' defeat. In an amazing display during the luckless 1980 season, season-ticket-holding fans of the New Orleans Saints football team began to appear at the stadium wearing paper bags to conceal their faces. As their team suffered loss after loss, more and more fans donned the bags until TV cameras were regularly able to record the extraordinary image of gathered masses of people shrouded in brown paper with nothing to identify them but the tips of their noses. I find it instructive that during a late-season contest, when it was clear that the Saints were at last going to win one, the fans discarded their bags and went public once more.

All this tells me that we purposefully manipulate the visibility of our connections with winners and losers in order to make ourselves look good to anyone who could view these connections. By showcasing the positive associations and burying the negative ones, we are trying to get observers to think more highly of us and to like us more. There are many ways we go about this, but one of the simplest and most pervasive is in the pronouns we use. Have you noticed, for example, how often after a home-team victory fans crowd into the range of a TV camera, thrust their index fingers high, and shout, "We're number one! We're number one!" Note that the call is not "They're number one" or even "Our team is number one." The pronoun is "we," designed to imply the closest possible identity with the team.

Note also that nothing similar occurs in the case of failure. No television viewer will ever hear the chant, "We're in last place! We're in last place!" Home-team defeats are the times for distancing oneself. Here "we" is not nearly as preferred as the insulating pronoun "they." To prove the point, I once did a small experiment in which students at Arizona State University were phoned and asked to describe the outcome of a football game their school team had played a few weeks earlier. Some of the students were asked the outcome of a certain game their team had lost; the other students were asked the outcome of a different game—one their team had won. My fellow researcher, Avril Thorne, and I simply listened to what was said and recorded the percentage of students who used the word "we" in their descriptions. When the results were tabulated, it was obvious that the students had tried to connect themselves to success by using the pronoun "we" to describe their school-team victory—"We beat Houston, seventeen to fourteen," or "We won." In the case of the lost game, however, "we" was rarely used. Instead, the students used terms designed to keep themselves separate from their vanquished team—"They lost to Missouri, thirty to twenty," or "I don't know the score, but Arizona State got beat." Perhaps the twin desires to connect ourselves to winners and to distance ourselves from losers were combined consummately in the remarks of one particular student. After dryly recounting the score of the home-team defeat—"Arizona State lost it, thirty to twenty"—he blurted in anguish, "*They* threw away *our* chance for a national championship!"[27]

If it is true that, to make ourselves look good, we try to bask in the reflected glory of the successes we are even remotely associated with, a provocative implication emerges: We will be most likely to use this approach when we feel that we don't look so good. Whenever our public image is damaged, we will experience an increased desire to restore that image by trumpeting our ties to successful others. At the same time, we will most scrupulously avoid publicizing our ties to failing others. Support for these ideas comes from the telephone study of Arizona State University students. Before being asked about the home-team victory or loss, they were given a test of their general knowledge. The test was rigged so that some of the students would fail badly while the others would do quite well.

So at the time they were asked to describe the football score,

LIKING

FIGURE 5–5

WHEE! WE!

When, after decades of failure, the 1980 Philadelphia Phillies won the World Series, 1.1 million people—in a city of 1.5 million—crowded the streets to shout "We're Number 1" as their heroes passed in a victory parade. (Source: Kluetmeier, Iooss, Sports Illustrated)

half of the students had experienced recent image damage from their failure of the test. These students later showed the greatest need to manipulate their connections with the football team to salvage their prestige. If they were asked to describe the team defeat, only 17 percent used the pronoun "we" in so doing. If, however, they were asked to describe the win, 41 percent said "we."

The story was very different, though, for the students who had done well on the general knowledge test. They later used "we" about equally, whether they were describing a home-team victory (25 percent) or defeat (24 percent). These students had bolstered their images through their own achievement and didn't need to do so through the achievement of others. This finding tells me that it is not when we have a strong feeling of recognized personal accomplishment that we will seek to bask in reflected glory. Instead, it will be when prestige (both public and private) is low that we will be intent upon using the successes of associated others to help restore image.

I think it revealing that the remarkable hubbub following the American hockey team victory in the 1980 Olympics came at a time of recently diminished American prestige. The U.S. government had been helpless to prevent both the holding of American hostages in Iran and the Soviet invasion of Afghanistan. It was a time when, as a citizenry, we needed the triumph of that hockey team and we needed to display or even manufacture our connections to it. We should not be surprised to learn, for instance, that outside the hockey arena, in the aftermath of the win over the Soviet team, scalpers were getting a hundred dollars a pair for ticket *stubs*.

Although the desire to bask in reflected glory exists to a degree in all of us, there seems to be something special about people who would wait in the snow to spend fifty dollars apiece for the shreds of tickets to a game they had not attended, presumably to "prove" to friends back home that they had been present at the big victory. Just what kind of people are they? Unless I miss my guess, they are not merely great sports *aficionados;* they are individuals with a hidden personality flaw—a poor self-concept. Deep inside is a sense of low personal worth that directs them to seek prestige not from the generation or promotion of their own attainments but from the generation or promotion of their associations with others of attainment. There are several varieties of this species that bloom throughout our culture. The persistent name-dropper is a classic example. So, too, is the rock-music groupie, who trades sexual favors for the right to tell girlfriends that she was "with" a famous musician for a time. No matter which form it takes, the behavior of such individuals shares a similar theme—the rather tragic view of accomplishment as deriving from outside the self.

Certain of these people work the association principle in a slightly different way. Instead of striving to inflate their visible connections to others of success, they strive to inflate the success of others they are visibly connected to. Although not exclusive to females, this approach seems to be favored by women whose roles have not allowed for careers outside the home. The clearest illustration is the notorious "stage mother," obsessed with securing stardom for her child. Another is the driven-woman-behind-the-successful-man character. In many occupations, the social standing of a wife is directly tied to the professional stature of her husband. The status-hungry woman in such a position frequently resorts to a continuing campaign of agitation designed to push her husband to greater and greater efforts. Physicians' wives often speak of the pressures to obtain personal prestige in this way. John Pekkanen, who authored the book *The Best Doctors in the U.S.*, reports that many enraged protests to his list came not from the physicians who were omitted but from their wives. In one instance that reveals the extent to which the principle of association dominates the thinking of some of these women, Pekkanen received a letter from a frantic wife along with her proof that her husband deserved to be on the list of best doctors. It was a photograph of the man with Merv Griffin.

❊

HOW TO SAY NO

Because liking can be increased by many means, a proper consideration of defenses against compliance professionals who employ the liking rule must, oddly enough, be a short one. It would be pointless to construct a horde of specific counter tactics to combat each of the myriad versions of the various ways to influence liking. There are simply too many routes to be blocked effectively with such a one-on-one strategy. Besides, several of the factors leading to liking—physical attractiveness, familiarity, association—have been shown to work unconsciously to produce their effects on us, making it unlikely that we could muster a timely protection against them.

Instead we need to consider a general approach, one that can be applied to any of the liking-related factors to neutralize their unwelcome influence on our compliance decisions. The secret to such an approach may lie in its timing. Rather than trying to recognize and prevent the action of liking factors before they have a chance to work on us, we might be well advised to let them work. Our vigilance should be directed not toward the things that may produce undue liking for a compliance practitioner but toward the fact that undue liking has been *produced*. The time to react protectively is when we feel ourselves liking the practitioner more than we should under the circumstances.

By concentrating our attention on the effect rather than the causes, we can avoid the laborious, nearly impossible task of trying to detect and deflect the many psychological influences on liking. Instead, we have to be sensitive to only one thing related to liking in our contacts with compliance practitioners: the feeling that we have come to like the practitioner more quickly or more deeply than we would have expected. Once we *notice* this feeling, we will have been tipped off that there is probably some tactic being used, and we can start taking the necessary countermeasures. Note that the strategy I am suggesting borrows much from the jujitsu style favored by the compliance professionals themselves. We don't attempt to restrain the influence of the factors that cause liking. Quite the contrary. We allow these factors to exert their force, and then we use that force in our campaign against them. The stronger the force, the more conspicuous it becomes and, consequently, the more subject to our alerted defenses.

Suppose, for example, we find ourselves bargaining on the price of a new car with Dealin' Dan, a candidate for Joe Girard's vacated "greatest car salesman" title. After talking a while and negotiating a bit, Dan wants to close the deal; he wants us to decide to buy the car. Before any such decision is made, it would be important to ask ourselves a crucial question, "In the twenty-five minutes I've known this guy, have I come to like him more than I would have expected?" If the answer is yes, we might want to reflect upon whether Dan behaved during those few minutes in ways that we know affect liking. We might recall that he had fed us (coffee and doughnuts) before launching into his pitch, that he had complimented us on our choice of options and color combinations, that he had made us laugh, that he had co-operated with us against the sales manager to get us a better deal.

Although such a review of events might be informative, it is not a necessary step in protecting ourselves from the liking rule. Once we discover that we have come to like Dan more than we would have expected to, we don't have to know why. The simple recognition of unwarranted liking should be enough to get us to react against it. One possible reaction would be to reverse the process and actively dislike Dan. But that might be unfair to him and contrary to our own interests. After all, some individuals are naturally likable, and Dan might just be one of them. It wouldn't be right to turn automatically against those compliance professionals who happen to be most likable. Besides, for our own sakes, we wouldn't want to shut ourselves off from business interactions with such nice people, especially when they may be offering us the best available deal.

I would recommend a different reaction. If our answer to the crucial question is "Yes, under the circumstances, I like this guy peculiarly well," this should be the signal that the time has come for a quick countermaneuver: Mentally separate Dan from that Chevy or Toyota he's trying to sell. It is vital to remember at this point that, should we decide for Dan's car, we will be driving *it,* not him, off the dealership lot. It is irrelevant to a wise automobile purchase that we find Dan likable because he is good-looking, claims an interest in our favorite hobby, is funny, or has relatives back where we grew up.

Our proper response, then, is a conscious effort to concentrate exclusively on the merits of the deal and car Dan has for us. Of course, in making a compliance decision, it is always a good idea to keep separate our feelings about the requester and the request. But once immersed in even a brief personal and sociable contact with a requester, that distinction is easy to forget. In those instances when we don't care one way or the other about a requester, forgetting to make the distinction won't steer us very far wrong. The big mistakes are likely to come when we are fond of the person making a request.

That's why it is so important to be alert to a sense of undue liking for a compliance practitioner. The recognition of that feeling can serve as our reminder to separate the dealer from the merits of the deal and to make our decision based on considerations related only to the latter. Were we all to follow this procedure, I am certain we would be much more pleased with the results of our exchanges with compliance professionals—though I suspect that Dealin' Dan would not.

6

AUTHORITY
Directed deference

❋

Suppose that while leafing through the newspaper, you notice an ad for volunteers to take part in a "study of memory" being done in the psychology department of a nearby university. Let's suppose further that, finding the idea of such an experiment intriguing, you contact the director of the study, a Professor Stanley Milgram, and make arrangements to participate in an hour-long session. When you arrive at the laboratory suite, you meet two men. One is the researcher in charge of the experiment, as is clearly evidenced by the gray lab coat he wears and the clipboard he carries. The other is a volunteer like yourself who seems average in all respects.

After initial greetings and pleasantries are exchanged, the researcher begins to explain the procedures to be followed. He says that the experiment is a study of how punishment affects learning and memory. Therefore, one participant will have the task of learning pairs of words in a long list until each pair can be recalled perfectly; this person is to be called the Learner. The other participant's job will be to test the Learner's memory and to deliver increasingly strong electric shocks for every mistake; this person will be designated the Teacher.

Naturally, you get a bit nervous at this news. And your apprehension increases when, after drawing lots with your partner, you find that you are assigned the Learner role. You hadn't expected the possibility of pain as part of the study, so you briefly consider leaving. But no, you think, there's plenty of time for that if need be and, besides, how strong a shock could it be?

After you have had a chance to study the list of word pairs, the researcher straps you into a chair and, with the Teacher looking on, attaches electrodes to your arm. More worried now about the effect of the shock, you inquire into its severity. The researcher's response is hardly comforting; he says that although the shocks can be extremely painful, they will cause you "no permanent tissue damage." With that, the researcher and the Teacher leave you alone and go to the next room, where the Teacher asks you the test questions through an intercom system and delivers electric punishment for every wrong response.

As the test proceeds, you quickly recognize the pattern that the Teacher follows: He asks the question and waits for your answer over the intercom. Whenever you err, he announces the voltage of the shock you are about to receive and pulls a level to deliver the punishment. The most troubling thing is that with each error you make, the shock increases by 15 volts.

The first part of the test progresses smoothly. The shocks are annoying but tolerable. Later on, though, as your mistakes accumulate and the shock voltages climb, the punishment begins to hurt enough to disrupt your concentration, which leads to more errors and ever more disruptive shocks. At the 75-, 90-, and 105-volt levels, the pain makes you grunt audibly. At 120 volts, you exclaim into the intercom that the shocks are *really* starting to hurt. You take one more punishment with a groan and decide that you can't take much more pain. After the Teacher delivers the 150-volt shock, you shout back into the intercom, "That's all! Get me out of here! Get me out of here, please! Let me out!"

But instead of the assurance you expect from the Teacher that he and the researcher are coming to release you, the Teacher

AUTHORITY

merely gives you the next test question to answer. Surprised and confused, you mumble the first answer to come into your head. It's wrong, of course, and the Teacher delivers a 165-volt shock. You scream at the Teacher to stop, to let you out. But he responds only with the next test question—and with the next slashing shock when your frenzied answer is incorrect. You can't hold down the panic any longer; the shocks are so strong now they make you writhe and shriek. You kick the wall, demand to be released, beg the Teacher to help you. But the test questions continue as before and so do the dreaded shocks—in searing jolts of 195, 210, 225, 240, 255, 270, 285, and 300 volts. You realize that you can't possibly answer the test correctly now, so you shout to the Teacher that you won't answer his questions any longer. Nothing changes; the Teacher interprets your failure to respond as an incorrect response and sends another bolt. The ordeal continues in this way until, finally, the power of the shocks stuns you into near-paralysis. You can no longer cry out, no longer struggle. You can only feel each terrible electric bite. Perhaps, you think, this total inactivity will cause the Teacher to stop. There can be no reason to continue this experiment. But he proceeds relentlessly, calling out the test questions, announcing the horrid shock levels (about 400 volts now), and pulling the levers. What must this man be like? you wonder in confusion. Why doesn't he help me? Why won't he stop?

For most of us, the above scenario reads like a bad dream. To recognize how nightmarish it is, though, we should understand that in most respects it is real. There was such an experiment—actually, a whole series—run by a psychology professor named Milgram in which participants in the Teacher role were willing to deliver continued, intense, and dangerous levels of shock to a kicking, screeching, pleading other person. Only one major aspect of the experiment was not genuine. No real shock was delivered; the Learner, the victim who repeatedly cried out in agony for mercy and release, was not a true subject but an actor who only pretended to be shocked. The actual purpose of Milgram's study, then, had nothing to do with the effects of punishment on learning and memory. Rather, it involved an entirely different question: When it is their job, how much suffering will ordinary people be willing to inflict on an entirely innocent other person?

The answer is most unsettling. Under circumstances mirroring precisely the features of the "bad dream," the typical Teacher was willing to deliver as much pain as was available to give. Rather than yield to the pleas of the victim, about two thirds of the subjects in Milgram's experiment pulled every one of the thirty shock switches in front of them and continued to engage the last switch (450 volts) until the researcher ended the experiment. More alarming still, not one of the forty subjects in this study quit his job as Teacher when the victim first began to demand his release; nor later, when he began to beg for it; nor even later, when his reaction to each shock had become, in Milgram's words, "definitely an agonized scream." Not until the 300-volt shock had been sent and the victim had "shouted in desperation that he would no longer provide answers to the memory test" did anyone stop—and even then, it was a distinct minority who did.

These results surprised everyone associated with the project, Milgram included. In fact, before the study began, he asked groups of colleagues, graduate students, and psychology majors at Yale University (where the experiment was performed) to read a copy of the experimental procedures and estimate how many subjects would go all the way to the last (450-volt) shock. Invariably, the answers fell in the 1–2 percent range. A separate group of thirty-nine psychiatrists predicted that only about one person in a thousand would be willing to continue to the end. No one, then, was prepared for the behavior patterns that the experiment actually produced.

How can we explain those alarming patterns? Perhaps, as some have argued, it has to do with the fact that the subjects were all males who are known as a group for their aggressive tendencies, or that the subjects didn't recognize the potential harm that such high shock voltages could cause, or that the subjects were a freakish collection of moral cretins who enjoyed the chance to inflict misery. But there is good evidence against each of these possibilities. First, the subjects' sex was shown by a later experiment to be irrelevant to their willingness to give all the

AUTHORITY

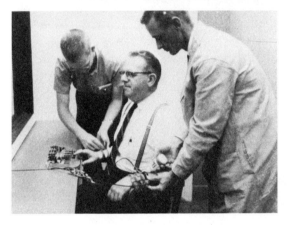

FIGURE 6–1

THE MILGRAM STUDY

The picture above shows the wicked-looking "shock generator" used in the experiment. The picture below shows the Learner (victim) being strapped into a chair and fitted with electrodes by the lab-coated experimenter and a true subject. (Source: Stanley Milgram, 1965. From the film Obedience, *distributed by the Pennsylvania University, PCR)*

shocks to the victim; female Teachers were just as likely to do so as the males in Milgram's initial study.

The explanation that subjects weren't aware of the potential physical danger to the victim was also examined in a subsequent experiment and found to be wanting. In that version, when the victim was instructed to announce that he had a heart condition and to declare that his heart was being affected by the shock— "That's all. Get me out of here. I told you I had heart trouble. My heart's starting to bother me. I refuse to go on. Let me out"—the results were the same as before; 65 percent of the subjects carried out their duties faithfully through the maximum shock.

Finally, the explanation that Milgram's subjects were a twisted, sadistic bunch not at all representative of the average citizen has proven unsatisfactory as well. The people who answered Milgram's newspaper ad to participate in his "memory" experiment represented a standard cross section of ages, occupations, and educational levels within our society. What's more, later on, a battery of personality scales showed these people to be quite normal psychologically, with not a hint of psychosis as a group. They were, in fact, just like you and me; or, as Milgram likes to term it, they *are* you and me. If he is right that his studies implicate us in their grisly findings, the unanswered question becomes an uncomfortably personal one: "What could make *us* do such things?"

Milgram is sure he knows the answer. It has to do, he says, with a deep-seated sense of duty to authority within us all. According to Milgram, the real culprit in the experiments was his subject's inability to defy the wishes of the boss of the study— the lab-coated researcher who urged and, if need be, directed the subjects to perform their duties, despite the emotional and physical mayhem they were causing.

The evidence supporting Milgram's obedience to authority explanation is strong. First, it is clear that, without the researcher's directives to continue, the subjects would have ended the experiment quickly. They hated what they were doing and agonized over their victim's agony. They implored the researcher to let them stop. When he refused, they went on, but in the process they trembled, they perspired, they shook, they stammered protests and additional pleas for the victim's release. Their fingernails dug into their own flesh; they bit their lips until they bled; they held their heads in their hands; some fell into fits of uncontrollable nervous laughter. As one outside observer to the experiment wrote:

> I observed a mature and initially poised businessman enter the laboratory smiling and confident. Within twenty minutes he was reduced to a twitching, stuttering wreck who was rapidly approaching a point of nervous collapse. He constantly pulled on his earlobe and twisted his hands. At one point he pushed his fist into his forehead and muttered: "Oh, God, let's stop it." And yet he continued to respond to every word of the experimenter and obeyed to the end.[1]

In addition to these observations, Milgram has provided even more convincing evidence for the obedience to authority interpretation of his subjects' behavior. In a later study, for instance, he had the researcher and the victim switch scripts so that the researcher told the Teacher to stop delivering shocks to the victim, while the victim insisted bravely that the Teacher continue. The result couldn't have been clearer; 100 percent of the subjects refused to give one additional shock when it was merely the fellow subject who demanded it. The identical finding appeared in another version of the experiment in which the researcher and fellow subject switched roles so that it was the researcher who was strapped into the chair and the fellow subject who ordered the Teacher to continue—over the protests of the researcher. Again, not one subject touched another shock lever.

The extreme degree to which subjects in Milgram's situation were attentive to the wishes of authority was documented in yet another variation of the basic study. In this case, Milgram presented the Teacher with two researchers, who issued contradictory orders; one ordered the Teacher to terminate the shocks when the victim cried out for release, while the other maintained that the experiment should go on. These conflicting instructions reliably produced what may have been the project's only humor: In tragicomic befuddlement and with eyes darting from one researcher to another, subjects would beseech the pair to agree on a

INFLUENCE

single command they could follow: "Wait, wait. Which is it going to be? One says stop, one says go. Which is it!?" When the researchers remained at loggerheads, the subjects tried frantically to determine who was the bigger boss. Failing this route to obedience with *the* authority, every subject finally followed his better instincts and ended the shocks. As in the other experimental variations, such a result would hardly be expected had the subjects' motivations involved some form of sadism or neurotic aggressiveness.[2]

To Milgram's mind, evidence of a chilling phenomenon emerges repeatedly from his accumulated data: "It is the extreme willingness of adults to go to almost any lengths on the command of an authority that constitutes the chief finding of the study." There are sobering implications of this finding for those concerned about the ability of another form of authority—government—to extract frightening levels of obedience from ordinary citizens.[3] Furthermore, the finding tells us something about the sheer strength of authority pressures in controlling our behavior. After witnessing Milgram's subjects squirming and sweating and suffering at their task, could anyone doubt the power of the force that held them there?

Whenever we are faced with so potent a motivator of human action, it is natural to expect that good reasons exist for the motivation. In the case of obedience to authority, even a brief consideration of human social organization offers justification aplenty. A multilayered and widely accepted system of authority confers an immense advantage upon a society. It allows the development of sophisticated structures for resource production, trade, defense, expansion, and social control that would otherwise be impossible. The other alternative, anarchy, is a state that is hardly known for its beneficial effects on cultural groups and one that the social philosopher Thomas Hobbes assures us would render life "solitary, poor, nasty, brutish, and short." Consequently, we are trained from birth that obedience to proper authority is right and disobedience is wrong. The essential message fills the parental lessons, the schoolhouse rhymes, stories, and songs of our childhood and is carried forward in the legal, military, and political systems we encounter as adults. Notions of

AUTHORITY

submission and loyalty to legitimate rule are accorded much value in each.

Religious instruction contributes as well. The very first book of the Bible, for example, describes how failure to obey the ultimate authority produced the loss of paradise for Adam, Eve, and the rest of the human race. Should that particular metaphor prove too subtle, just a bit further into the Old Testament we can read—in what might be the closest biblical representation of the Milgram experiment—the respectful account of Abraham's willingness to plunge a dagger through the heart of his young son, because God, without any explanation, ordered it. We learn in this story that the correctness of an action was not adjudged by such considerations as apparent senselessness, harmfulness, injustice, or usual moral standards, but by the mere command of a higher authority. Abraham's tormented ordeal was a test of obedience, and he—like Milgram's subjects, who perhaps had learned an early lesson from him—passed.

Stories like those of Abraham and Milgram's subjects can tell us much about the power of and value for obedience in our culture. In another sense, however, they may be misleading as to the way obedience typically occurs. We rarely agonize to such a degree over the pros and cons of authority's demands. In fact, our obedience frequently takes place in a *click, whirr* fashion, with little or no conscious deliberation. Information from a recognized authority can provide us a valuable shortcut for deciding how to act in a situation.

After all, as Milgram himself suggests, conforming to the dictates of authority figures has always had genuine practical advantages for us. Early on, these people (for example, parents, teachers) knew more than we did, and we found that taking their advice proved beneficial—partly because of their greater wisdom and partly because they controlled our rewards and punishments. As adults, the same benefits persist for the same reasons, though the authority figures now appear as employers, judges, and government leaders. Because their positions speak of superior access to information and power, it makes great sense to comply with the wishes of properly constituted authorities. It makes so much sense, in fact, that we often do so when it makes no sense at all.

This paradox is, of course, the same one that attends all

major weapons of influence. In this instance, once we realize that obedience to authority is mostly rewarding, it is easy to allow ourselves the convenience of automatic obedience. The simultaneous blessing and bane of such blind obedience is its mechanical character. We don't have to think; therefore, we don't. Although such mindless obedience leads us to appropriate action in the great majority of cases, there will be conspicuous exceptions—because we are reacting rather than thinking.

Let's take an example from one facet of our lives where authority pressures are visible and strong: medicine. Health is enormously important to us. Thus, physicians, who possess large amounts of knowledge and influence in this vital area, hold the position of respected authorities. In addition, the medical establishment has a clearly terraced power and prestige structure. The various kinds of health workers well understand the level of their jobs in this structure; and they well understand, too, that the M.D. sits at the top. No one may overrule the doctor's judgment in a case, except perhaps, another doctor of higher rank. As a consequence, a long-established tradition of automatic obedience to a doctor's orders has developed among health-care staffs.

The worrisome possibility arises, then, that when a physician makes a clear error, no one lower in the hierarchy will *think* to question it—precisely because, once a legitimate authority has given an order, subordinates stop *thinking* in the situation and start reacting. Mix this kind of *click, whirr* response into a complex hospital environment and mistakes are certain. Indeed, a recent study by the U.S. Health Care Financing Administration shows that, for patient medication alone, the average hospital has a 12 percent daily error rate. Errors in the medicine patients receive can occur for a variety of reasons. However, a book entitled *Medication Errors: Causes and Prevention* by two Temple University pharmacy professors, Michael Cohen and Neil Davis, attributes much of the problem to the mindless deference given the "boss" of the patient's case: the attending physician. According to Professor Cohen, "in case after case, patients, nurses, pharmacists, and other physicians do not question the prescription." Take, for example, the strange case of the "rectal earache" reported by Cohen and Davis. A physician ordered ear drops to be administered to the right ear of a patient suffering pain and infection there. But instead of writing out completely the location "right ear" on the prescription, the doctor abbreviated it so that the instructions read "place in R ear." Upon receiving the prescription, the duty nurse promptly put the required number of ear drops into the patient's anus.

Obviously, rectal treatment of an earache made no sense. Yet neither the patient nor the nurse questioned it. The important lesson of this story is that in many situations where a legitimate authority has spoken, what would otherwise make sense is irrelevant. In these instances, we don't consider the situation as a whole but attend and respond to only one aspect of it.[4]

Wherever our behaviors are governed in such an unthinking manner, we can be confident that there will be compliance professionals trying to take advantage. We can stay within the field of medicine and see that advertisers have frequently harnessed the respect accorded to doctors in our culture by hiring actors to play the roles of doctors speaking on behalf of the product. My favorite example is a TV commercial featuring actor Robert Young counseling people against the dangers of caffeine and recommending caffeine-free Sanka brand coffee. The commercial was highly successful, selling so much coffee that it was played for years in several versions. But why should this commercial prove so effective? Why on earth would we take Robert Young's word for the health consequences of decaffeinated coffee? Because—as the advertising agency that hired him knew perfectly well—he is associated in the minds of the American public with Marcus Welby, M.D., the role he played in an earlier long-running television series. Objectively it doesn't make sense to be swayed by the comments of a man we know to be just an actor who used to play a doctor. But, as a practical matter, that man moved the Sanka.

INFLUENCE

FIGURE 6–2

DR. WELBY, WE PRESUME

An example from the classic Sanka Brand advertising campaign featuring Robert Young. (Courtesy of General Foods Corporation)

AUTHORITY

✻

CONNOTATION, NOT CONTENT

From the first time I saw it, the most intriguing feature for me in the Robert Young Sanka commercial was its ability to use the influence of the authority principle without ever providing a real authority. The appearance of authority was enough. This tells us something important about unthinking reactions to authority figures. When in a *click, whirr* mode, we are often as vulnerable to the *symbols* of authority as to the *substance*.

There are several kinds of symbols that can reliably trigger our compliance in the absence of the genuine substance of authority. Consequently, they are employed extensively by those compliance professionals who are short on substance. Con artists, for example, drape themselves with the titles, clothes, and trappings of authority. They love nothing more than to emerge elegantly dressed from a fine automobile and to introduce themselves to their prospective "mark" as Doctor or Judge or Professor or Commissioner Someone. They understand that when they are so equipped, their chances for compliance are greatly increased. Each of these three types of symbols of authority has its own story and is worth a separate look.

Titles

Titles are simultaneously the most difficult and the easiest symbols of authority to acquire. To earn one normally takes years of work and achievement. Yet it is possible for somebody who has put in none of this effort to adopt the mere label and receive a kind of automatic deference. As we have seen, TV-commercial actors and con artists do it successfully all the time.

I recently talked with a friend—a faculty member at a well-known eastern university—who provided a telling illustration of how our actions are frequently more influenced by a title than by the nature of the person claiming it. My friend travels quite a bit and often finds himself chatting with strangers in bars, restaurants, and airports. He says that he has learned through much experience never to use his title—professor—during these conversations. When he does, he reports, the tenor of the interaction changes immediately. People who have been spontaneous and interesting conversation partners for the prior half hour become respectful, accepting, and dull. His opinions that earlier might have produced a lively exchange now usually generate extended (and highly grammatical) statements of accord. Annoyed and slightly bewildered by the phenomenon—because, as he says, "I'm still the same guy they've been talking to for the past thirty minutes, right?"—my friend now regularly lies about his occupation in such situations.

What a refreshing shift from the more typical pattern in which certain compliance practitioners lie about titles they *don't* truly have. In either direction, however, such practiced dishonesty makes the same point about the sufficiency of a mere symbol of authority to influence behavior.

I wonder whether my professor friend—who is physically somewhat short—would be so eager to hide his title if he knew that, besides making strangers more accommodating, it also makes them see him as taller. Studies investigating the way in which authority status affects perceptions of size have found that prestigious titles lead to height distortions. In one experiment conducted on five classes of Australian college students, a man was introduced as a visitor from Cambridge University in England. However, his status at Cambridge was represented differently in each of the classes. To one class, he was presented as a student; to a second class, a demonstrator; to another, a lecturer; to yet another, a senior lecturer; to a fifth, a professor. After he left the room, each class was asked to estimate his height. It was found that with each increase in status, the same man grew in perceived height by an average of a half inch, so that as the "professor" he was seen as two and a half inches taller than as the "student."[5]

It is worth the time for a small detour to pursue this interesting connection between status and perceived size, since it shows up in a variety of ways. In judging the size of coins, for example, children most overestimate the size of the more valuable coins. And adults are just as guilty of such distortions. In one study, college students drew cards that had monetary values printed on them ranging from $3.00 to $−3.00; they won or lost the amount shown on the cards they picked. Afterward, they were asked to rate the size of each card. Even though all cards were exactly the same size, those that had the more extreme values— positive or negative—were seen as physically larger. Thus it is not necessarily the pleasantness of a thing that makes it seem bigger to us, it is its importance.[6]

Because we see size and status as related, it is possible for certain individuals to benefit by substituting the former for the latter. In some animal societies, where the status of a male is assigned on the basis of dominance, size is an important factor in determining which male will achieve which status level in the group.[7] Usually, in combat with a rival, the larger and more powerful male wins. To avoid the harmful effects to the group of such physical conflict, however, many species have adopted methods that frequently involve more form than fracas. The two males confront each other with showy aggression displays that invariably include size-enhancing tricks. Various mammals arch their backs and bristle their coats; fish extend their fins and puff themselves up with water; birds unfurl and flutter their wings. Very often, this exhibition alone is enough to send one of the histrionic warriors into retreat, leaving the contested status position to his seemingly larger and stronger rival.

Fur, fins, and feathers. Isn't it interesting how these most delicate of parts can be exploited to give the impression of substance and weight? There are two lessons for us here. One is specific to the association between size and status. The connection of those two things can be profitably employed by individuals who are able to fake the first to gain the appearance of the second. This is precisely why con men, even those of average or slightly above-average height, commonly wear lifts in their shoes.

The other lesson is more general: The outward signs of power and authority frequently may be counterfeited with the flimsiest of materials. Let's return to the realm of titles for an example—an example that involves what, in several ways, is the scariest experiment I know. A group of researchers, comprised of doctors and nurses with connections to three midwestern hospitals, became increasingly concerned with the extent of mechanical obedience to doctors' orders on the part of nurses. It seemed to the researchers that even highly trained and skilled nurses were not using that training or skill sufficiently to check on a doctor's judgment; instead, when confronted with a physician's directives, they would simply defer.

Earlier, we saw how this process accounted for the case of the rectally administered ear drops. But the midwestern researchers took things several steps further. First, they wanted to find out whether such cases were isolated incidents or representative of a widespread phenomenon. Second, they wanted to examine the problem in the context of a serious treatment error—the gross overprescription of an unauthorized drug to a hospital patient. Finally, they wanted to see what would happen if they physically removed the authority figure from the situation and substituted an unfamiliar voice on the phone, offering only the frailest evidence of authority—the claimed title "doctor."

To twenty-two separate nurses' stations on various surgical, medical, pediatric, and psychiatric wards, one of the researchers made an identical phone call in which he identified himself as a hospital physician and directed the answering nurse to give twenty milligrams of a drug (Astrogen) to a specific ward patient. There were four excellent reasons for a nurse's caution in response to this order: (1) The prescription was transmitted by phone, in direct violation of hospital policy. (2) The medication itself was unauthorized; Astrogen had not been cleared for use nor placed on the ward stock list. (3) The prescribed dosage was obviously and dangerously excessive. The medication containers clearly stated that the "maximum daily dose" was only ten milligrams, half of what had been ordered. (4) The directive was given by a man the nurse had never met, seen, or even talked with before on the phone. Yet, in 95 percent of the instances, the nurses went straightway to the ward medicine cabinet, where they secured the ordered dosage of Astrogen and started for the patient's room to administer it. It was at this point that they were stopped by a secret observer, who revealed the nature of the experiment.

The results are frightening, indeed. That 95 percent of regular staff nurses complied unhesitatingly with a patently improper instruction of this sort must give us all great reason for concern as potential hospital patients. Given the recent U.S. Health Care Financing Administration estimate of a 12 percent daily medication error rate in American hospitals, stays of longer than a week make it likely that we will be recipients of such an error. What the midwestern study shows is that the mistakes are hardly limited to trivial slips in the administration of harmless ear drops or the like, but extend to grave and dangerous blunders.

In interpreting their unsettling findings, the researchers came to an instructive conclusion:

> In a real-life situation corresponding to the experimental one, there would, in theory, be two professional intelligences, the doctor's and the nurse's, working to ensure that a given procedure be undertaken in a manner beneficial to the patient or, at the very least, not detrimental to him. The experiment strongly suggests, however, that one of these intelligences is, for all practical purposes, nonfunctioning.[8]

It seems that, in the face of a physician's directives, the nurses unhooked their "professional intelligences" and moved to a *click, whirr* form of responding. None of their considerable medical training or knowledge was engaged in the decision of what to do. Instead, because obedience to legitimate authority had always been the most preferred and efficient action in their work setting, they had become willing to err on the side of automatic obedience. It is all the more instructive that they had traveled so far in this direction that their error had come not in response to genuine authority but to its most easily falsified symbol—a bare title.[9]

Clothes

A second kind of authority symbol that can trigger our mechanical compliance is clothing. Though more tangible than a title, the cloak of authority is every bit as fakable. Police bunco files bulge with records of con artists whose artistry includes the quick change. In chameleon style, they adopt the hospital white, priestly black, army green, or police blue that the situation requires for maximum advantage. Only too late do their victims realize that the garb of authority is hardly its guarantee.

A series of studies by social psychologist Leonard Bickman gives an indication of how difficult it can be to resist requests that come from figures in authority attire. Bickman's basic procedure was to ask passersby on the street to comply with some sort of odd request (to pick up a discarded paper bag, to stand on the other side of a bus-stop sign). In half of the instances, the requester—a young man—was dressed in normal street clothes; the rest of the time, he was dressed in a security guard's uniform. Regardless of the type of request, many more people obeyed the requester when he wore the guard costume.

Especially revealing was one version of the experiment in which the requester stopped pedestrians and pointed to a man standing by a parking meter fifty feet away. The requester, whether dressed normally or as a security guard, always said the same thing to the pedestrian: "You see that guy over there by the meter? He's overparked but doesn't have any change. Give him a dime!" The requester then turned a corner and walked away so that by the time the pedestrian reached the meter, the requester was out of sight. The power of his uniform lasted, however, even after he was long gone: Nearly all the pedestrians complied with his directive when he had worn the guard costume, but fewer than half did so when he had dressed normally. It is interesting to note that later on, Bickman found college students able to guess with considerable accuracy the percentage of compliance that had occurred in the experiment when the requester wore street clothes (50 percent vs. the actual 42 percent); yet the students greatly underestimated the percentage of compliance when he was in uniform (63 percent vs. the actual 92 percent).[10]

Less blatant in its connotation than a uniform, but nonetheless effective, is another kind of attire that has traditionally bespoken authority status in our culture: the well-tailored business suit. It, too, can evoke a telling form of deference from total strangers. Research conducted in Texas, for instance, arranged for a thirty-one-year-old man to violate the law by crossing the street against the traffic light on a variety of occasions. In half of the cases, he was dressed in a freshly pressed business suit and tie;

on the other occasions, he wore a work shirt and trousers. The researchers watched from a distance and counted the number of pedestrians waiting at the corner who followed the man across the street. Like the children of Hamelin who crowded after the Pied Piper, three and a half times as many people swept into traffic behind the suited jaywalker. In this case, though, the magic came not from his pipe but his pinstripes.[11]

It is noteworthy that the two types of authority apparal shown by the above research to be influential—the guard uniform and business suit—are combined deftly by confidence men in a fraud called the bank-examiner scheme. The target of the swindle can be anyone, but elderly persons living alone are preferred. The con begins when a man dressed in a properly conservative three-piece business suit appears at the door of a likely victim. Everything about his clothing sends a message of propriety and respectability. The white shirt is starched; the wingtip shoes glow darkly. His suit is not trendy but classic: The lapels are three inches wide—no more, no less; the cloth is heavy and substantial, even in July; the tones are muted, business blue, business gray, business black.

He explains to his intended victim—perhaps a widow he secretly followed home from the bank a day or two earlier—that he is a professional bank examiner who, in the course of auditing the books of her bank, has found some seeming irregularities. He thinks he has spotted the culprit, a bank officer who is regularly doctoring reports of transactions in certain accounts. He says that the widow's account may be one of these, but he can't be sure until he has hard evidence. Therefore, he has come to ask for her cooperation. Would she help out by withdrawing her savings so a team of examiners and responsible bank officials can trace the record of the transaction as it passes across the suspect's desk?

Often the appearance and presentation of the "bank examiner" are so impressive that the victim never thinks to check on their validity with even a simple phone call. Instead, she drives to the bank, withdraws all her money, and returns home with it to wait with the "examiner" for word on the success of the trap. When the message comes, it is delivered by a uniformed bank guard, who arrives after closing hours to announce that all is well—apparently the widow's account was not one of those being tampered with. Greatly relieved, the "examiner" offers gracious thanks and, since the bank is now conveniently closed, instructs the guard to return the lady's money to the vault, to save her the trouble of doing so the next day. With smiles and handshakes all around, the guard takes the funds and leaves the "examiner" to express a few more minutes of thanks before he, too, exits. Naturally, as the victim eventually discovers, the "guard" is no more a guard than the "examiner" is an examiner. What they are is a pair of bunco artists who have recognized the capacity of carefully counterfeited uniforms to click us into mesmerized compliance with "authority."

Trappings

Aside from its function in uniforms, clothing can symbolize a more generalized type of authority when it serves an ornamental purpose. Finely styled and expensive clothes carry an aura of status and position, as do trappings such as jewelry and cars. The last of these status symbols is particularly interesting in the United States, where "the American love affair with the automobile" gives it unusual significance.

According to the findings of a study done in the San Francisco Bay area, owners of prestige autos receive a special kind of deference from us. The experimenters discovered that motorists would wait significantly longer before honking their horns at a new, luxury car stopped in front of a green traffic light than at an older, economy model. The motorists had little patience with the economy-car driver: Nearly all sounded their horns, and the majority of these did so more than once; two simply rammed into his rear bumper. So intimidating was the aura of the prestige automobile, however, that 50 percent of the motorists waited respectfully behind it, never touching their horns until it drove on.[12]

Later on, the researchers asked college students what they would have done in such situations. Compared to the true findings of the experiment, the students consistently underestimated the time it would take them to honk at the luxury car. The male students were especially inaccurate, feeling that they would honk faster at the prestige- than the economy-car driver; of course, the study itself showed just the opposite. Note the similarity of this pattern to much other research on authority pressures. As in Milgram's research, the midwestern hospital-nurses' study, and the security-guard-uniform experiment, people were unable to predict correctly how they or others would react to authority influence. In each instance, the effect of such influence was grossly underestimated. This property of authority status may account for much of its success as a compliance device. Not only does it work forcefully on us, but it also does so unexpectedly.

✵

HOW TO SAY NO

One protective tactic we can use against authority status is to remove its element of surprise. Because we typically misperceive the profound impact of authority (and its symbols) on our actions, we are at the disadvantage of being insufficiently cautious about its presence in compliance situations. A fundamental form of defense against this problem, therefore, is a heightened awareness of authority power. When this awareness is coupled with a recognition of how easily authority symbols can be faked, the benefit will be a properly guarded approach to situations involving authority-influence attempts.

Sounds simple, right? And in a way it is. A better understanding of the workings of authority influence should help us resist it. Yet there is a perverse complication—the familiar one inherent in all weapons of influence: We shouldn't want to resist altogether, or even most of the time. Generally, authority figures know what they are talking about. Physicians, judges, corporate executives, legislative leaders, and the like have typically gained their positions because of superior knowledge and judgment. Thus, as a rule, their directives offer excellent counsel. The trick is to be able to recognize without much strain or vigilance when authority promptings are best followed and when they should be resisted.

INFLUENCE

Posing two questions to ourselves can help enormously to accomplish this trick. The first is to ask, when we are confronted with what appears to be an authority figure's influence attempt, "Is this authority truly an expert?" The question is helpful because it focuses our attention on a pair of crucial pieces of information: the authority's credentials and the relevance of those credentials to the topic at hand. By orienting in this simple way toward the *evidence* for authority status, we can avoid the major pitfalls of automatic deference. An illustration or two is in order.

Let's examine the highly successful Robert Young Sanka-coffee commercial in this light. If, rather than responding to his "Marcus Welby, M.D." association, people had focused on Mr. Young's actual status as an authority, I am confident that the commercial would not have had so long and productive a run. Obviously, Robert Young does not possess a physician's training or knowledge. We all know that. What he does possess, however, is a physician's *title*, "M.D." Now, clearly, it is an empty title, connected to him in our minds through the device of play-acting. We all know that, too. But isn't it fascinating how, when we are *whirring* along, what is obvious often doesn't matter unless we pay specific attention to it?

That is why the "Is this authority truly an expert?" question can be so valuable: It brings our attention to the obvious. It channels us effortlessly away from a focus on possibly meaningless symbols to a consideration of genuine authority credentials. What's more, the question impels us to distinguish between relevant authorities and irrelevant authorities. And this is a distinction that is easy to forget when the push of authority pressure is combined with the rush of modern life. The Texas pedestrians who bustled into city traffic behind a business-suited jaywalker offer a prime example. Even if the man had been the business authority his clothes suggested he might be, he was unlikely to be a greater authority on crossing the street than other people, including those who followed him into traffic.

Still, they did follow, as if his label, "authority," overwhelmed the vital difference between relevant and irrelevant forms. Had they bothered to ask themselves whether he represented a true expert in the situation, someone whose actions reflected superior knowledge there, I expect the result would have been quite different. The same process applies to Robert Young, a man who is not without expertise. He has fashioned a long career with many achievements in a difficult business. But his skills and knowledge are as an actor, not a doctor. When, in viewing the famous coffee commercial, we focus on his true credentials, we will realize quickly that he should be no more believed than any other successful actor who claims that Sanka is healthy.

Suppose, though, we are confronted with an authority we determine *is* a relevant expert. Before submitting to authority influence, it would be wise to ask a second simple question: "How truthful can we expect the expert to be here?" Authorities, even the best informed, may not present their information honestly to us. Therefore we need to consider their trustworthiness in the situation. In fact, most of the time, we do. We allow ourselves to be much more swayed by experts who seem to be impartial than by those who have something to gain by convincing us; and this has been shown by research to be true around the world.[13] By wondering how an expert stands to benefit from our compliance, we give ourselves another safety net against undue and automatic influence. Even knowledgeable authorities in a field will not persuade us until we are satisfied that their messages represent the facts faithfully.

When asking ourselves about such a person's trustworthiness, we should keep in mind a little tactic compliance practitioners often use to assure us of their sincerity: They will seem to argue to a degree against their own interests. Correctly done, this can be a subtly effective device for proving their honesty. Perhaps they will mention a small shortcoming in their position or product ("Oh, the disadvantages of Benson & Hedges"). Invariably, though, the drawback will be a secondary one that is easily overcome by more significant advantages—"Listerine, the taste you hate three times a day"; "Avis: We're number two, but we try harder"; "L'oréal, a bit more expensive and worth it." By establishing their basic truthfulness on minor issues, the compliance professionals who use this ploy can then be more believable when stressing the important aspects of their argument.[14]

I have seen this approach used with devastating effect in a

place that few of us recognize as a compliance setting: the restaurant. It is no secret that because of shamelessly low wages, servers in restaurants must supplement their earnings with tips. Leaving the sine qua non of good service aside, the most successful waiters and waitresses know certain tricks for increasing tips. They also know that the larger a customer's bill, the larger the amount of money likely to come to them in a standard gratuity. In these two regards, then—building the size of the customer's charge and building the percentage of that charge that is given as a tip—servers regularly act as compliance agents.

Hoping to find out how they operate, I applied for waiter openings at several fairly expensive restaurants. Without experience, though, the best I could do was to land a busboy job that, as things turned out, provided me a propitious vantage point from which to watch and analyze the action. Before long, I realized what the other employees already knew—that the most successful waiter in the place was Vincent, who somehow arranged for patrons to order more and tip higher than for anyone else; in fact, the other servers were not even close to him in weekly earnings.

So I began to linger in my duties around Vincent's tables to observe his style. I quickly learned that his style was to have no single style. He had a repertoire of them, each ready to be called on under the appropriate circumstances. When the customers were a family, he was effervescent—even slightly clownish—directing his remarks as often to the children as to the adults. With a young couple on a date, he became formal and a bit imperious in an attempt to intimidate the young man (to whom he spoke exclusively) into ordering and tipping lavishly. With an older, married couple, he retained the formality but dropped the superior air in favor of a respectful orientation to both members of the couple. Should the patron be dining alone, Vincent selected a friendly demeanor—cordial, conversational, and warm.

But Vincent reserved the trick of seeming to argue against his own interests for large parties of eight to twelve people. Here his technique was veined with genius. When it was time for the first person, normally a lady, to order, he went into his act. No matter what she selected, Vincent reacted identically: His brow furrowed, his hand hovered above his order pad, and after looking quickly over his shoulder for the manager, he leaned conspiratorially toward the table to report for all to hear, "I'm afraid that is not as good tonight as it normally is. Might I recommend instead the _____ or the _____?" (Here Vincent suggested a pair of menu items that were fifty cents or so less expensive than the dish the patron had selected initially.) "They are both excellent tonight."

With this single maneuver, Vincent engaged several important principles of influence. First, even those who did not take his suggestions felt that Vincent had done them a favor by offering valuable information to help them order. Everyone felt grateful, and consequently the rule for reciprocity would work in his favor when it came time to decide on his gratuity. But besides hiking the percentage of his tip, Vincent's maneuver also placed him in a favorable position to increase the size of the table's order. It established him as an authority on the current stores of the house; he clearly knew what was and wasn't good that night. Moreover—and this is where seeming to argue against his own interests came in—it proved him to be a trustworthy informant because he recommended dishes that were slightly *less* expensive than originally ordered. Rather than trying to line his own pockets, he seemed to have the customers' best interests at heart.

To all appearances, he was at once knowledgeable and honest, a combination that gave him great credibility. And Vincent was quick to exploit the advantage of this credible image. When the party had finished giving their food orders, he would say, "Very well, and would you like me to suggest or select some wine to go with your meals?" As I watched the scene repeated almost nightly, there was a notable consistency to the customers' reactions—smiles, nods, and for the most part, general assent.

Even from the distance of my vantage point, one could read their thoughts from their faces. "Sure," they seemed to say, "you know what's good here, and you're obviously on our side. Tell us what to get." Looking pleased, Vincent, who did know his vintages, would respond with some excellent (and costly) choices. He was similarly persuasive when it came time for dessert decisions. Patrons who otherwise would have passed up the dessert course or shared with a friend were swayed to partake fully by Vincent's rapturous descriptions of the Baked Alaska and chocolate mousse. Who, after all, is more believable than a demonstrated expert of proven sincerity?

By combining the factors of reciprocity and credible authority into a single, elegant maneuver, Vincent was able to inflate substantially both the percentage of his tip and the base charge on which it was figured. His proceeds from this trick were handsome, indeed. But notice that much of his profit came from an apparent lack of concern for personal profit. Seeming to argue against his financial interests served those interests extremely well.

In sum, then, when faced with an authority-influence attempt, we would do well to ask ourselves what real, rather than symbolic, evidence exists that the authority figure is a relevant expert. Even when we are satisfied that the expertise is genuine, though, we should also wonder about the authority's trustworthiness in the situation. Concerning this second question of trustworthiness, our suspicions should be aroused when we find certain compliance professionals appearing to argue counter to their own interests. To paraphrase a centuries-old admonition: When they are describing the quality of their products, "Beware sneaks baring rifts."

7

SCARCITY
The rule of the few

✳

The city of Mesa, Arizona, is a suburb in the Phoenix area where I live. Perhaps the most notable features of Mesa are its sizable Mormon population—next to that of Salt Lake City, the largest in the world—and a huge Mormon temple located on exquisitely kept grounds in the center of the city. Although I had appreciated the landscaping and architecture from a distance, I had never been interested enough in the temple to go inside until the day I read a newspaper article. It told of a special inner sector of Mormon temples to which no one has access but faithful members of the Church. Even potential converts must not see it. There is one exception to the rule, however. For a few days immediately after a temple is newly constructed, nonmembers are allowed to tour the entire structure, including the otherwise restricted section.

The newspaper story reported that the Mesa temple had recently been refurbished and that the renovations had been extensive enough to classify it as "new" by Church standards. Thus, for the next several days only, non-Mormon visitors could see the temple area traditionally banned to them. I remember quite well the effect of the article on me: I immediately resolved to take a tour. But when I phoned a friend to ask if he wanted to come along, I came to understand something that changed my decision just as quickly.

After declining the invitation, my friend wondered why *I* seemed so intent on a visit. I was forced to admit that, no, I had never been inclined toward the idea of a temple tour before, that I had no questions about the Mormon religion I wanted answered, that I had no general interest in architecture of houses of worship, and that I expected to find nothing more spectacular or stirring than I might see at a number of other temples, churches, or cathedrals in the area. It became clear as I spoke that the special lure of the temple had a sole cause: If I did not experience the restricted sector shortly, I would never again have the chance. Something that, on its own merits, held little appeal for me had become decidedly more attractive merely because it would soon become unavailable.

Since that encounter with the scarcity principle—that opportunities seem more valuable to us when their availability is limited—I have begun to notice its influence over a whole range of my actions. For instance, I routinely will interrupt an interesting face-to-face conversation to answer the ring of an unknown caller. In such a situation, the caller has a compelling feature that my face-to-face partner does not: potential unavailability. If I don't take the call, I might miss it (and the information it carries) for good. Never mind that the ongoing conversation may be highly engaging or important—much more than I could reasonably expect an average phone call to be. With each unanswered ring, the phone interaction becomes less retrievable. For that reason and for that moment, I want it more than the other.

I count myself far from alone in this weakness. Almost everyone is vulnerable to the scarcity principle in some form. Take as evidence what happens at singles bars as closing time approaches and as chances to meet suitable members of the opposite sex become scarcer. At three separate times during the evening—three and a half hours, two hours, and a half hour be-

SCARCITY

fore closing—researchers in Virginia randomly selected customers at several bars and asked them to rate the attractiveness of the
opposite-sex individuals present. Contrary to what one might
expect, the romantic possibilities still remaining only a half hour
before closing were judged as the best-looking by far. How
might we account for this surprising finding? It could be argued,
for example, that the influence of greater amounts of alcohol
causes everybody and everything to seem more pleasant-looking
by night's end. Or it might be that the truly beautiful people
don't come out until late; if so, the study's results were not
drink-distorted but accurate.

Although possible, these explanations do not stand up well
under close scrutiny. For example, the researchers found that the
women who were present at the bars just before closing looked
best only to the male patrons; similarly, the late-staying men
looked best only to the female customers. Thus it was not true
that people *generally* were more attractive or seemed more attractive late in the evening. Instead, only those who were potential
romantic partners grew "better-looking" as the night wore on.[1]

A more satisfying explanation of the patrons' ratings can be
found in the scarcity principle: Opposite-sex individuals look
better near closing time because the chances to meet them are
rapidly dwindling. And anything that is becoming less available
seems more attractive.

Collectors of everything from baseball cards to antiques are
keenly aware of the influence of the scarcity principle in determining the worth of an item. As a rule, if it is rare or becoming
rare, it is more valuable. Especially enlightening as to the importance of scarcity in the collectibles market is the phenomenon of
the "precious mistake." Flawed items—a blurred stamp or a
double-struck coin—are sometimes the most valued of all. Thus
a stamp carrying a three-eyed likeness of George Washington is
anatomically incorrect, aesthetically unappealng, and yet highly
sought after. There is instructive irony here: Imperfections that
would otherwise make for rubbish, make for prized possessions
when they bring along an abiding scarcity.

With the scarcity principle operating so powerfully on the
worth we assign things, it is natural that compliance professionals will do some related operating of their own. Probably the

INFLUENCE

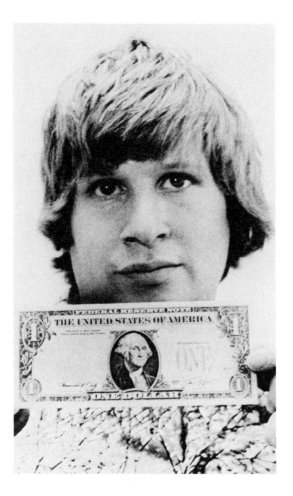

FIGURE 7–1

FORTUNATE FLAWS

Barry Faintich holds a dollar bill he purchased from a bank teller for $400. Even at that price, Mr. Faintich, co-owner of the Midwest Money Co., is no fool. The bill was erroneously printed with no serial numbers or government seals, making it far more valuable than the price he paid. (Source: UPI)

most straightforward use of the scarcity principle occurs in the "limited-number" tactic, when the customer is informed that a certain product is in short supply that cannot be guaranteed to last long. During the time I was researching compliance strategies by infiltrating various organizations, I saw the limited-number tactic employed repeatedly in a range of situations: "There aren't more than five convertibles with this engine left in the state. And when they're gone, that's it, 'cause we're not making 'em anymore." "This is one of only two unsold corner lots in the entire development. You wouldn't want the other one; it's got a nasty east–west exposure." "You may want to think seriously about buying more than one case today because production is backed way up and there's no telling when we'll get any more in."

Sometimes the limited-number information was true, sometimes it was wholly false. But in each instance, the intent was to convince customers of an item's scarcity and thereby increase its immediate value in their eyes. I admit to developing a grudging admiration for the practitioners who made this simple device work in a multitude of ways and styles. I was most impressed, however, with a particular version that extended the basic approach to its logical extreme by selling a piece of merchandise at its scarcest point—when it seemingly could no longer be had. The tactic was played to perfection in one appliance store I investigated, where 30 to 50 percent of the stock was regularly listed as on sale. Suppose a couple in the store seemed from a distance to be moderately interested in a certain sale item. There are all sorts of cues that tip off such interest—closer-than-normal examination of the appliance, a casual look at any instruction booklets associated with the appliance, discussions held in front of the appliance, but no attempt to seek out a salesperson for further information. After observing the couple so engaged, a salesperson might approach and say, "I see you're interested in this model here, and I can understand why; it's a great machine at a great price. But, unfortunately, I sold it to another couple not more than twenty minutes ago. And, if I'm not mistaken, it was the last one we had."

The customers' disappointment registers unmistakably. Because of its lost availability, the appliance jumps suddenly in attractiveness. Typically, one of the customers asks if there is any chance that an unsold model still exists in the store's back room, or warehouse, or other location. "Well," the salesperson allows, "that is possible, and I'd be willing to check. But do I understand that this is the model you want and if I can get it for you at this price, you'll take it?" Therein lies the beauty of the technique. In accord with the scarcity principle, the customers are asked to commit to buying the appliance when it looks least available—and therefore most desirable. Many customers do agree to a purchase at this singularly vulnerable time. Thus, when the salesperson (invariably) returns with the news that an additional supply of the appliance has been found, it is also with a pen and sales contract in hand. The information that the desired model is in good supply may actually make some customers find it less attractive again.[2] But by then, the business transaction has progressed too far for most people to renege. The purchase decision made and committed to publicly at an earlier, crucial point still holds. They buy.

Related to the limited-number technique is the "deadline" tactic in which some official time limit is placed on the customer's opportunity to get what the compliance professional is offering. Much like my experience with the Mormon temple's inner sanctum, people frequently find themselves doing what they wouldn't particularly care to do, simply because the time to do so is shrinking. The adept merchandiser makes this tendency pay off by arranging and publicizing customer deadlines—witness the collage of such newspaper ads in Figure 7-3—that generate interest where none may have existed before. Concentrated instances of this approach often occur in movie advertising. In fact, I recently noticed that one theater owner, with remarkable singleness of purpose, had managed to invoke the scarcity principle three separate times in just five words that read "Exclusive, limited engagement ends soon!"

A variant of the deadline tactic is much favored by some face-to-face, high-pressure sellers because it carries the purest form of decision deadline: right now. Customers are often told that unless they make an immediate decision to buy, they will have to purchase the item at a higher price or they will be unable

Swindled

By Peter Kerr
New York Times

NEW YORK — Daniel Gulban doesn't remember how his life savings disappeared.

He remembers the smooth voice of a salesman on the telephone. He remembers dreaming of a fortune in oil and silver futures. But to this day, the 81-year-old retired utility worker does not understand how swindlers convinced him to part with $18,000.

"I just wanted to better my life in my waning days," said Gulban, a resident of Holder, Fla. "But when I found out the truth, I couldn't eat or sleep. I lost 30 pounds. I still can't believe I would do anything like that."

Gulban was the victim of a what law enforcement officials call a "boiler-room operation," a ruse that often involves dozens of fast-talking telephone salesmen crammed into a small room where they call thousands of customers each day. The companies snare hundreds of millions of dollars each year from unsuspecting customers, according to a U.S. Senate subcommittee on investigations, which issued a report on the subject last year.

"They use an impressive Wall Street address, lies and deception to get individuals to sink their money into various glamorous-sounding schemes," said Robert Abrams, the New York State attorney general, who has pursued more than a dozen boiler-room cases in the past four years. "The victims are sometimes persuaded to invest the savings of a lifetime."

Orestes J. Mihaly, the New York assistant attorney general in charge of the bureau of investor protection and securities, said the companies often operate in three stages. First, Mihaly said, comes the "opening call," in which a salesman identifies himself as representing a company with an impressive-sounding name and address. He will simply ask the potential customer to receive the company's literature.

A second call involves a sales pitch, Mihaly said. The salesman first describes the great profits to be made and then tells the customer that it is no longer possible to invest. The third call gives the customer a chance to get in on the deal, he said, and is offered with a great deal of urgency.

"The idea is to dangle a carrot in front of the buyer's face and then take it away," Mihaly said. "The aim is to get someone to want to buy quickly, without thinking too much about it." Sometimes, Mihaly said, the salesman will be out of breath on the third call and will tell the customer that he "just came off the trading floor."

Such tactics convinced Gulban to part with his life savings. In 1979, a stranger called him repeatedly and convinced Gulban to wire $1,756 to New York to purchase silver, Gulban said. After another series of telephone calls the salesman cajoled Gulban into wiring more than $6,000 for crude oil. He eventually wired an additional $9,740, but his profits never arrived.

"My heart sank," Gulban recalled. "I was not greedy. I just hoped I would see better days." Gulban never recouped his losses.

FIGURE 7–2

THE SCARCITY SCAM

Note how the scarcity principle was employed during the second and third phone calls to cause Mr. Gulban to "buy quickly without thinking too much about it." Click, blur. *(Source: Peter Kerr,* The New York Times*)*

to purchase it at all. A prospective health-club member or automobile buyer might learn that the deal offered by the salesperson is good only for that one time; should the customer leave the premises, the deal is off. One large child-portrait photography company urges parents to buy as many poses and copies as they can afford because "stocking limitations force us to burn the unsold pictures of your children within twenty-four hours." A door-to-door magazine solicitor might say that salespeople are in the customer's area for just a day; after that, they—and the customer's chance to buy their magazine package—will be long gone. A home vacuum-cleaner operation I infiltrated instructed its sales trainees to claim, "I have so many other people to see that I have the time to visit a family only once. It's company policy that even if you decide later that you want this machine, I can't come back and sell it to you." This, of course, is nonsense; the company and its representatives are in the business of making sales, and any customer who called for another visit would be accommodated gladly. As the company sales manager impressed on his trainees, the true purpose of the can't-come-back claim has nothing to do with reducing overburdened sales schedules. It is to "keep the prospects from taking the time to think the deal over by scaring them into believing they can't have it later, which makes them want it now."

PSYCHOLOGICAL REACTANCE

The evidence, then, is clear. Compliance practitioners' reliance on scarcity as a weapon of influence is frequent, wide-ranging, systematic, and diverse. Whenever such is the case with a weapon of influence, we can feel assured that the principle involved has notable power in directing human action. In the instance of the scarcity principle, that power comes from two major sources. The first is familiar. Like the other weapons of influence, the scarcity principle trades on our weakness for shortcuts. The weakness is, as before, an *enlightened* one. In this case, because we know that the things that are difficult to possess are

SCARCITY

FIGURE 7–3

DON'T WAIT!

*Last chance to read this now before you turn the
page. (Source: Robert B. Cialdini)*

typically better than those that are easy to possess, we can often
use an item's availability to help us quickly and correctly decide
on its quality. Thus, one reason for the potency of the scarcity
principle is that, by following it, we are usually and efficiently
right.[3]

In addition, there is a unique, secondary source of power
within the scarcity principle: As opportunities become less available, we lose freedoms; and we *hate* to lose the freedoms we already have. This desire to preserve our established prerogatives is

INFLUENCE

the centerpiece of psychological reactance theory, developed by psychologist Jack Brehm to explain the human response to diminishing personal control. According to the theory, whenever free choice is limited or threatened, the need to retain our freedoms makes us desire them (as well as the goods and services associated with them) significantly more than previously. So when increasing scarcity—or anything else—interferes with our prior access to some item, we will *react against* the interference by wanting and trying to possess the item more than before.[4]

As simple as the kernel of the theory seems, its shoots and roots curl extensively through much of the social environment. From the garden of young love to the jungle of armed revolution to the fruits of the marketplace, impressive amounts of our behavior can be explained by examining for the tendrils of psychological reactance. Before beginning such an examination, though, it would be helpful to know when people first show the desire to fight against restrictions of their freedoms.

Child psychologists have traced the tendency back to the start of the third year of life—a year independently indentified as a problem by parents and widely known to them as "the terrible twos." Most parents can attest to the development of a decidedly more contrary style in their children around this period. Two-year-olds seem masters of the art of resistance to outside, especially parental, pressure: Tell them one thing, they do the opposite; give them one toy, they want another; pick them up against their will, they wriggle and squirm to be put down; put them down against their will, they claw and struggle to be carried.

One Virginia-based study nicely captured the terrible twos style among boys who averaged twenty-four months in age. The boys accompanied their mothers into a room containing two equally attractive toys. The toys were always arranged so that one stood next to a transparent Plexiglas barrier and the other stood behind the barrier. For some of the boys, the Plexiglas sheet was only a foot tall—forming no real barrier to the toy behind, since the boys could easily reach over the top. For the other boys, however, the Plexiglas was two feet tall, effectively blocking the boys' access to one toy unless they went around the barrier. The researchers wanted to see how quickly the toddlers would make contact with the toys under these conditions. Their findings were clear. When the barrier was too small to restrict access to the toy behind it, the boys showed no special preference for either of the toys; on the average, the toy next to the barrier was touched just as quickly as the one behind. But when the barrier was big enough to be a true obstacle, the boys went directly to the obstructed toy, making contact with it three times faster than with the unobstructed toy. In all, the boys in this study demonstrated the classic terrible twos' response to a limitation of their freedom: outright defiance.[5]

Why should psychological reactance emerge at the age of two? Perhaps the answer has to do with a crucial change that most children go through around this time. It is then that they first come to a full recognition of themselves as individuals. No longer do they view themselves as mere extensions of the social milieux but rather as identifiable, singular, and separate.[6] This developing concept of autonomy brings naturally with it the concept of freedom. An independent being is one with choices; and a child with the newfound realization that he or she is such a being will want to explore the length and breadth of the options. Perhaps we should be neither surprised nor distressed, then, when our two-year-olds strain incessantly against our will. They have come to a recent and exhilarating perspective on themselves as free-standing human entities. Vital questions of volition, entitlements, and control now need to be asked and answered within their small minds. The tendency to fight for every liberty and against every restriction might be best understood as a quest for information. By testing severely the limits of their freedoms (and coincidentally, the patience of their parents), the children are discovering where in their worlds they can expect to be controlled and where they can expect to be in control. As we will see later, the wise parent provides highly consistent information.

Although the terrible twos may be the most noticeable age of psychological reactance, we show the strong tendency to react against restrictions on our freedoms of action throughout our lives. One other age does stand out, however, as a time when this tendency takes an especially rebellious form: teenage. Like the twos, this is a period characterized by an emerging sense of individuality. For teenagers, the emergence is out of the role of child, with all of its attendant parental control, and toward the role of adult, with all of its attendant rights and duties. Not surprisingly, adolescents tend to focus less on the duties than on the rights they feel they have as young adults. Not surprisingly, again, imposing traditional parental authority at these times is often counterproductive; the teenager will sneak, scheme, and fight to resist such attempts at control.

Nothing illustrates the boomerang quality of parental pressure on adolescent behavior quite so clearly as a phenomenon known as the "Romeo and Juliet effect." As we know, Romeo Montague and Juliet Capulet were the ill-fated Shakespearean characters whose love was doomed by a feud between their families. Defying all parental attempts to keep them apart, the teenagers won a lasting union in their tragic act of twin suicide, an ultimate assertion of free will.

The intensity of the couple's feelings and actions has always been a source of wonderment and puzzlement to observers of the play. How could such inordinate devotion develop so quickly in a pair so young? A romantic might suggest rare and perfect love. A social scientist, though, might point to the role of parental interference and the psychological reactance it can produce. Perhaps the passion of Romeo and Juliet was not initially so consuming that it transcended the extensive barriers erected by the families. Perhaps, instead, it was fueled to a white heat by the placement of those barriers. Could it be that had the youngsters been left to their own devices, their inflamed devotion would have amounted to no more than a flicker of puppy love?

Because the story is fiction, such questions are, of course, hypothetical, and any answers to them are speculative. However, it is possible to ask and answer with more certainty similar questions about modern-day Romeos and Juliets. Do couples suffering parental interference react by committing themselves more firmly to the partnership and falling more deeply in love? According to a study done with 140 Colorado couples, that is exactly what they do. In fact, the researchers found that although parental interference was linked to some problems in the relationship—the partners viewed one another more critically and reported a greater number of negative behaviors in the other—

that interference also made the pair feel greater love and desire for marriage. During the course of the study, as parental interference intensified, so did the love experience; and when the interference weakened, romantic feelings actually cooled.[7]

For twos and teens, then, psychological reactance flows across the broad surface of experience, always turbulent and forceful. For most of the rest of us, the pool of reactant energy lies quiet and covered, erupting geyserlike only on occasion. Still, these eruptions manifest themselves in a variety of fascinating ways that are of interest not only to the student of human behavior but to lawmakers and policymakers as well.

For instance, there's the odd case of Kennesaw, Georgia, the town that on June 1, 1982, enacted a law requiring every adult resident to own a gun and ammunition, under penalty of six months in jail and a two-hundred-dollar fine. All the features of the Kennesaw gun law make it a prime target for psychological reactance: The freedom that the law restricts is an important, long-standing one to which most American citizens feel entitled. Furthermore, the law was passed by the Kennesaw City Council with a minimum of public input. Reactance theory would predict that under these circumstances few of the adults in the town of fifty-four hundred would obey. Yet newspaper reports testified that three to four weeks after passage of the law, firearms sales in Kennesaw were—no pun intended—booming.

How are we to make sense of this apparent contradiction of the reactance principle? By looking a bit more closely at those who were buying Kennesaw's guns. Interviews with Kennesaw store owners revealed that the gun buyers were not town residents at all, but visitors, many of them lured by publicity to purchase their initial gun in Kennesaw. Donna Green, proprietor of a shop described in one newspaper article as a virtual "grocery store of firearms," summed it up: "Business is great. But they're almost all being bought by people from out of town. We've only had two or three local people buy a gun to comply with the law." After passage of the law, then, gun buying had become a frequent activity in Kennesaw, but not among those it was intended to cover; they were massively noncompliant. Only those individuals whose freedom in the matter had not been restricted by the law had the inclination to live by it.

INFLUENCE

A similar situation arose a decade earlier and several hundred miles to the south of Kennesaw, when Dade County (containing Miami), Florida, imposed an antiphosphate ordinance prohibiting the use—and possession!—of laundry or cleaning products containing phosphates. A study done to determine the social impact of the law discovered two parallel reactions on the part of Miami residents. First, in what seems a Florida tradition, many Miamians turned to smuggling. Sometimes with neighbors and friends in large "soap caravans," they drove to nearby counties to load up on phosphate detergents. Hoarding quickly developed; and in the rush of obsession that frequently characterizes hoarders, families were reported to boast of twenty-year supplies of phosphate cleaners.

The second reaction to the law was more subtle and more general than the deliberate defiance of the smugglers and hoarders. Spurred by the tendency to want what they could no longer have, the majority of Miami consumers came to see phosphate cleaners as better products than before. Compared to Tampa residents, who were not affected by the Dade County ordinance, the citizens of Miami rated phosphate detergents as gentler, more effective in cold water, better whiteners and fresheners, more powerful on stains. After passage of the law, they had even come to believe that phosphate detergents poured more easily than did the Tampa consumers.[8]

This sort of response is typical of individuals who have lost an established freedom and is crucial to an understanding of how psychological reactance and scarcity work on us. When our freedom to have something is limited, the item becomes less available, and we experience an increased desire for it. However, we rarely recognize that psychological reactance has caused us to want the item more; all we know is that we *want* it. Still, we need to make sense of our desire for the item, so we begin to assign it positive qualities to justify the desire. After all, it is natural to suppose that if one feels drawn to something, it is because of the merit of the thing. In the case of the Dade County antiphosphate law—and in other instances of newly restricted availability—that is a faulty supposition. Phosphate detergents clean, whiten, and pour no better after they are banned than before. We just assume they do because we find that we desire them more.

SCARCITY

*   *   *

The tendency to want what has been banned and therefore to presume that it is more worthwhile is not limited to such commodities as laundry soap. In fact, the tendency is not limited to commodities at all but extends to restrictions on information. In an age when the ability to acquire, store, and manage information is becoming increasingly the determinant of wealth and power, it is important to understand how we typically react to attempts to censor or otherwise constrain our access to information. Although much data exist on our reactions to various kinds of potentially censorable material—media violence, pornography, radical political rhetoric—there is surprisingly little evidence as to our reactions to the act of censoring them. Fortunately, the results of the few studies that have been done on the topic are highly consistent. Almost invariably, our response to the banning of information is a greater desire to receive that information and a more favorable attitude toward it than before the ban.[9]

The intriguing thing about the effects of censoring information is not that audience members want to have the information more than they did before; that seems natural. Rather, it is that they come to believe in the information more, even though they haven't received it. For example, when University of North Carolina students learned that a speech opposing coed dorms on campus would be banned, they became more opposed to the idea of coed dorms. Thus, without ever hearing the speech, they became more sympathetic to its argument. This raises the worrisome possibility that especially clever individuals holding a weak or unpopular position can get us to agree with that position by arranging to have their message restricted. The irony is that for such people—members of fringe political groups, for example—the most effective strategy may not be to publicize their unpopular views but to get those views officially censored and then to publicize the censorship. Perhaps the authors of this country's Constitution were acting as much as sophisticated social psychologists as staunch civil libertarians when they wrote the remarkably permissive free-speech provision of the First Amendment. By refusing to restrain freedom of speech, they may have been attempting to minimize the chance that new political notions would win support via the irrational course of psychological reactance.

Of course, political ideas are not the only kind that are susceptible to restriction. Access to sexually relevant material is frequently limited. Although not as sensational as the occasional police crackdowns on "adult" bookstores and theaters, regular pressure is applied by parents and by citizens' groups to censor the sexual content of educational material ranging from sex education and hygiene texts to books on the shelves of school libraries. Both sides in the struggle seem to be well intentioned, and the issues are not simple, since they involve such matters as morality, art, parental control over the schools, and First Amendment freedoms. But from a purely psychological point of view, those favoring strict censorship may wish to examine closely the results of a study done on Purdue University undergraduates.[10] The students were shown some advertisements for a novel. For half the students, the advertising copy included the statement, "a book for adults only, restricted to those 21 years and over"; the other half of the students read about no such age restriction on the book. When the researchers later asked the students to indicate their feelings toward the book, they discovered the same pair of reactions we have noted with other bans: Those who learned of the age restriction (1) wanted to read the book more and (2) believed that they would like the book more than did those who thought their access to the book was unlimited.

It might be argued that although these results may be true for a small sample of sexually inclined college students, they would not apply to students in junior and senior high schools, where the sex curricula battles are actually being waged. Two factors make me doubt such an argument. First, developmental psychologists report that as a general style, the desire to oppose adult control begins quite soon in adolescence, around the start of the teenage years. Nonscientific observers have also noted the early rise of these strong oppositional tendencies. Shakespeare, scholars tell us, placed Romeo and Juliet at the ages of fifteen and thirteen years, respectively. Second, the pattern of reactions exhibited by the Purdue students is not unique and thus can't be attributed to any great preoccupation with sex that college students may have. The pattern is common to externally imposed restrictions in general. Limiting access to the book had the same effects as did banning phosphate detergent in Florida or censoring a speech in North Carolina: The people involved came to want the restricted item more and, as a result, came to feel more favorable toward it.

Those who support the official banning of sexually relevant materials from school curricula have the avowed purpose of reducing the orientation of the society, especially its youth, toward eroticism. In the light of the Purdue study and in the context of other research on the effects of imposed restraints, one must wonder whether official censorship as a means may not be antithetical to the goal. If we are to believe the implications of the research, then the censorship is likely to increase the desire of students for sexual material and, consequently, to cause them to view themselves as the kind of individuals who like such material.

The term "official censorship" usually makes us think of bans on political or sexual material; yet there is another common sort of official censorship that we don't think of in the same way, probably because it occurs after the fact. Often in a jury trial, a piece of evidence or testimony will be introduced, only to be ruled inadmissible by the presiding judge, who may then admonish the jurors to disregard that evidence. From this perspective, the judge may be viewed as a censor, though the form of censorship is odd. The presentation of the information to the jury is not banned—it's too late for that—it's the jury's use of the information that is banned. How effective are such instructions from a judge? And is it possible that, for jury members who feel it is their right to consider all the available information, declarations of inadmissibility may actually cause psychological reactance, leading the jurors to use the evidence to a greater extent?

These were some of the questions asked in a large-scale jury-research project conducted by the University of Chicago Law School. One reason the results of the Chicago jury project are informative is that the participants were individuals who were actually on jury duty at the time and who agreed to be members of "experimental juries" formed by the researchers. These experimental juries then heard tapes of evidence from previous trials and deliberated as if they were deciding the case. In the study most relevant to our interest in official censorship, thirty such juries heard the case of a woman who was injured by a car driven by a careless male defendant. The first finding of the study was no surprise: When the driver said he had liability insurance, the jurors awarded his victim an average of four thousand dollars more than when he said he had no insurance (thirty-seven thousand dollars vs. thirty-three thousand dollars). Thus, as insurance companies have long suspected, juries make larger awards to victims if an insurance company will have to pay. The second finding of the study is the fascinating one, though. If the driver said he was insured *and* the judge ruled that evidence inadmissible (directing the jury to disregard it), the instruction to disregard had a boomerang effect, causing an average award of forty-six thousand dollars. So when certain juries learned that the driver was insured, they increased the damage payment by four thousand dollars. But when other juries were told officially that they must not use that information, they used it still more, increasing the damage payment by thirteen thousand dollars. It appears, then, that even proper, official censorship in a courtroom setting creates problems for the censor. We react to information restriction there, as usual, by valuing the banned information more than ever.[11]

The realization that we value limited information allows us to apply the scarcity principle to realms beyond material commodities. The principle works for messages, communications, and knowledge, too. Taking this perspective, we can see that information may not have to be censored for us to value it more; it need only be scarce. According to the scarcity principle, then, we will find a piece of information more persuasive if we think we can't get it elsewhere. This idea that exclusive information is more persuasive information is central to the thinking of two psychologists, Timothy Brock and Howard Fromkin, who have developed a "commodity theory" analysis of persuasion.[12]

The strongest support I know for Brock and Fromkin's theory comes from a small experiment done by a student of mine. At the time, the student was also a successful businessman, the owner of a beef-importing company, who had returned to school to get advanced training in marketing. After we talked in my office one day about scarcity and exclusivity of information, he decided to do a study using his sales staff. The company's cus-

tomers—buyers for supermarkets or other retail food outlets—
were phoned as usual by a salesperson and asked for a purchase
in one of three ways. One set of customers heard a standard sales
presentation before being asked for their orders. Another set of
customers heard the standard sales presentation plus information
that the supply of imported beef was likely to be scarce in the
upcoming months. A third group received the standard sales presentation and the information about a scarce supply of beef, too;
however, they also learned that the scarce-supply news was not
generally available information—it had come, they were told,
from certain exclusive contacts that the company had. Thus the
customers who received this last sales presentation learned that
not only was the availability of the product limited, so also was
the news concerning it—the scarcity double whammy.

The results of the experiment quickly become apparent
when the company salespeople began to urge the owner to buy
more beef because there wasn't enough in the inventory to keep
up with all the orders they were receiving. Compared to the customers who got only the standard sales appeal, those who were
also told about the future scarcity of beef bought more than
twice as much. But the real boost in sales occurred among the
customers who heard of the impending scarcity via "exclusive"
information. They purchased six times the amount that the customers who received only the standard sales pitch did. Apparently the fact that the news carrying the scarcity of information
was itself scarce made it especially persuasive.[13]

※

OPTIMAL CONDITIONS

Much like the other effective weapons of influence, the scarcity
principle is more effective at some times than at other times. An
important practical problem, then, is to find out when scarcity
works best on us. A great deal can be learned in this regard from
an experiment devised by social psychologist Stephen Worchel.[14]
The basic procedure used by Worchel and his research team was
simple: Participants in a consumer-preference study were given a

chocolate-chip cookie from a jar and asked to taste and rate its quality. For half of the raters, the jar contained ten cookies; for the other half, it contained just two. As we might expect from the scarcity principle, when the cookie was one of the only two available, it was rated more favorably than when it was one of ten. The cookie in short supply was rated as more desirable to eat in the future, more attractive as a consumer item, and more costly than the identical cookie in abundant supply.

Although this pattern of results provides a rather striking validation of the scarcity principle, it doesn't tell us anything we don't already know. Once again, we see that a less-available item is more desired and valued. The real worth of the cookie study comes from two additional findings. Let's take them one at a time, as each deserves a thorough consideration.

The first of these noteworthy results involved a small variation in the experiment's basic procedure. Rather than rating the cookies under conditions of constant scarcity, some participants were first given a jar of ten cookies that was then replaced by a jar of two cookies. Thus, before taking a bite, certain of the participants saw their abundant supply of cookies reduced to a scarce supply. Other participants, however, knew only scarcity of supply from the outset, since the number of cookies in their jars was left at two. With this procedure, the researchers were seeking to answer a question about types of scarcity: Do we value more those things that have recently become less available to us, or those things that have always been scarce? In the cookie experiment, the answer was plain. The drop from abundance to scarcity produced a decidedly more positive reaction to the cookies than did constant scarcity. This was true for all the ratings but can be seen most easily in the cost per pound participants estimated that the cookies were worth (sixty-one cents vs. fifty-one cents).

The idea that newly experienced scarcity is the more powerful kind applies to situations well beyond the bounds of the cookie study. For example, social scientists have determined that such scarcity is a primary cause of political turmoil and violence. Perhaps the most prominent proponent of this argument is James C. Davies, who states that we are most likely to find revolutions where a period of improving economic and social conditions is followed by a short, sharp reversal in those conditions. Thus it is not the traditionally most downtrodden people—who have come to see their deprivation as part of the natural order of things— who are especially liable to revolt. Instead, revolutionaries are more likely to be those who have been given at least some taste of a better life. When the economic and social improvements they have experienced and come to expect suddenly become less available, they desire them more than ever and often rise up violently to secure them.[15]

Davies has gathered persuasive evidence for his novel thesis from a range of revolutions, revolts, and internal wars, including the French, Russian, and Egyptian revolutions as well as such domestic uprisings as Dorr's Rebellion in nineteenth-century Rhode Island, the American Civil War, and the urban black riots of the 1960s. In each case, a time of increasing well-being preceded a tight cluster of reversals that burst into violence.

The racial conflict in America's cities during the mid-1960s represents a case in point that many of us can recall. At the time, it was not uncommon to hear the question, "Why now?" It didn't seem to make sense that within their three-hundred-year history, most of which had been spent in servitude and much of the rest in privation, American blacks would choose the socially progressive sixties in which to revolt. Indeed, as Davies points out, the two decades after the start of World War II had brought dramatic political and economic gains to the black population. In 1940, blacks faced stringent legal restrictions in such areas as housing, transportation, and education; moreover, even with the same amount of education, the average black family earned only a bit more than half of its counterpart white family. Fifteen years later, much had changed. Federal legislation had struck down as unacceptable formal and informal attempts to segregate blacks in schools, public places, housing, and employment settings. Large economic advances had been made, too; black family income had risen from 56 percent to 80 percent of that of a comparably educated white family.

But then, according to Davies's analysis of social conditions, this rapid progress was stymied by events that soured the heady optimism of previous years. First, political and legal change proved substantially easier to enact than social change. Despite all the progressive legislation of the forties and fifties, blacks perceived that most neighborhoods, jobs, and schools remained segregated. Thus the Washington-based victories came to feel like defeats at home. For example, in the four years following the U.S. Supreme Court's 1954 decision to integrate all public schools, blacks were the targets of 530 acts of violence (direct intimidation of black children and parents, bombings, and burnings) designed to prevent school integration. This violence generated the perception of another sort of setback in black progress. For the first time since well before World War II, when lynchings had occurred at an average rate of seventy-eight per year, blacks had to be concerned about the basic safety of their families. The new violence was not limited to the education issue, either. Peaceful civil-rights demonstrations of the time were frequently confronted by hostile crowds—and police.

Still another type of downturn occurred—in pocketbook progress. In 1962, the income of a black family had slid back to 74 percent of that of a similarly educated white family. By Davies's argument, the most illuminating aspect of this 74 percent figure is not that it represented a long-term increase in prosperity from pre-1940s levels but that it represented a short-term decline from the flush mid-1950s levels. In the next year came the Birmingham riots and, in staccato succession, scores of violent demonstrations, building toward the major upheavals of Watts, Newark, and Detroit.

In keeping with a distinct historial pattern of revolution, blacks in the United States were more rebellious when their prolonged progress was curtailed somewhat than they were before it began. This pattern offers a valuable lesson for would-be rulers: When it comes to freedoms, it is more dangerous to have given for a while than never to have given at all. The problem for a government that seeks to improve the political and economic status of a traditionally oppressed group is that, in so doing, it establishes freedoms for the group where none existed before. And should these now *established* freedoms become less available, there will be an especially hot variety of hell to pay.

The lesson applies as well to the politics of family as country. The parent who grants privileges or enforces rules erratically invites rebelliousness by unwittingly establishing freedoms for the child. The parent who only sometimes prohibits between-meal sweets may create for the child the freedom to have such snacks. At that point, enforcing the rule becomes a much more difficult and explosive matter because the child is no longer merely lacking a never-possessed right but is losing an established one. As we have seen in the case of political freedoms and (especially pertinent to the present discussion) chocolate-chip cookies, people see a thing as more desirable when it has recently become less available than when it has been scarce all along. We should not be surprised, then, when research shows that parents who enforce discipline inconsistently produce generally rebellious children. [16]

Let's look back to the cookie study for another insight into the way we react to scarcity. We've already seen from the results of that study that scarce cookies were rated higher than abundant cookies and that newly scarce cookies were rated higher still. Staying with the newly scarce cookies now, there was a certain cookie that was the highest rated of all: those that became less available because of a demand for them.

Remember that in the experiment the participants who experienced new scarcity had been given a jar of ten cookies that was then replaced with a jar of only two cookies. Actually, the researchers did this in one of two ways. To certain participants, it was explained that some of their cookies had to be given away to other raters to supply the demand for cookies in the study. To another set of participants, it was explained that their number of cookies had to be reduced because the researcher had simply made a mistake and given them the wrong jar initially. The results showed that those whose cookies became scarce through the process of social demand liked them significantly more than those whose cookies became scarce by mistake. In fact, the cookies made less available through social demand were rated the most desirable of any in the study.

This finding highlights the importance of competition in the pursuit of limited resources. Not only do we want the same item more when it is scarce, we want it most when we are in competition for it. Advertisers often try to exploit this tendency in us. In their ads, we learn that "popular demand" for an item is so great that we must "hurry to buy," or we see a crowd pressing against the doors of a store before the start of a sale, or we watch a flock of hands quickly deplete a supermarket shelf of a product. There is more to such images than the idea of ordinary social proof. The message is not just that the product is good because other people think so but also that we are in direct competition with those people for it.

The feeling of being in competition for scarce resources has powerfully motivating properties. The ardor of an indifferent lover surges with the appearance of a rival. It is often for reasons of strategy, therefore, that romantic partners reveal (or invent) the attentions of a new admirer. Salespeople are taught to play the same game with indecisive customers. For example, a Realtor who is trying to sell a house to a "fence-sitting" prospect will sometimes call the prospect with news of another potential buyer who has seen the house, liked it, and is scheduled to return the following day to talk about terms. When wholly fabricated, the new bidder is commonly described as an outsider with plenty of money: "an out-of-state investor buying for tax purposes" and "a physician and his wife moving into town" are favorites. The tactic, called in some circles "goosing 'em off the fence," can work devastatingly well. The thought of losing out to a rival frequently turns a buyer from hesitant to zealous.

There is something almost physical about the desire to have a contested item. Shoppers at big close-out or bargain sales report being caught up emotionally in the event. Charged by the crush of competitors, they swarm and struggle to claim merchandise they would otherwise disdain. Such behavior brings to mind the "feeding frenzy" of wild, indiscriminate eating among animal groups. Commercial fishermen exploit this phenomenon by throwing a quantity of loose bait to large schools of certain fish. Soon the water is a roiling expanse of thrashing fins and snapping mouths competing for the food. At this point, the fishermen save time and money by dropping unbaited lines into the water, since the crazed fish will bite ferociously at anything now, including bare metal hooks.

There is a noticeable parallel between the ways that commercial fishermen and department stores generate a competitive

SCARCITY

FIGURE 7–4

CONTAGIOUS COMPETITIVENESS

A disgruntled store employee steps through the aftermath of a closeout sporting-shoe sale, where customers are reported to have "gone wild, grabbing and struggling with one another over shoes whose sizes they had sometimes not yet seen." (Source: UPI)

fury in those they wish to hook. To attract and arouse the catch, fishermen scatter some loose bait called chum. For similar reasons, department stores holding a bargain sale toss out a few especially good deals on prominently advertised items called loss leaders. If the bait, of either form, has done its job, a large and eager crowd forms to snap it up. Soon, in the rush to score, the group becomes agitated, nearly blinded, by the adversarial nature of the situation. Human and fish alike lose perspective on what they want and begin striking at whatever is being contested. One wonders whether the tuna flapping on a dry deck with only a bare hook in its mouth shares the what-hit-me bewilderment of the shopper arriving home with only a load of department store bilge.

Lest we believe that the competition-for-limited-resources-fever occurs only in such unsophisticated forms of life as tuna and bargain-basement shoppers, we should examine the story behind a remarkable purchase decision made in 1973 by Barry Diller, who was vice president for prime-time programming at the American Broadcasting Company. He agreed to pay $3.3 million for a single television showing of the movie *The Poseidon Adventure*. The figure is noteworthy in that it greatly exceeded the highest price ever previously paid for a one-time movie showing: $2 million for *Patton*. In fact, the payment was so excessive that ABC figured to lose $1 million on the *Poseidon* showing. As NBC vice president for special programs, Bill Storke, declared at the time, "There's no way they can get their money back, no way at all."

How could an astute and experienced businessman like Diller go for a deal that would produce an expected loss of a million dollars? The answer may lie in a second noteworthy aspect of the sale: It was the first time that a motion picture had been offered to the networks in an open-bid auction. Never before had the three major commercial networks been forced to battle for a scarce resource in quite this way. The novel idea of a competitive auction was the brainchild of the movie's flamboyant showman-producer, Irwin Allen, and a 20th Century-Fox vice president, William Self, who must have been ecstatic about the outcome. But how can we be sure that it was the auction format that generated the spectacular sales price rather than the blockbuster quality of the movie itself?

Some comments from the auction participants provide impressive evidence. First came a statement from the victor, Barry Diller, intended to set future policy for his network. In language sounding as if it could have escaped only from between clenched teeth, he said, "ABC has decided regarding its policy for the future that it would never again enter into an auction situation."

Even more instructive are the remarks of Diller's rival, Robert
Wood, then president of CBS Television, who nearly lost his
head and outbid his competitors at ABC and NBC:

> We were very rational at the start. We priced the movie
> out, in terms of what it could bring in for us, then allowed a
> certain value on top of that for exploitation.
>
> But then the bidding started. ABC opened with two mil-
> lion. I came back with two point four. ABC went to two
> point eight. And the fever of the thing caught us. Like a guy
> who had lost his mind, I kept bidding. Finally, I went to three
> point two; and there came a moment when I said to myself,
> "Good grief, if I get it, what the heck am I going to do with
> it?" When ABC finally topped me, my main feeling was re-
> lief.
>
> It's been very educational.[17]

According to interviewer Bob MacKenzie, when Wood
made his "It's been very educational" statement, he was smiling.
We can be sure that when ABC's Diller made his "never again"
announcement, he was not. Both men had clearly learned something from the "Great *Poseidon* Auction." But for one, there had
been a $1 million tuition charge. Fortunately, there is a valuable
but drastically less expensive lesson here for us, too. It is instructive to note that the smiling man was the one who had *lost* the
highly sought-after prize. As a general rule, whenever the dust
settles and we find losers looking and speaking like winners (and
vice versa), we should be especially wary of the conditions that
kicked up the dust—in the present case, open competition for a
scarce resource. As the TV executives now know, extreme caution is advised whenever we encounter the devilish construction
of scarcity plus rivalry.

※

HOW TO SAY NO

It is easy enough to feel properly warned against scarcity pressures; but it is substantially more difficult to act on that warning. Part of the problem is that our typical reaction to scarcity hinders our ability to think. When we watch something we want become less available, a physical agitation sets in. Especially in those cases involving direct competition, the blood comes up, the focus narrows, and emotions rise. As this visceral current advances, the cognitive, rational side retreats. In the rush of arousal, it is difficult to be calm and studied in our approach. As CBS-TV's president, Robert Wood, commented in the wake of his *Poseidon* adventure, "You get caught up in the mania of the thing, the acceleration of it. Logic goes right out the window."

Here's our predicament, then: Knowing the causes and workings of scarcity pressures may not be sufficient to protect us from them because knowing is a cognitive thing, and cognitive processes are suppressed by our emotional reaction to scarcity. In fact, this may be the reason for the great effectiveness of scarcity tactics. When they are employed properly, our first line of defense against foolish behavior—a thoughtful analysis of the situation—becomes less likely.

If, because of brain-clouding arousal, we can't rely on our knowledge about the scarcity principle to stimulate properly cautious behavior, what can we use? Perhaps, in fine jujitsu style, we can use the arousal itself as our prime cue. In this way we can turn the enemy's strength to our advantage. Rather than relying on a considered, cognitive analysis of the entire situation, we might simply tune ourselves to the internal, visceral sweep for our warning. By learning to flag the experience of heightening arousal in a compliance situation, we can alert ourselves to the possibility of scarcity tactics there and to the need for caution.

But suppose we accomplish this trick of using the rising tide of arousal as a signal to calm ourselves and to proceed with care. What then? Is there any other piece of information we can use to help make a proper decision in the face of scarcity? After all, merely recognizing that we ought to move carefully doesn't tell us the direction in which to move; it only provides the necessary context for a thoughtful decision.

Fortunately, there is information available on which we can base thoughtful decisions about scarce items. It comes, once again, from the chocolate-chip-cookie study, where the researchers uncovered something that seems strange but rings true regarding scarcity: Even though the scarce cookies were rated as significantly more desirable, they were not rated as any bettertasting than the abundant cookies. So despite the increased yearning that scarcity caused (the raters said they wanted to have more of the scarce cookies in the future and would pay a greater price for them), it did not make the cookies taste one whit better. Therein lies an important insight. The joy is not in *experiencing* a scarce commodity but in *possessing* it. It is important that we not confuse the two.

Whenever we confront the scarcity pressures surrounding some item, we must also confront the question of what it is we want from the item. If the answer is that we want the thing for the social, economic, or psychological benefits of possessing something rare, then, fine; scarcity pressures will give us a good indication of how much we would want to pay for it—the less available it is, the more valuable to us it will be. But very often we don't want a thing purely for the sake of owning it. We want it, instead, for its utility value; we want to eat it or drink it or touch it or hear it or drive it or otherwise *use* it. In such cases it is vital to remember that scarce things do not taste or feel or sound or ride or work any better because of their limited availability.

Although this is a simple point, it can often escape us when we experience the heightened desirability that scarce items naturally possess. I can cite a family example. My brother Richard supported himself through school by employing a compliance trick that cashed in handsomely on the tendency of most people to miss that simple point. In fact, his tactic was so effective that he had to work only a few hours each weekend for his money, leaving the rest of the time free for his studies.

Richard sold cars, but not in a showroom nor on a car lot. He would buy a couple of used cars sold privately through the newspaper on one weekend and, adding nothing but soap and water, would sell them at a decided profit through the newspaper on the following weekend. To do this, he had to know three things. First, he had to know enough about cars to buy those that were offered for sale at the bottom of their blue-book price range but could be legitimately resold for a higher price. Second, once he got the car, he had to know how to write a newspaper ad that would stimulate substantial buyer interest. Third, once a buyer arrived, he had to know how to use the scarcity principle to generate more desire for the car than it perhaps deserved. Richard knew how to do all three. For our purposes, though, we need to examine his craft with just the third.

For a car he had purchased on the prior weekend, he would place an ad in the Sunday paper. Because he knew how to construct a good ad, he usually received an array of calls from potential buyers on Sunday morning. Each prospect who was interested enough to want to see the car was given an appointment time—*the same appointment time.* So if six people were scheduled, they were all scheduled for, say, two o'clock that afternoon. This little device of simultaneous scheduling paved the way for later compliance because it created an atmosphere of competition for a limited resource.

Typically, the first prospect to arrive would begin a studied examination of the car and would engage in standard car-buying behavior, such as pointing out any blemishes or deficiencies or asking if the price was negotiable. The psychology of the situation changed radically, however, when the second buyer drove up. The availability of the car to either prospect suddenly became limited by the presence of the other. Often the earlier arrival, inadvertently stoking the sense of rivalry, would assert his right to primary consideration. "Just a minute, now. I was here first." If he didn't assert that right, Richard would do it for him. Addressing the second buyer, Richard would say, "Excuse me, but this other gentleman was here before you. So can I ask you to wait on the other side of the driveway for a few minutes until he's finished looking at the car? Then, if he decides he doesn't want it or if he can't make up his mind, I'll show it to you."

Richard claims it was possible to watch the agitation grow on the first buyer's face. His leisurely assessment of the car's pros and cons had suddenly become a now-or-never, limited-time-only rush to decision over a contested resource. If he didn't decide for the car—at Richard's asking price—in the next few minutes, he might lose it for good to that . . . that . . . lurking newcomer over there. For his part, the second buyer would be equally agitated by the combination of rivalry and restricted availability. He would pace on the periphery, visibly straining to get at this now more desirable hunk of metal. Should two-o'clock appointment number one fail to buy or even fail to decide quickly enough, two-o'clock appointment number two was ready to pounce.

If these conditions alone were not enough to secure a favorable purchase decision immediately, the trap snapped surely shut as soon as the third two-o'clock appointment arrived on the scene. According to Richard, stacked-up competition was usually too much for the first prospect to bear. He would end the pressure quickly by either agreeing to Richard's price or by leaving abruptly. In the latter instance, the second arrival would strike at the chance to buy out of a sense of relief coupled with a new feeling of rivalry with that . . . that . . . lurking newcomer over there.

All those buyers who contributed to my brother's college education failed to recognize a fundamental fact about their purchases: The increased desire that spurred them to buy had little to do with the merits of the car. That failure of recognition occurred for two reasons. First, the situation Richard arranged for them produced an emotional reaction that made it difficult for them to think straight. Second, as a consequence, they never stopped to think that the reason they wanted the car in the first place was to use it, not merely to have it. And the competition-for-a-scarce-resource pressures Richard applied affected only their desire to have the car in the sense of possessing it. Those pressures did not affect the value of the car in terms of the real purpose for which they had wanted it.

Should we find ourselves beset by scarcity pressures in a compliance situation, then, our best response would occur in a two-stage sequence. As soon as we feel the tide of emotional arousal that flows from scarcity influences, we should use that rise in arousal as a signal to stop short. Panicky, feverish reactions have no place in wise compliance decisions. We need to calm ourselves and regain a rational perspective. Once that is done, we can move to the second stage by asking ourselves why we want the item under consideration. If the answer is that we want it primarily for the purpose of owning it, then we should use its availability to help gauge how much we want to spend for it. However, if the answer is that we want it primarily for its function (that is, we want something good to drive, drink, eat, etc.), then we must remember that the item under consideration will function equally well whether scarce or plentiful. Quite simply, we need to recall that the scarce cookies didn't taste any better.

INSTANT INFLUENCE
Primitive consent for an
automatic age

✺

Back in the 1960s a man named Joe Pine hosted a rather remarkable TV talk show that was syndicated from California. The program was made distinctive by Pine's caustic and
confrontational style with his guests—for the most part, a collection of exposure-hungry entertainers, would-be celebrities, and
representatives of fringe political or social organizations. The
host's abrasive approach was designed to provoke his guests into
arguments, to fluster them into embarrassing admissions, and
generally to make them look foolish. It was not uncommon for
Pine to introduce a visitor and launch immediately into an attack
on the individual's beliefs, talent, or appearance. Some people
claimed that Pine's acid personal style was partially caused by a
leg amputation that had embittered him to life; others said no,
that he was just vituperous by nature.

One evening rock musician Frank Zappa was a guest on the
show. This was at a time in the sixties when very long hair on

men was still unusual and controversial. As soon as Zappa had been introduced and seated, the following exchange occurred:

PINE: I guess your long hair makes you a girl.

ZAPPA: I guess your wooden leg makes you a table.

Aside from containing what may be my favorite ad-lib, the above dialogue illustrates a fundamental theme of this book: Very often in making a decision about someone or something, we don't use all the relevant available information, we use, instead, only a single, highly representative piece of the total. And an isolated piece of information, even though it normally counsels us correctly, can lead us to clearly stupid mistakes—mistakes that, when exploited by clever others, leave us looking silly or worse.

At the same time, a complicating companion theme has been present throughout this book: Despite the susceptibility to stupid decisions that accompanies a reliance on a single feature of the available data, the pace of modern life demands that we frequently use this shortcut. Recall that early in Chapter 1, our shortcut approach was likened to the automatic responding of lower animals, whose elaborate behavior patterns could be triggered by the presence of a lone stimulus feature—a "cheep-cheep" sound, a shade of red breast feather, or a specific sequence of light flashes. The reason infrahumans must often rely on such solitary stimulus features is their restricted mental capability. Their small brains cannot begin to register and process all the relevant information in their environments. So these species have evolved special sensitivities to certain aspects of the information. Because those selected aspects of information are normally enough to cue a correct response, the system is usually very efficient: Whenever a female turkey hears "cheep-cheep," *click, whirr,* out rolls the proper maternal behavior in a mechanical fashion that conserves much of her limited brainpower for dealing with the variety of other situations and choices she must face in her day.

We, of course, have vastly more effective brain mechanisms than mother turkeys, or any other animal group, for that matter.

EPILOGUE

We are unchallenged in the ability to take into account a multitude of relevant facts and, consequently, to make good decisions. Indeed, it is this information-processing advantage over other species that has helped make us the dominant form of life on the planet.

Still, we have our capacity limitations, too; and, for the sake of efficiency, we must sometimes retreat from the time-consuming, sophisticated, fully informed brand of decision-making to a more automatic, primitive, single-feature type of responding. For instance, in deciding whether to say yes or no to a requester, it is clear that we frequently pay attention to but one piece of the relevant information in the situation. We have been exploring several of the most popular of the single pieces of information that we use to prompt our compliance decisions. They are the most popular prompts precisely because they are the most reliable ones, those that normally point us toward the correct choice. That is why we employ the factors of reciprocation, consistency, social proof, liking, authority, and scarcity so often and so automatically in making our compliance decisions. Each, by itself, provides a highly reliable cue as to when we will be better off saying yes than no.

We are likely to use these lone cues when we don't have the inclination, time, energy, or cognitive resources to undertake a complete analysis of the situation. Where we are rushed, stressed, uncertain, indifferent, distracted, or fatigued, we tend to focus on less of the information available to us. When making decisions under these circumstances, we often revert to the rather primitive but necessary single-piece-of-good-evidence approach.[1] All this leads to a jarring insight: With the sophisticated mental apparatus we have used to build world eminence as a species, we have created an environment so complex, fast-paced, and information-laden than we must increasingly deal with it in the fashion of the animals we long ago transcended.

John Stuart Mill, the British economist, political thinker, and philosopher of science, died a little more than a hundred years ago. The year of his death (1873) is important because he is reputed to have been the last man to know everything there was to know in the world. Today, the notion that one of us could be aware of all known facts is only laughable. After eons of slow accumulation, human knowledge has snowballed into an era of momentum-fed, multiplicative, monstrous expansion. We now live in a world where most of the information is less than fifteen years old.[2] In certain fields of science alone (for example, physics), knowledge is said to double every eight years.[3] And the scientific information explosion is not limited to such arcane arenas as molecular chemistry or quantum physics but extends to everyday areas of knowledge where we strive to keep ourselves current—health, child development, nutrition, and the like. What's more, this rapid growth is likely to continue, since 90 percent of all scientists who have ever lived are working today.

Apart from the streaking advance of science, things are quickly changing much closer to home. In his book *Future Shock,* Alvin Toffler provided early documentation of the unprecedented and increasing rapidity of modern daily life: We travel more and faster; we relocate more frequently to new residences, which are built and torn down more quickly; we contact more people and have shorter relationships with them; in the supermarket, car showroom, and shopping mall, we are faced with an array of choices among styles and products that were unheard of the previous year and may well be obsolete or forgotten by the next. Novelty, transience, diversity, and acceleration are acknowledged as prime descriptors of civilized existence.

This avalanche of information and choices is made possible by burgeoning technological progress. Leading the way are developments in our ability to collect, store, retrieve, and communicate information. At first, the fruits of such advances were limited to large organizations—government agencies or powerful corporations. For example, speaking as chairman of Citicorp, Walter Wriston could say of his company, "We have tied together a data base in the world that is capable of telling almost anyone in the world, almost anything, immediately."[4] But now, with further developments in telecommunication and computer technology, access to such staggering amounts of information is falling within the reach of individual citizens. Extensive cable and satellite television systems provide one route for that information into the average home.

EPILOGUE

The other major route is the personal computer. In 1972, Norman Macrae, an editor of *The Economist,* speculated prophetically about a time in the future:

> The prospect is, after all, that we are going to enter an age when any duffer sitting at a computer terminal in his laboratory or office or public library or home can delve through unimaginable increased mountains of information in mass-assembly data banks with mechanical powers of concentration and calculation that will be greater by a factor of tens of thousands than was ever available to the human brain of even an Einstein.[5]

One short decade later, *Time* magazine signaled that Macrae's future age had arrived by naming a machine, the personal computer, as its Man of the Year. *Time*'s editors defended their choice by citing the consumer "stampede" to purchase small computers and by arguing that "America [and], in a larger perspective, the entire world will never be the same." Macrae's vision is now being realized. Millions of ordinary "duffers" are sitting at machines with the potential to present and analyze enough data to bury an Einstein.

Because technology can evolve much faster than we can, our natural capacity to process information is likely to be increasingly inadequate to handle the surfeit of change, choice, and challenge that is characteristic of modern life. More and more frequently, we will find ourselves in the position of the lower animals—with a mental apparatus that is unequipped to deal thoroughly with the intricacy and richness of the outside environment. Unlike the animals, whose cognitive powers have always been relatively deficient, we have created our own deficiency by constructing a radically more complex world. But the consequence of our new deficiency is the same as that of the animals' long-standing one. When making a decision, we will less frequently enjoy the luxury of a fully considered analysis of the total situation but will revert increasingly to a focus on a single, usually reliable feature of it.

When those single features are truly reliable, there is nothing

inherently wrong with the shortcut approach of narrowed attention and automatic response to a particular piece of information.
The problem comes when something causes the normally trustworthy cues to counsel us poorly, to lead us to erroneous actions
and wrongheaded decisions. As we have seen, one such cause is
the trickery of certain compliance practitioners who seek to
profit from the rather mindless and mechanical nature of shortcut
response. If, as seems true, the frequency of shortcut response is
increasing with the pace and form of modern life, we can be sure
that the frequency of this trickery is destined to increase as well.

What can we do about the expected intensified attack on our
system of shortcuts? More than evasive action, I would urge
forceful counterassault. There is an important qualification, however. Compliance professionals who play fairly by the rules of
shortcut response are not to be considered the enemy; on the
contrary, they are our allies in an efficient and adaptive process of
exchange. The proper targets for counteraggression are only
those individuals who falsify, counterfeit, or misrepresent the evidence that naturally cues our shortcut responses.

Let's take an illustration from what is perhaps our most frequently used shortcut. According to the principle of social proof,
we often decide to do what other people like us are doing. It
makes all kinds of sense since, most of the time, an action that is
popular in a given situation is also functional and appropriate.
Thus, an advertiser who, without using deceptive statistics, provides information that a brand of toothpaste is the largest selling
or fastest growing has offered us valuable evidence about the
quality of the product and the probability that we will like it.
Provided that we are in the market for a tube of good toothpaste,
we might want to rely on that single piece of information, popularity, to decide to try it. This strategy will likely steer us right,
will unlikely steer us far wrong, and will conserve our cognitive
energies for dealing with the rest of our increasingly information-laden, decision-overloaded environment. The advertiser
who allows us to use effectively this efficient strategy is hardly
our antagonist but rather must be considered a cooperating
partner.

The story becomes quite different, however, should a com-

EPILOGUE

pliance practitioner try to stimulate a shortcut response by giving us a fraudulent signal for it. The enemy is the advertiser who seeks to create an image of popularity for a brand of toothpaste by, say, constructing a series of staged "unrehearsed-interview" commercials in which an array of actors posing as ordinary citizens praise the product. Here, where the evidence of popularity is counterfeit, we, the principle of social proof, and our shortcut response to it, are all being exploited. In an earlier chapter, I recommended against the purchase of any product featured in a faked "unrehearsed-interview" ad, and I urged that we send the product manufacturers letters detailing the reason and suggesting that they dismiss their advertising agency. I would recommend extending this aggressive stance to any situation in which a compliance professional abuses the principle of social proof (or any other weapon of influence) in this manner. We should refuse to watch TV programs that use canned laughter. If we see a bartender beginning a shift by salting his tip jar with a bill or two of his own, he should get none from us. If, after waiting in line outside a nightclub, we discover from the amount of available space that the wait was designed to impress passersby with false evidence of the club's popularity, we should leave immediately and announce our reason to those still in line. In short, we should be willing to use boycott, threat, confrontation, censure, tirade, nearly anything, to retaliate.

I don't consider myself pugnacious by nature, but I actively advocate such belligerent actions because in a way I am at war with the exploiters—we all are. It is important to recognize, however, that their motive for profit is not the cause for hostilities; that motive, after all, is something we each share to an extent. The real treachery, and the thing we cannot tolerate, is any attempt to make their profit in a way that threatens the reliability of our shortcuts. The blitz of modern daily life demands that we have faithful shortcuts, sound rules of thumb to handle it all. These are not luxuries any longer; they are out-and-out necessities that figure to become increasingly vital as the pulse of daily life quickens. That is why we should want to retaliate whenever we see someone betraying one of our rules of thumb

INFLUENCE

for profit. We want that rule to be as effective as possible. But to the degree that its fitness for duty is regularly undercut by the tricks of a profiteer, we naturally will use it less and will be less able to cope efficiently with the decisional burdens of our day. We cannot allow that without a fight. The stakes have gotten too high.

NOTES

※

CHAPTER 1 (pp. 15–28)

1. Honest, this animal researcher's name is Fox. See his 1974 monograph for a complete description of the turkey and polecat experiment.

2. Sources for the Robin and Bluethroat information are Lack (1943) and Peiponen (1960), respectively.

3. Although several important similarities exist between this kind of automatic responding in humans and lower animals, there are some important differences as well. The automatic behavior sequences of humans tend to be learned rather than inborn, more flexible than the lock-step patterns of the lower animals, and responsive to a larger number of triggers.

4. Perhaps the common "because . . . just because" response of children asked to explain their behavior can be traced to their shrewd recognition of the unusual amount of power adults appear to assign to the raw word *because*.

The reader who wishes to find a more systematic treatment of Langer's Xerox study and her conceptualization of it can do so in Langer (1978).

5. Sources for the Photuris and the blenny information are Lloyd (1965) and Eibl-Eibesfeldt (1958), respectively. As exploitative as these creatures seem, they are topped in this respect by an insect known as the rove beetle. By using a variety of triggers involving smell and touch, the rove beetles get two species of ants to protect, groom, and feed them as larvae and to harbor them for the

winter as adults. Responding mechanically to the beetles' trick trigger features, the ants treat the beetles as though they were fellow ants. Inside the ant nests, the beetles respond to their hosts' hospitality by eating ant eggs and young, yet they are never harmed (Hölldobler, 1971).

6. These studies are reported by Kenrick and Gutierres (1980), who warn that the unrealistically attractive people portrayed in the popular media (for example, actors, actresses, models) may cause us to be less satisfied with the looks of the genuinely available romantic possibilities around us. The most recent work of these authors takes their argument a step farther, showing that exposure to the exaggerated sexual attractiveness of nude pinup bodies (in such magazines as *Playboy* and *Playgirl*) causes people to become less pleased with the sexual desirability of their current spouse or live-in mate (Kenrick, Gutierres, & Goldberg, 1983).

CHAPTER 2 (pp. 29–65)

1. A formal description of the greeting-card study is provided in Kunz and Woolcott (1976).

2. Certain societies have formalized the rule into ritual. Consider for example the *Vartan Bhanji,* an institutionalized custom of the gift exchange common to parts of Pakistan and India. In commenting upon the *Vartan Bhanji,* Gouldner (1960) remarks:

> It is . . . notable that the system painstakingly prevents the total elimination of outstanding obligations. Thus, on the occasion of a marriage, departing guests are given gifts of sweets. In weighing them out, the hostess may say, 'These five are yours,' meaning 'These are a repayment for what you formerly gave me,' and then she adds an extra measure, saying, 'These are mine.' On the next occasion, she will receive these back along with an additional measure which she later returns, and so on.

3. The quote is from Leakey and Lewin (1978).

4. For a fuller discussion, see Tiger and Fox (1971).

5. The experiment is reported formally in Regan (1971).

6. The statement appears in Mauss (1954).

7. Surprise is an effective compliance producer in its own right. People who are surprised by a request will often comply because they are momentarily unsure of themselves and, consequently, influenced easily. For example, the social psychologists Stanley Milgram and John Sabini (1975) have shown that people riding on the New York subway were twice as likely to give up their seats to a person who surprised them with the request "Excuse me. May I have your seat?" than to one who forewarned them first by mentioning to a fellow

NOTES

passenger that he was thinking of asking for someone's seat (56 percent vs. 28 percent).

8. It is interesting that a cross-cultural study has shown that those who break the reciprocity rule in the reverse direction—by giving without allowing the recipient an opportunity to repay—are also disliked for it. This result was found to hold for each of the three nationalities investigated—Americans, Swedes, and Japanese. See Gergen et al. (1975) for an account of the study.

9. According to the data of the Pittsburgh study, this reluctance to ask for help when it cannot be repaid is equally strong for both sexes (Greenberg and Shapiro, 1971).

10. To convince ourselves that this result was no fluke, we conducted two more experiments testing the effectiveness of the rejection-then-retreat trick. Both showed results similar to the first experiment. See Cialdini et al. (1975) for the details of all three.

11. The Israeli study was conducted in 1979 by Schwartzwald, Raz, and Zvibel.

12. The *TV Guide* article appeared in December 1978.

13. The source for the quotes is Magruder (1974).

14. *Consumer Reports,* January 1975, p. 62.

15. Another way of gauging the effectiveness of a request technique is to examine the bottom-line proportion of individuals who, after being asked, complied with the request. Using such a measure, the rejection-then-retreat procedure was more than four times more effective than the procedure of asking for the smaller request only. See Miller et al. (1976) for a complete description of the study.

16. The blood-donation study was reported by Cialdini and Ascani (1976).

17. The UCLA study was performed by Benton, Kelley, and Liebling in 1972.

18. A variety of other business operations use the no-cost information offer extensively. Pest-exterminator companies, for instance, have found that most people who agree to a free home examination give the extermination job to the examining company, provided they are convinced that it is needed. They apparently feel an obligation to give their business to the firm that rendered the initial, complimentary service. Knowing that such customers are unlikely to comparison-shop for this reason, unscrupulous pest-control operators will take advantage of the situation by citing higher-than-competitive prices for work commissioned in this way.

INFLUENCE

CHAPTER 3 (pp. 66–114)

1. The racetrack study was done twice, with the same results, by Knox and Inkster (1968).

2. It is important to note that the collaboration was not always intentional. The American investigators defined collaboration as "any kind of behavior which helped the enemy" and it thus included such diverse activities as signing peace petitions, running errands, making radio appeals, accepting special favors, making false confessions, informing on fellow prisoners, or divulging military information.

3. The Schein quote comes from his 1956 article "The Chinese Indoctrination Program for Prisoners of War: A Study of Attempted Brainwashing."

4. See Greene (1965) for the source of this advice.

5. Freedman and Fraser published their data in the *Journal of Personality and Social Psychology,* in 1966.

6. The quote comes from Freedman and Fraser (1966).

7. See Segal (1954) for the article from which this quote originates.

8. See Jones and Harris (1967).

9. It is noteworthy that the housewives in this study (Kraut, 1973) heard that they were considered charitable at least a full week before they were asked to donate to the Multiple Sclerosis Association.

10. From "How to begin retailing," Amway Corporation.

11. See Deutsch and Gerard (1955).

12. From Whiting, Kluckhohn, and Anthony (1958).

13. From Gordon and Gordon (1963).

14. The survey was conducted by Walker (1967).

15. The electric-shock experiment was published seven years after the Aronson and Mills (1959) study by Gerard and Mathewson (1966).

16. Young (1965) conducted this research.

17. The robot study is reported fully in Freedman (1965).

18. The reader who wishes stronger evidence for the action of the low-ball tactic than my subjective observations in the car showroom may refer to a pair of articles that attest to its effectiveness under controlled, experimental conditions: Cialdini et al. (1978) and Burger and Petty (1981).

19. A formal report of the energy-conservation project appears in Pallak et al. (1980).

NOTES

20. It is not altogether unusual for even some of our most familiar quotations to be truncated by time in ways that greatly modify their character. For example, it is not *money* that the Bible claims as the root of all evil, it is *the love of money*. So as not to be guilty of the same sort of error myself, I should note that the Emerson quote from *Self-reliance* is somewhat longer and substantially more textured than I have reported. In full, it reads, "A foolish consistency is the hobgoblin of little minds adored by little statesmen, and philosophers, and divines."

21. See Zajonc (1980) for a summary of this evidence.

22. This is not to say that what we feel about an issue is always different from or always to be trusted more than what we think about it. However, the data are clear that our emotions and beliefs often do not point in the same direction. Therefore, in situations involving a decisional commitment likely to have generated supporting rationalizations, feelings may well provide the truer counsel. This would be especially so when, as in the question of Sara's happiness, the fundamental issue at hand concerns an emotion.

CHAPTER 4 (pp. 115–162)

1. The general evidence regarding the facilitative effect of canned laughter on responses to humor comes from such studies as Smyth and Fuller (1972), Fuller and Sheehy-Skeffinton (1974), and Nosanchuk and Lightstone (1974), the last of which contains the indication that canned laughter is most effective for poor material.

2. The researchers who infiltrated the Graham Crusade and who provided the quote are Altheide and Johnson (1977).

3. See Bandura, Grusec, and Menlove (1967) and Bandura and Menlove (1968) for full descriptions of the dog-phobia treatment.
Any reader who doubts that the seeming appropriateness of an action is importantly influenced by the number of others performing it might try a small experiment. Stand on a busy sidewalk, pick out an empty spot in the sky or on a tall building, and stare at it for a full minute. Very little will happen around you during that time—most people will walk past without glancing up, and virtually no one will stop to stare with you. Now, on the next day, go to the same place and bring along four friends to look upward too. Within sixty seconds, a crowd of passersby will have stopped to crane their necks skyward with the group. For those pedestrians who do not join you, the pressure to look up at least briefly will be nearly irresistible; if your experiment brings the same results as the one performed by three New York social psychologists, you and your friends will cause 80 percent of all passersby to lift their gaze to your empty spot (Milgram, Bickman, & Berkowitz, 1967).

4. Other research besides O'Connor's (1972) suggests that there are two sides to the filmed-social-proof coin, however. The dramatic effect of filmed

INFLUENCE

depictions on what children find appropriate has been a source of great distress for those concerned with frequent instances of violence and aggression on television. Although the consequences of televised violence on the aggressive actions of children are far from simple, the data from a well-controlled experiment by psychologists Robert Liebert and Robert Baron (1972) have an ominous look. Some children were shown excerpts from a television program in which people intentionally harmed another. Afterward, these children were significantly more harmful toward another child than were children who had watched a nonviolent television program (a horserace). The finding that seeing others perform aggressively led to more aggression on the part of the young viewers held true for the two age groups tested (five-to-six-year-olds and eight-to-nine-year-olds) and for both girls and boys.

5. An engagingly written report of their complete findings is presented in Festinger, Riecken, and Schachter's (1956) book *When Prophecy Fails*.

6. Perhaps because of the quality of ragged desperation with which they approached their task, the believers were wholly unsuccessful at enlarging their number. Not a single convert was gained. At that point, in the face of the twin failures of physical and social proof, the cult quickly disintegrated. Less than three weeks after the date of the predicted flood, group members were scattered and maintaining only sporadic communication with one another. In one final—and ironic—disconfirmation of prediction, it was the movement that perished in the flood.

Ruin has not always been the fate of doomsday groups whose predictions proved unsound, however. When such groups have been able to build social proof for their beliefs through effective recruitment efforts, they have grown and prospered. For example, when the Dutch Anabaptists saw their prophesied year of destruction, 1533, pass uneventfully, they became rabid seekers after converts, pouring unprecedented amounts of energy into the cause. One extraordinarily eloquent missionary, Jakob van Kampen, is reported to have baptized one hundred persons in a single day. So powerful was the snowballing social evidence in support of the Anabaptist position that it rapidly overwhelmed the disconfirming physical evidence and turned two thirds of the population of Holland's great cities into adherents.

7. From Rosenthal's *Thirty-eight Witnesses,* 1964.

8. This quote comes from Latané and Darley's award-winning book (1968), where they introduced the concept of pluralistic ignorance.

The potentially tragic consequences of the pluralistic ignorance phenomenon are starkly illustrated in a UPI news release from Chicago:

> A university coed was beaten and strangled in daylight hours near one of the most popular tourist attractions in the city, police said Saturday.
>
> The nude body of Lee Alexis Wilson, 23, was found Friday in dense shrubbery alongside the wall of the Art Institute by a 12-year-old boy playing in the bushes.

NOTES

Police theorized she may have been sitting or standing by a fountain in the Art Institute's south plaza when she was attacked. The assailant apparently then dragged her into the bushes. She apparently was sexually assaulted, police said.

Police said thousands of persons must have passed the site and one man told them he heard a scream about 2 P.M. but did not investigate *because no one else seemed to be paying attention.*

9. The New York "seizure" and "smoke" emergency studies are reported by Darley and Latané (1968) and Latané and Darley (1968), respectively. The Toronto experiment was performed by Ross (1971). The Florida studies were published by Clark and Word in 1972 and 1974.

10. See a study by Latané and Rodin (1969) showing that groups of strangers help less in an emergency than groups of acquaintances.

11. The wallet study was conducted by Hornstein et al. (1968).

12. The sources of these statistics are articles by Phillips in 1979 and 1980.

13. The newspaper story data are reported by Phillips (1974), while the TV story data come from Bollen and Phillips (1982).

14. These new data appear in Phillips (1983).

15. The quote is from *The International Cyclopedia of Music and Musicians,* 1964, which Sabin edited.

16. From Hornaday (1887).

CHAPTER 5 (pp. 163–202)

1. The Canadian election study was reported by Efran and Patterson (1976). Data of this sort give credence to the claim of some Richard Nixon backers that the failure that contributed most to the loss of the 1960 TV debates with John F. Kennedy—and thereby to the election—was the poor performance of Nixon's makeup man.

2. The quote is from Monahan (1941).

3. This finding—that attractive defendants, even when they are found guilty, are less likely to be sentenced to prison—helps explain one of the more fascinating experiments in criminology I have heard of (Kurtzburg et al., 1968). Some New York City jail inmates with facial disfigurements were given plastic surgery while incarcerated; others with similar disfigurements were not. Furthermore, some of each of these two groups of criminals were given services (for example, counseling and training) designed to rehabilitate them to society. One year after their release, a check of the records revealed that (except for heroin addicts) those given the cosmetic surgery were significantly less likely to have returned to jail. The most interesting feature of this finding was that it was equally true for those criminals who had not received the traditional rehabilita-

INFLUENCE

tive services as for those who had. Apparently, some criminologists then argued, when it comes to ugly inmates, prisons would be better off to abandon the costly rehabilitation treatments they typically provide and offer plastic surgery instead; the surgery seems to be at least as effective and decidedly less expensive.

The importance of the newer, Pennsylvania data (Stewart, 1980) is its suggestion that the argument for surgery as a means of rehabilitation may be faulty. Making an ugly criminal more attractive may not reduce the chances that he will commit another crime; it may only reduce his chances of being sent to jail for it.

4. The negligence-award study was done by Kulka and Kessler (1978), the helping study by Benson et al. (1976), and the persuasion study by Chaiken (1979).

5. For example, see the studies by Dion (1972) and Rich (1975).

6. The dime-request experiment was conducted by Emswiller et al. (1971) while the petition-signing experiment was done by Suedfeld et al. (1971).

7. The insurance sales data were reported by Evans (1963). More recent work suggests yet another reason for caution when dealing with similar requesters: We typically underestimate the degree to which similarity affects our liking for another (Gonzales et al., 1983).

8. See Drachman et al. (1978) for a complete description of the findings.

9. The Minnesota study was published by Aronson and Linder in 1965. It should be noted that the tactic of describing someone in unfavorable and then in favorable terms is advisable only when the description is accidently overheard. Several experiments done after the Minnesota study have shown that evaluations presented directly to another do not generate more liking when they begin with criticism. See the research by Taylor et al. (1969), Mettee (1971), and Hewitt (1972). In face-to-face situations, then, where off-the-bat negativity is likely to be regarded as offensive and inappropriate, our best strategy is probably Joe Girard's.

10. The mirror study was performed by Mita et al. (1977).

11. For general evidence regarding the positive effect of familiarity on attraction, see Zajonc (1968). For more specific evidence of this effect on our response to politicians, the research of Joseph Grush is enlightening and sobering (Grush et al., 1978; Grush, 1980) in documenting a strong connection between amount of media exposure and a candidate's chances of winning an election.

12. See Wilson (1979).

13. For an especially thorough examination of this issue see Stephan (1978).

14. The evidence of the tendency of ethnic groups to stay with their own

NOTES

in school comes from Gerard and Miller (1975). The evidence for the dislike of things repeatedly presented under unpleasant conditions comes from such studies as Burgess and Sales (1971), Zajonc et al. (1974) and Swap (1977).

15. From Aronson (1975).

16. A fascinating description of the entire boys'-camp project, called the "Robbers' Cave Experiment," can be found in Sherif et al. (1961).

17. The Carlos example comes once again from Aronson's initial report in his 1975 article. However, additional reports by Aronson and by others have shown similarly encouraging results. A representative list would include Johnson and Johnson (1975), DeVries and Slavin (1978), Cook (1978), and Aronson, Bridgeman, and Geffner (1978a, b).

18. For a careful examination of the possible pitfalls of cooperative learning approaches, see Rosenfield and Stephan (1981).

19. In truth, little in the way of combat takes place when the salesman enters the manager's office under such circumstances. Often, because the salesman knows exactly the price below which he cannot go, he and the boss don't even speak. In one car dealership I infiltrated while researching this book, it was common for a salesman to have a soft drink or cigarette in silence while the boss continued working at his desk. After a seemly time, the salesman would loosen his tie and return to his customers, looking weary but carrying the deal he had just "hammered out" for them—the same deal he had in mind before entering the boss's office.

20. For experimental evidence of the validity of Shakespeare's observation, see Manis et al. (1974).

21. A review of research supporting this statement is provided by Lott and Lott (1965).

22. See the study by Miller et al. (1966) for evidence.

23. The study was done by Smith and Engel (1968).

24. To demonstrate that the principle of association also works for unpleasant experiences, Razran (1940) included in his experiment a condition in which certain participants had putrid odors piped into the room while they were shown the political slogans. In this case, approval ratings for the slogans declined.

25. The Georgia study was done by Rosen and Tesser (1970).

26. From Asimov (1975).

27. Both the sweat-shirt and the pronoun experiments are reported fully in Cialdini et al. (1976).

INFLUENCE

CHAPTER 6 (pp. 203–228)

1. The quote is from Milgram's 1963 article in the *Journal of Abnormal and Social Psychology.*

2. All of these variations on the basic experiment, as well as several others, are presented in Milgram's highly readable book *Obedience to Authority,* 1974.

3. In fact, Milgram first began his investigations in an attempt to understand how the German citizenry could have participated in the concentration-camp destruction of millions of innocents during the years of Nazi ascendancy. After testing his experimental procedures in the United States, he had planned to take them to Germany, a country whose populace he was sure would provide enough obedience for a full-blown scientific analysis of the concept. That first eye-opening experiment in New Haven, Connecticut, however, made it clear that he could save his money and stay close to home. "I found so much obedience," he has said, "I hardly saw the need of taking the experiment to Germany."

More telling evidence, perhaps, of a willingness within the American character to submit to authorized command comes from a national survey taken after the trial of Lieutenant William Calley, who ordered his soldiers to kill the inhabitants—from the infants and toddlers through their parents and grandparents—of My Lai, Vietnam. A majority of Americans (51 percent) responded that if so ordered, in a similar context, they too would shoot all the residents of a Vietnamese village. The pollsters concluded, "Our data suggest that many Americans feel they have no right to resist authoritative demands. They regard Calley's actions at My Lai as normal, even desirable, because [they think] he performed them in obedience to legitimate authority." See Kelman and Lawrence (1972) for the full survey results.

4. We are not the only species to give sometimes wrongheaded deference to those in authority positions. In monkey colonies, where rigid dominance hierarchies exist, beneficial innovations (like learning how to use a stick to bring food into the cage area) do not spread quickly through the group unless they are taught first to a dominant animal. When a lower animal is taught the new concept first, the rest of the colony remains mostly oblivious to its value. One study, cited by Ardry (1970), on the introduction of new food tastes to Japanese monkeys provides a nice illustration. In one troop, a taste for caramels was developed by introducing this new food into the diet of young peripherals, low on the status ladder. The taste for caramels inched slowly up the ranks: A year and a half later, only 51 percent of the colony had acquired it, and still none of the leaders. Contrast this with what happened in a second troop where wheat was introduced first to the leader: Wheat eating—to this point unknown to these monkeys—spread through the whole colony within four hours.

5. The experiment was performed by Wilson (1968).

6. The study on children's judgments of coins was done by Bruner and

NOTES

Goodman (1947). The study on college students' judgments was done by Dukes and Bevan (1952). In addition to the relationship between importance (status) and perceived size that both of these experiments show, there is even some evidence that the importance we assign to our identity is reflected in the size of a frequent symbol of that identity: our signature. The psychologist Richard Zweigenhaft (1970) has collected data suggesting that as a man's sense of his own status grows, so does the size of his signature. This finding may give us a secret way of discovering how the people around us view their own status and importance: Simply compare the size of their signature to that of their other handwriting.

7. Subhumans are not alone in this regard, even in modern times. For example, since 1900 the U.S. presidency has been won by the taller of the major-party candidates in eighteen of the twenty-one elections.

8. From Hofling et al. (1966).

9. Additional data collected in the same study suggest that nurses may not be conscious of the extent to which the title Doctor sways their judgments and actions. A separate group of thirty-three nurses and student nurses were asked what they would have done in the experimental situation. Contrary to the actual findings, only two predicted that they would have given the medication as prescribed.

10. See Bickman (1974) for a complete account of this research.

11. This experiment was conducted by Lefkowitz, Blake, and Mouton (1955).

12. The horn-honking study was published in 1968 by Anthony Doob and Alan Gross.

13. For evidence, see Choo (1964) and McGuinnies and Ward (1980).

14. See Settle and Gorden (1974).

CHAPTER 7 (pp.229–260)

1. According to the researchers, the singles-bar experiment (Pennebaker et al., 1979) got its inspiration from the title of a song by country-and-western music artist Mickey Gilley, "Don't the Girls All Get Prettier at Closing Time?"

2. See Schwartz (1980) for evidence of such a process.

3. Without wishing to minimize the advantages of this type of shortcut or the dangers associated with it, I should note that these advantages and dangers are essentially the same ones we have examined in previous chapters. Accordingly, I will not focus on this theme in the remainder of the present chapter, except to say at this point that the key to using properly the shortcut feature of scarcity is to be alert to the distinction between naturally occurring, honest scarcity and the fabricated variety favored by certain compliance practitioners.

INFLUENCE

4. The original reactance-theory formulation appeared in Brehm (1966); an updated version appears in Brehm and Brehm (1981).

5. Brehm and Weintraub (1977) did the barrier experiment. It should be noted that two-year-old girls in the study did not show the same resistant response to the large barrier as did the boys. This does not seem to be because girls don't oppose attempts to limit their freedoms. Instead, it appears that they are primarily reactant to restrictions that come from other people rather than from physical barriers (Brehm, 1983).

6. For descriptions of the two-year-old's change in self-perception, see Mahler et al. (1975), Lewis and Brooks-Gunn (1979), Brooks-Gun and Lewis (1982), and Levine (1983).

7. The occurrence of the Romeo and Juliet effect should not be interpreted as a warning to parents to be always accepting of their teenagers' romantic choices. New players at this delicate game are likely to err often and consequently would benefit from the direction of an adult with greater perspective and experience. In providing such direction, parents should recognize that teenagers, who see themselves as young adults, will not respond well to control attempts that are typical of parent-child relationships. Especially in the clearly adult arena of mating, adult tools of influence (preference and persuasion) will be more effective than traditional forms of parental control (prohibitions and punishments). Although the experience of the Montague and Capulet families is an extreme example, heavy-handed restrictions on a young romantic alliance may well turn it clandestine, torrid, and sad.

A full description of the Colorado couples study can be found in Driscoll et al. (1972).

8. See Mazis (1975) and Mazis et al. (1973) for formal reports of the phosphate study.

9. For evidence, see Ashmore et al. (1971), Wicklund and Brehm (1974), Worchel and Arnold (1973), and Worchel et al. (1975).

10. The Purdue study was done by Zellinger et al. (1974).

11. The University of Chicago jury experiment on inadmissible evidence was reported by Broeder (1959).

12. The initial statements of commodity theory appeared in Brock (1968) and Fromkin and Brock (1971).

13. For ethical reasons, the information provided to the customers was always true. There *was* an impending beef shortage and this news had, indeed, come to the company through its exclusive sources. See Knishinsky (1982) for full details of the project.

14. Worchel et al. (1975).

15. See Davies (1962, 1969).

NOTES

16. See Lytton (1979) and Rosenthal and Robertson (1959).

17. The quote comes from MacKenzie (1974).

EPILOGUE (pp. 261–268)

1. For evidence of such perceptual and decisional narrowing see Berkowitz (1967), Cohen (1978), Easterbrook (1959), Hockey and Hamilton (1970), Mackworth (1965), Milgram (1970), and Tversky and Kahnemann (1974).

2. See West (1981).

3. From Crane (1972).

4. Quoted in the PBS-TV documentary *The Information Society*.

5. From Macrae (1972).

BIBLIOGRAPHY

✳

Altheide, D. L., and J. M. Johnson. "Counting Souls: A Study of Counseling at Evangelical Crusades." *Pacific Sociological Review*, 20 (1977): 323–48.

Ardry, R. *The Social Contract*. New York: Atheneum, 1970.

Aronson, E. "The Jigsaw Route to Learning and Liking." *Psychology Today*, Feb. 1975.

Aronson, E., D. L. Bridgeman, and R. Geffner. "The Effects of a Cooperative Classroom Structure on Students' Behavior and Attitudes," *Social Psychology of Education: Theory and Research*, ed. D. Bar-Tal and L. Saxe. New York: Halstead Press, 1978.

———."Interdependent Interactions and Prosocial Behavior." *Journal of Research and Development in Education*, 12 (1978): 16–27.

Aronson, E., and D. L. Linder. "Gain and Loss of Esteem as Determinants of Interpersonal Attractiveness." *Journal of Experimental Social Psychology*, 1 (1965): 156–71.

Aronson, E., and J. Mills. "The Effect of Severity of Initiation on Lik-

BIBLIOGRAPHY

ing for a Group." *Journal of Abnormal and Social Psychology,* 59 (1959): 177–81.

Aronson, E., et al. *The Jigsaw Classroom.* Beverly Hills: Sage Publications, 1978.

Ashmore, R. D., V. Ramchandra, and R. A. Jones. "Censorship as an Attitude Change Induction." Paper presented at Eastern Psychological Association meetings, New York, April 1971.

Asimov, I. "The Miss America Pageant." *TV Guide,* Aug. 30, 1975.

Bandura, A., J. E. Grusec, and F. L. Menlove. "Vicarious Extinction of Avoidance Behavior." *Journal of Personality and Social Psychology,* 5 (1967): 16–23.

Bandura, A., and F. L. Menlove. "Factors Determining Vicarious Extinction of Avoidance Behavior Through Symbolic Modeling." *Journal of Personality and Social Psychology,* 8 (1968): 99–108.

Benson, P. L., S. A. Karabenic, and R. M. Lerner. "Pretty Pleases: The Effects of Physical Attractiveness on Race, Sex, and Receiving Help." *Journal of Experimental Social Psychology,* 12 (1976): 409–15.

Benton, A. A., H. H. Kelley, and B. Liebling. "Effects of Extremity of Offers and Concession Rate on the Outcomes of Bargaining." *Journal of Personality and Social Psychology,* 24 (1972): 73–83.

Berkowitz, L., and R. W. Buck. "Impulsive Aggression: Reactivity to Aggressive Cues Under Emotional Arousal." *Journal of Personality and Social Psychology,* 35 (1967): 415–24.

Bickman, L. "The Social Power of a Uniform." *Journal of Applied Social Psychology,* 4 (1974): 47–61.

Bollen, K. A., and D. P. Phillips. "Imitative Suicides: A National Study of the Effects of Television News Stories." *American Sociological Review,* 47 (1982): 802–09.

Brehm, J. W. *A Theory of Psychological Reactance.* New York: Academic Press, 1966.

Brehm, S. S. "Psychological Reactance and the Attractiveness of Unattainable Objects: Sex Differences in Children's Responses to an Elimination of Freedom." *Sex Roles,* 7 (1981): 937–49.

Brehm, S. S., and J. W. Brehm. *Psychological Reactance.* New York: Academic Press, 1981.

Brehm, S. S., and M. Weintraub. "Physical Barriers and Psychological Reactance: Two-year-olds' Responses to Threats to Freedom." *Journal of Personality and Social Psychology,* 35 (1977): 830–36.

Brock, T. C. "Implications of Commodity Theory for Value Change," *Psychological Foundations of Attitudes*, ed. A. G. Greenwald, T. C. Brock, and T. M. Ostrom. New York: Academic Press, 1968.

Broeder, D. "The University of Chicago Jury Project." *Nebraska Law Review*, 38 (1959): 760–74.

Brooks-Gunn, J., and M. Lewis. "The Development of Self-Knowledge," *The Child*, ed. C. B. Kopp and J. B. Krakow. Reading, Mass.: Addison-Wesley, 1982.

Bruner, J. S., and C. C. Goodman. "Value and Need as Organizing Factors in Perception." *Journal of Abnormal and Social Psychology*, 42 (1947): 33–44.

Burger, J. M., and R. E. Petty. "The Low-Ball Compliance Technique: Task or Person Commitment?" *Journal of Personality and Social Psychology*, 40 (1981): 492–500.

Burgess, T., and S. Sales. "Attitudinal Effects of 'Mere Exposure': A Reevaluation." *Journal of Experimental Social Psychology*, 7 (1971): 461–72.

Chaiken, S. "Communicator Physical Attractiveness and Persuasion." *Journal of Personality and Social Psychology*, 37 (1979): 1387–97.

Choo, T. "Communicator Credibility and Communication Discrepancy as Determinants of Opinion Change." *Journal of Social Psychology*, 64 (1964): 1–20.

Cialdini, R. B., and K. Ascani. "Test of a Concession Procedure for Inducing Verbal, Behavioral, and Further Compliance with a Request to Give Blood." *Journal of Applied Psychology*, 61 (1976): 295–300.

Cialdini, R. B., et al. "Basking in Reflected Glory: Three (Football) Field Studies." *Journal of Personality and Social Psychology*, 34 (1976): 366–75.

Cialdini, R. B., et al. "The Low-Ball Procedure for Producing Compliance: Commitment, Then Cost." *Journal of Personality and Social Psychology*, 36 (1978): 463–76.

Cialdini, R. B., et al. "Reciprocal Concessions Procedure for Inducing Compliance: The Door-in-the-Face Technique." *Journal of Personality and Social Psychology*, 31 (1975): 206–15.

Clark, R. D., III, and L. E. Word. "Where Is the Apathetic Bystander? Situational Characteristics of the Emergency." *Journal of Personality and Social Psychology*, 29 (1974): 279–87.

BIBLIOGRAPHY

————. "Why Don't Bystanders Help? Because of Ambiguity?" *Journal of Personality and Social Psychology*, 24 (1972): 392–400.

Cohen, M., and N. Davis. *Medication Errors: Causes and Prevention.* Philadelphia: G. F. Stickley, 1981.

Cohen, S. "Environmental Load and the Allocation of Attention," *Advances in Environmental Psychology*, Vol. 1, ed. A. Baum, J. E. Singer, and S. Valins. New York: Halstead Press, 1978.

Cook, S. W. "Interpersonal and Attitudinal Outcomes in Cooperating Interracial Groups." *Journal of Research and Development in Education*, 12 (1978): 97–113.

Crane, D. *Invisible Colleges.* Chicago: University of Chicago Press, 1972.

Darley, J. M., and B. Latané. "Bystandar Intervention in Emergencies: Diffusion of Responsibility." *Journal of Personality and Social Psychology*, 8 (1968): 377–83.

Davies, J. C. "The J-Curve of Rising and Declining Satisfactions as a Cause of Some Great Revolutions and a Contained Rebellion," *Violence in America*, ed. H. D. Graham and T. R. Gurr. New York: Signet Books, 1969.

————. "Toward a Theory of Revolution." *American Sociological Review*, 27 (1962): 5–19.

Deutsch, M., and H. B. Gerard, "A Study of Normative and Informational Social Influences upon Individual Judgment." *Journal of Abnormal and Social Psychology*, 51 (1955): 629–36.

De Vries, D. L., and R. E. Slavin. "Teams-Games-Tournaments (TGT): Review of Ten Classroom Experiments." *Journal of Research and Development in Education*, 12 (1978): 28–38.

Dion, K. K. "Physical Attractiveness and Evaluation of Children's Transgressions." *Journal of Personality and Social Psychology*, 24 (1972): 207–13.

Doob, A. N., and A. E. Gross. "Status of Frustrator as an Inhibitor of Horn-Honking Responses." *Journal of Social Psychology*, 76 (1968): 213–18.

Drachman, D., A., deCarufel, and C. A. Inkso. "The Extra Credit Effect in Interpersonal Attraction." *Journal of Experimental Social Psychology*, 14 (1978): 458–67.

Driscoll, R., K. E. Davies, and M. E. Lipetz. "Parental Interference and Romantic Love: The Romeo and Juliet Effect." *Journal of Personality and Social Psychology*, 24 (1972): 1–10.

Dukes, W. F., and W. Bevan. "Accentuation and Response Variability in the Perception of Personally Relevant Objects." *Journal of Personality*, 20 (1952): 457–65.

Easterbrook, J. A. "The Effects of Emotion on Cue Utilization and the Organization of Behavior." *Psychological Review*, 66 (1959): 183–201.

Efran, M. G., and E.W.J. Patterson. "The Politics of Appearance." Unpublished manuscript, University of Toronto, 1976.

Eibl-Eibesfeldt, I. "Der Fisch *Aspidontus taeniatus* als Machahmer des Putzers *Labroides dimidiatus*." *Zeitschrift fuer Tierpsychologie*, 16 (1959): 19–25.

Emswiller, T., K. Deaux, and J. E. Willits. "Similarity, Sex, and Requests for Small Favors." *Journal of Applied Social Psychology*, 1 (1971): 284–91.

Evans, F. B. *American Behavioral Scientist*, 6:7 (1963): 76–79.

Festinger, L., H. W. Riecken, and S. Schachter. *When Prophecy Fails*. Minneapolis: University of Minnesota Press, 1956.

Fox, M. W. *Concepts in Ethology: Animal and Human Behavior*. Minneapolis: University of Minnesota Press, 1974.

Freedman, J. L. "Long-term Behavioral Effects of Cognitive Dissonance." *Journal of Experimental Social Psychology*, 4 (1966): 195–203.

———, and S. C. Fraser. "Compliance Without Pressure: The Foot-in-the-Door Technique." *Journal of Personality and Social Psychology*, 4 (1966): 195–203.

Fromkin, H. L., and T. C. Brock. "A Commodity Theory Analysis of Persuasion." *Representative Research in Social Psychology*, 2 (1971): 47–57.

Fuller, R.G.C., and A. Sheehy-Skeffinton. "Effects of Group Laughter on Responses to Humorous Materials: A Replication and Extension." *Psychological Reports*, 35 (1974): 531–34.

Gerard, H. B., and G. C. Mathewson. "The Effects of Severity of Initiation on Liking for a Group: A Replication." *Journal of Experimental Social Psychology*, 2 (1966): 278–87.

Gerard, H. B., and N. Miller. *School Desegregation*. New York: Plenum, 1975.

Gergen, K., et al. "Obligation, Donor Resources, and Reactions to Aid in Three Cultures." *Journal of Personality and Social Psychology*, 31 (1975): 390–400.

BIBLIOGRAPHY

Gonzales, M. H., et al. "Interactional Approach to Interpersonal Attraction." *Journal of Personality and Social Psychology*, 44 (1983): 1192–97.

Gordon, R. E., and K. Gordon. *The Blight on the Ivy*. Englewood Cliffs, N.J.: Prentice-Hall, 1963.

Gouldner, A. W. "The Norm of Reciprocity: A Preliminary Statement." *American Sociological Review*, 25 (1960): 161–78.

Green, F. "The 'Foot-in-the-Door' Technique." *American Salesman*, 10 (1965): 14–16.

Greenberg, M. S., and S. P. Shapiro. "Indebtedness: An Adverse Aspect of Asking for and Receiving Help." *Sociometry*, 34 (1971): 290–301.

Grush, J. E. "Impact of Candidate Expenditures, Regionality, and Prior Outcomes on the 1976 Democratic Presidential Primaries." *Journal of Personality and Social Psychology*, 38 (1980): 337–47.

———, K. L. McKeough, and R. F. Ahlering. "Extrapolating Laboratory Exposure Experiments to Actual Political Elections." *Journal of Personality and Social Psychology*, 36 (1978): 257–70.

Hockey, G.R.J., and P. Hamilton. "Arousal and Information Selection in Short-term Memory." *Nature*, 226 (1970): 866–67.

Hofling, C. K., et al. "An Experimental Study of Nurse-Physician Relationships." *Journal of Nervous and Mental Disease*, 143 (1966): 171–80.

Hölldobler, B. "Communication Between Ants and Their Guests." *Scientific American*, 198 (Jan.) (1971): 68–76.

Hornaday, W. T. "The Extermination of the American Bison, with a Sketch of Its Discovery and Life History." *Smithsonian Report*, 1887, Part II, 367–548.

Hornstein, H. A., E. Fisch, and M. Holmes. "Influence of a Model's Feeling About His Behavior and His Relevance as a Comparison Other on Observers' Helping Behavior." *Journal of Personality and Social Psychology*, 10 (1968): 222–26.

Johnson, D. W., and R. T. Johnson. *Learning Together and Learning Alone*. Englewood Cliffs, N.J.: Prentice-Hall, 1975.

Jones, E. E., and V.E. Harris. "The Attribution of Attitudes." *Journal of Experimental Social Psychology*, 3 (1967): 1–24.

Jones, E. E., and C. Wortman. *Ingratiation: An Attributional Approach*. Morristown, N.J.: General Learning Corp., 1973.

Kelman, J., and L. Lawrence. "Assignment of Responsibility in the Case of Lt. Calley: Preliminary Report on a National Survey." *Journal of Social Issues*, 28:1 (1978).

Kenrick, D. T., and S. E. Gutierres. "Contrast Effects in Judgments of Attractiveness: When Beauty Becomes a Social Problem." *Journal of Personality and Social Psychology*, 38 (1980): 131–40.

————, and L. Goldberg. "Influence of Popular Erotica on Attraction Toward the Mundane Nude Body." Unpublished manuscript, Arizona State University, 1983.

Knishinsky, A. "The Effects of Scarcity of Material and Exclusivity of Information on Industrial Buyer Perceived Risk in Provoking a Purchase decision." Doctoral dissertation, Arizona State University, 1982.

Knox, R. E., and J. A. Inkster. "Postdecisional Dissonance at Post Time." *Journal of Personality and Social Psychology*, 8 (1968): 319–23.

Kraut, R. E. "Effects of Social Labeling on Giving to Charity." *Journal of Experimental Social Psychology*, 9 (1973): 551–62.

Kulka, R. A., and J. R. Kessler. "Is Justice Really Blind? The Effect of Litigant Physical Attractiveness on Judicial Judgment." *Journal of Applied Social Psychology*, 4 (1978): 336–81.

Kunz, P. R., and M. Woolcott. "Season's Greetings: From My Status to Yours." *Social Science Research*, 5 (1976): 269–78.

Kurtzburg, R. L., H. Safar, and N. Cavior. "Surgical and Social Rehabilitation of Adult Offenders." *Proceedings of the 76th Annual Convention of the American Psychological Association*, 3 (1968): 649–50.

Lack, D. *The Life of the Robin*. London: Cambridge University Press, 1943.

Langer, E. "Rethinking the Role of Thought in Social Interaction," *New Directions in Attribution Research*, Vol. 2., ed. Harvey, Ickes, and Kidd. Potomac, Md.: Lawrence Erlbaum Associates, 1978.

Latané, B., and J. M. Darley. "Group Inhibition of Bystander Intervention in Emergencies." *Journal of Personality and Social Psychology*, 10 (1968): 215–21.

————. *The Unresponsive Bystander: Why Doesn't He Help?* New York: Appleton-Century-Crofts, 1968.

Latané, B., and J. Rodin. "A Lady in Distress: Inhibiting Effects of Friends and Strangers on Bystander Intervention." *Journal of Experimental Social Psychology*, 5 (1969): 189–202.

BIBLIOGRAPHY

Leakey, R., and R. Lewin. *People of the Lake.* New York: Anchor Press/Doubleday, 1978.

Lefkowitz, M., R. R. Blake, and J. S. Mouton. "Status Factors in Pedestrian Violation of Traffic Signals." *Journal of Abnormal and Social Psychology*, 51 (1955): 704–06.

Levine, L. E. "Mine: Self-Definition in Two-Year-Old Boys." *Developmental Psychology*, 19 (1983): 544–49.

Lewis, M., and J. Brooks-Gunn. *Social Cognition and the Acquisition of Self.* New York: Plenum, 1979.

Liebert, R., and R. A. Baron. "Some Immediate Effects of Televised Violence on Children's Behavior." *Developmental Psychology*, 6 (1972): 469–75.

Lloyd, J. E. "Aggressive Mimicry in *Photuris:* Firefly *Femme Fatales.*" *Science*, 149 (1965): 653–54.

Lott, A. J., and B. E. Lott. "Group Cohesiveness as Interpersonal Attraction: A Review of Relationships with Antecedent and Consequent Variables." *Psychological Bulletin*, 64 (1965): 259–309.

Lytton, J. "Correlates of Compliance and the Rudiments of Conscience in Two-Year-Old Boys." *Canadian Journal of Behavioral Science*, 9 (1979): 242–51.

McGuinnies, E., and C. D. Ward. "Better Liked Than Right: Trustworthiness and Expertise as Factors in Credibility." *Personality and Social Psychology Bulletin*, 6 (1980): 467–72.

MacKenzie, B. "When Sober Executives Went on a Bidding Binge." *TV Guide*, June 22, 1974.

Mackworth, N. H. "Visual Noise Causes Tunnel Vision." *Psychonomic Science*, 3 (1965): 67–68.

Macrae, N. "Multinational Business." *The Economist* (London), Jan. 22, 1972.

Magruder, J. S. *An American Life: One Man's Road to Watergate.* New York: Atheneum, 1974.

Mahler, M. S., F. Pine, and A. Bergman. *The Psychological Birth of the Infant.* New York: Basic Books, 1975.

Manis, M., S. D. Cornell, and J. C. Moore. "Transmission of Attitude Relevant Information Through a Communication Chain." *Journal of Personality and Social Psychology*, 30 (1974): 81–94.

Mauss, Marcel. *The Gift*, trans. I. G. Cunnison. London: Cohen and West, 1954.

INFLUENCE

Mazis, M. B. "Antipollution Measures and Psychological Reactance Theory: A Field Experiment." *Journal of Personality and Social Psychology*, 31 (1975): 654–66.

———, R. B. Settle, and D. C. Leslie. "Elimination of Phosphate Detergents and Psychological Reactance." *Journal of Marketing Research*, 10 (1973): 390–95.

Milgram, S. "Behavioral Study of Obedience." *Journal of Abnormal and Social Psychology*, 67 (1963): 371–78.

———. "The Experience of Living in Cities." *Science*, 13 (1970): 1461–68.

———. *Obedience to Authority*. New York: Harper and Row, 1974.

———, L. Bickman, and O. Berkowitz. "Note on the Drawing Power of Crowds of Different Size." *Journal of Personality and Social Psychology*, 13 (1969): 79–82.

Milgram, S., and J. Sabini. "On Maintaining Norms: A Field Experiment in the Subway." Unpublished manuscript, City University of New York, 1975.

Miller, N., et al. "Similarity, Contrast, and Complementarity in Friendship Choice." *Journal of Personality and Social Psychology*, 3 (1966): 3–12.

Miller, R. L., et al. "Perceptual Contrast Versus Reciprocal Concession as Mediators of Induced Compliance." *Canadian Journal of Behavioral Science*, 8 (1976): 401–09.

Mita, T. H., M. Dermer, and J. Knight. "Reversed Facial Images and the Mere Exposure Hypothesis." *Journal of Personality and Social Psychology*, 35 (1977): 597–601.

Monahan, F. *Women in Crime*. New York: Ives Washburn, 1941.

Nosanchuk, T. A., and J. Lightstone. "Canned Laughter and Public and Private Conformity." *Journal of Personality and Social Psychology*, 29 (1974): 153–56.

O'Connor, R. D. "Relative Efficacy of Modeling, Shaping, and the Combined Procedures for Modification of Social Withdrawal." *Journal of Abnormal Psychology*, 79 (1972): 327–34.

Packard, V. *The Hidden Persuaders*. New York: D. McKay Co., 1957.

Pallak, M. S., D. A. Cook, and J. J. Sullivan. "Commitment and Energy Conservation." *Applied Social Psychology Annual*, 1 (1980): 235–53.

BIBLIOGRAPHY

Peiponen, V. A. "Verhaltensstudien am blaukehlchen." *Ornis Fennica*, 37 (1960): 69–83.

Pekkanen, J. *The Best Doctors in the U.S.* New York: Seaview Books, 1971.

Pennebaker, J. W., et al. "Don't the Girls Get Prettier at Closing Time." *Personality and Social Psychology Bulletin*, 5 (1979): 122–25.

Phillips, D. P. "Airplane Accidents, Murder, and the Mass Media: Towards a Theory of Imitation and Suggestion." *Social Forces*, 58 (1980): 1001–24.

———. "The Impact of Mass Media Violence on U.S. Homicides." *American Sociological Review*, 48 (1983): 560–68.

———. "The Influence of Suggestion on Suicide: Substantive and Theoretical Implications of the Werther Effect." *American Sociological Review*, 39 (1974): 340–54.

———. "Suicide, Motor Vehicle Fatalities, and the Mass Media: Evidence Toward a Theory of Suggestion." *American Journal of Sociology*, 84 (1979): 1150–74.

Razran, G.H.S. "Conditioned Response Changes in Rating and Appraising Sociopolitical Slogans." *Psychological Bulletin*, 37 (1940): 481.

———. "Conditioning Away Social Bias by the Luncheon Technique." *Psychological Bulletin*, 35 (1938): 693.

Regan, D. T. "Effects of a Favor and Liking on Compliance." *Journal of Experimental Social Psychology*, 7 (1971): 627–39.

Rich, J. "Effects of Children's Physical Attractiveness on Teachers' Evaluations." *Journal of Educational Psychology*, 67 (1975): 599–609.

Rosen, S., and A. Tesser. "On the Reluctance to Communicate Undesirable Information: The MUM Effect." *Sociometry*, 33 (1970): 253–63.

Rosenfield, D., and W. G. Stephan. "Intergroup Relations Among Children," *Developmental Social Psychology*, ed. S. Brehm, S. Kassin, and F. Gibbons. New York: Oxford University Press, 1981.

Rosenthal, A. M. *Thirty-eight Witnesses*. New York: McGraw-Hill, 1964.

Rosenthal, M. J., E. Ni, and R. E. Robertson. "A Study of Mother-Child Relationships in the Emotional Disorders of Children." *Genetic Psychology Monographs*, 60 (1959): 65–116.

Ross, A. S. "Effect of Increased Responsibility on Bystander Intervention: The Presence of Children." *Journal of Personality and Social Psychology*, 19 (1971): 306–10.

Russell, D. "Leave It to the Merry Prankster, the Artful Dodger, and the Body Puncher," *TV Guide*, Dec. 16, 1978.

Sabin, R. *The International Cyclopedia of Music and Musicians*. New York: Dodd, Mead, 1964.

Schwarzwald, J., M. Raz, and M. Zvibel. "The Efficacy of the Door-in-the-Face Technique When Established Behavioral Customs Exist." *Journal of Applied Social Psychology*, 9 (1979): 576–86.

Schein, E. "The Chinese Indoctrination Program for Prisoners of War: A Study of Attempted 'Brainwashing.'" *Psychiatry*, 19 (1956): 149–72.

Schwarz, N. "Experimentelle Untersuchungen zur Reduktion durch Freiheitswerderstellung." Doctoral dissertation, Universität Mannheim, 1980.

Segal, H. A. "Initial Psychiatric Findings of Recently Repatriated Prisoners of War." *American Journal of Psychiatry*, 61 (1954): 358–63.

Settle, R. B., and L. L. Gorden. Attribution Theory and Advertiser Credibility. *Journal of Marketing Research*, 11 (1974): 181–85.

Sherif, M., et al. *Intergroup Conflict and Cooperation: The Robbers' Cave Experiment*. Norman, Okla. University of Oklahoma Institute of Intergroup Relations, 1961.

Smith, G. H., and R. Engel. "Influence of a Female Model on Perceived Characteristics of an Automobile." *Proceedings of the 76th Annual Convention of the American Psychological Association*, 3 (1968): 681–82.

Smith, M. M., and R. G. C. Fuller. "Effects of Group Laughter on Responses to Humorous Materials." *Psychological Reports*, 30 (1972): 132–34.

Stephan, W. G. "School Desegregation: An Evaluation of Predictions Made in *Brown* v. *Board of Education*." *Psychological Bulletin*, 85 (1978): 217–38.

Stewart, J. E., II. "Defendant's Attractiveness as a Factor in the Outcome of Trials." *Journal of Applied Social Psychology*, 10 (1980): 348–61.

Suedfeld, P., S. Bochner, and C. Matas. "Petitioner's Attire and Petition Signing by Peace Demonstrators: A Field Experiment." *Journal of Applied Social Psychology.*, 1 (1971): 278–83.

BIBLIOGRAPHY

Swap, W. C. "Interpersonal Attraction and Repeated Exposure to Rewards and Punishers." *Personality and Social Psychology Bulletin*, 3 (1977): 248–51.

Tiger, L., and R. Fox. *The Imperial Animal*. New York: Holt, Rinehart & Winston, 1971.

Toffler, A. *Future Shock*. New York: Random House, 1970.

Tversky, A., and D. Kahnemann. "Judgment Under Uncertainty: Heuristics and Biases." *Science*, 185 (1974): 1124–31.

Walker, M. G. "Organizational Type, Rites of Incorporation, and Group Solidarity: A Study of Fraternity Hell Week." Doctoral dissertation, University of Washington, 1967.

West, C. K. *The Social and Psychological Distortion of Information*. Chicago: Nelson-Hall, 1981.

Whiting, J.W.M., R. Kluckhohn, and A. Anthony. "The Function of Male Initiation Cermonies at Puberty," *Readings in Social Psychology*, ed. E. E. Maccoby, T. M. Newcomb, and E. L. Hartley. New York: Holt, 1958.

Whitney, R. A., T. Hubin, and J. D. Murphy. *The New Psychology of Persuasion and Motivation in Selling*. Englewood Cliffs, N.J.: Prentice-Hall, 1965.

Wicklund, R. A., and J. C. Brehm. Cited in Wicklund, R. A. *Freedom and Reactance*. Potomac, Md.: Lawrence Erlbaum Associates, 1974.

Wilson, P. R. "The Perceptual Distortion of Height as a Function of Ascribed Academic Status." *Journal of Social Psychology*, 74 (1968): 97–102.

Wilson, W. R. "Feeling More Than We Can Know: Exposure Effects Without Learning." *Journal of Personality and Social Psychology*, 37 (1979): 811–21.

Worchel, S., and S. E. Arnold. "The Effects of Censorship and the Attractiveness of the Censor on Attitude Change." *Journal of Experimental Social Psychology*, 9 (1973): 365–77.

———, and M. Baker. "The Effect of Censorship on Attitude Change: The Influence of Censor and Communicator Characteristics." *Journal of Applied Social Psychology*, 5 (1975): 222–39.

Worchel, S., J. Lee, and A. Adewole. "Effects of Supply and Demand on Ratings of Object Value." *Journal of Personality and Social Psychology*, 32 (1975): 906–14.

Young, F. W. *Initiation Ceremonies*. New York: Bobbs-Merrill, 1965.

Zajonc, R. B. "The Attitudinal Effects of Mere Exposure." *Journal of Personality and Social Psychology Monographs*, 9:2 (part 2) (1968).

————. "Feeling and Thinking: Preferences Need No Inferences." *American Psychologist*, 35 (1980): 151–75.

————, H. Markus, and W. R. Wilson. "Exposure Effects and Associative Learning." *Journal of Experimental Social Psychology*, 10 (1974): 248–63.

Zellinger, D. A., et al. "A Commodity Theory Analysis of the Effects of Age Restrictions on Pornographic Materials." Institute for Research in the Behavioral, Economic and Management Sciences, Purdue University, Paper No. 440, 1974.

Zweigenhaft, R. L. "Signature Size: A Key to Status Awareness." *Journal of Social Psychology*, 81 (1970): 49–54.

INDEX

※

INDEX

INDEX

INDEX

INDEX

INDEX

INDEX

About the author

Robert B. Cialdini received his M.A. and Ph.D. degrees from the University of North Carolina at Chapel Hill, where his training concentrated on the persuasion process. He continued his studies in experimental psychology under a National Science Foundation Postdoctoral Fellowship at Columbia University. Currently a full professor of psychology at Arizona State University in Tempe, he has served as an associate editor of the *Journal of Personality and Social Psychology*.